SUE VI DE TO

HEALTHY

HAPPY EATING
for all blood types

FOOD THERAPY FOR ALLERGIES,
SLIMMING, HEALING & ENERGY

ANDERSON
PUBLISHING

Publishing Manager: Lindy Anderson
P O Box 23505 Claremont 7735
Tel/fax 021 671 1742
lindy@andersonpublishing.co.za
First published in Cape Town in 2004
ISBN 0 - 9584583 - 8 - 3

ANDERSON PUBLISHING

Text, photography, layout and design by Sue Visser
Camera : SONY DIGITAL CYBER-SHOT DSC-S50

Disclaimer

The information in this book should not be regarded as medical advice. Consult a registered health practitioner for the correct diagnosis and a suitable medication or treatment for your condition. The author and publisher disclaim all responsibility for liability, loss or risk, personal or otherwise, which may be incurred as a consequence, directly or indirectly, of the use and application of any of the contents of this book.

Special precautions

Certain foods or herbs may enhance the effect of medications or could interfere with them. People with a gluten intolerance should exclude all gluten including wheat, rye, oats, barley, etc. regardless of blood type choices. Avoid dairy products if a casein allergy is present. Some individuals may still be allergic to a few of the foods that are recommended for their blood type.

Contents

A special dedication to my parents

Healthy and happy at 90!

Their secret? Healthy eating habits, fresh air and exercise. Mom (81) and Dad (90) are both blood type O. They hike, garden, camp out in the desert twice a year and swim or surf in the sea a few times a week. They maintain a happy, positive attitude and are full of love and concern for everybody.

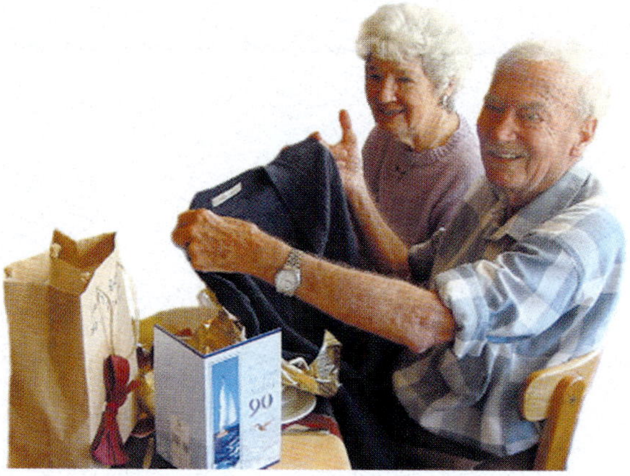

1 Know your body

Please note that this information should not be used to diagnose, treat or cure a condition. Consult your doctor or an experienced practitioner, especially if you are pregnant, breast-feeding, epileptic, diabetic or have blood pressure or heart complaints. (See page 2.)

Different bodies, different blood

We come in all shapes and sizes. Our rate of metabolism varies as does our tolerance to certain foods. Eating food that does not suit your blood type is one of the most fundamental causes of ill health.

Blood type testing techniques

Most people do not know their blood type, let alone their secretor status. Use the simple techniques in this chapter to determine your blood type or take blood and saliva tests.

Blood type A, B, AB and O

Determine your secretor status. General characteristics and eating guidelines for the four basic blood types and their secretor variants are included in this chapter.

Using food therapeutically

We have been told about the damaging effects of certain foods. Now learn how to use food to heal, cleanse and rejuvenate your body according to your biochemical individuality as well as your blood type attributes.

Kitchen remedies

Herbal remedies from the kitchen can be used as antibiotics, hormone balancers, remedies for colds and flu, arthritis, diabetes, etc.

A unique bunch of individuals

These carrots all grew from one packet of seeds in the same ground but they are not the same size. Each one of us comes in a different shape and size because we are born with a unique genetic structure. This is why our food and lifestyles affect us in different ways. Not everybody gets healthy or loses weight by eating exactly the same food. You are not only what you eat or think; you also have to consider your inherited blood type and metabolic characteristics. These are the factors that determine your build, what type of food suits you and even how you think or react in your daily life!

What you eat can cause disease

When we learn more about how unique we are, it becomes quite obvious that we have different metabolic rates and nutritional requirements. We also have different types of blood and this determines our basic food tolerances. There is no point in taking pills to cure the ills that have been caused by eating incorrectly. It is far better to cut out the offending food and not have to take endless medications or surrender to surgery. We need to eat healthy food that is beneficial to our blood type in the correct quantities and proportions.

Confront the cause of the problem

Today diseases such as diabetes, arthritis, cancer, obesity and immune disorders increase in direct proportion to regular consumption of grains, starches, meats and other foods that are not suited to individual blood types. There is, however, ample scientific proof that diseases can be prevented, if not cured, by eating foods that agree with your basic inherited blood type: A, B, AB or O. Only then can we really benefit from health and detoxification regimens and take herbal remedies or additional supplementation effectively.

You are what you eat but...

What are the negative effects of eating "wrong" for your blood type?

Incorrect or unsuitable eating does not always mean a diet of junk food. Ironically, many healthy foods can make you ill. Foods that clash with your blood type are often the regular choices of nutritionists or naturopaths. Lectins found in these foods are the substances that make cells stick to each other or bond to toxic substances. (See page 7.) Lectins are blood-type specific. The same food can be harmful, neutral or beneficial to people of blood type: A, B, AB or O, regardless of the vitamin, fibre or protein content. "Healthy", yet unsuitable foods may also cause organ enlargement and damage to the gut lining because they stimulate the formation of polyamines, the groups of amino acids that your system can't handle. (See page 7.) A balanced diet for your blood type does not encourage weight gain, heart problems, diabetes, mucous, arthritis, autoimmune disorders or cancer.

Incorrect eating affects our immunity, weight, kidneys, brain and hormones

A lifetime of incorrect eating takes its toll on every aspect of your constitution. By the age of 70, most people only have 25% of their kidney function, due to the clogging effect that lectins have in the bloodstream and on the kidneys. This means that 75% of the blood cannot be adequately cleansed of toxins or metabolic waste and acidic residues.

Senile dementia and Alzheimer's disease are linked to the destruction of neural pathways in the brain caused by lectins in foods that cause cell agglutination. A consuming foods that do not suit your blood type can impair your brain function.

Wheat lectins can damage pancreatic functions in later life. Many foods contain substances that mimic the roles of insulin, causing one to gain weight and become insulin resistant. To a blood type that does not tolerate soya, the estrogenic effect can overwhelm the normal functioning of the thyroid gland or cause some forms of cancer.

The immune system is provoked by food lectins and it produces antibodies that attack the cells and tissues of your own body. This causes autoimmune disorders such as arthritis, Addison's disease or fibromyalgia. Lectins from your favourite foods can block digestive hormones, cause leaky gut, interfere with protein digestion and impair the absorption of vital nutrients found in other foods.

Different body types, different blood types, different antigens

Dr Peter J D'Adamo's research

Hundreds of common diseases can be cured by simply eating and living according to your blood type. Dr Peter J D'Adamo and his father initiated and developed this logical and very effective therapeutic system. His scientific studies are well documented with thousands of case histories. Some therapists have managed to restore as well as maintain the health of their patients by using Dr D'Adamo's dietary guidelines. He has produced many excellent reference books and runs a very helpful and interactive website. (See page 160). To fully benefit from the blood-type style of eating, we need to become familiar with his terminology.

Secretors and non-secretors

There are two blood-type variants within the four blood types of: A, B, AB and O. Each type either has only blood-based antigens (sub-type 1) or they also secrete antigens (sub-type 2) that come from saliva and digestive juices. Thus, we have two A types, two B's, AB's and two O's.

Body types: ectomorph, mesomorph or endomorph

We need to consider our body type as it determines the metabolic rate.
1 An endomorph is a person with a large frame and a slow metabolic rate. They are usually calm, passive individuals who gain weight easily when they eat too much. They have a well-rounded appearance.
2 A mesomorph has a medium-sized frame, an average build and is reasonably active. Moderation and routine suit them best. Most mesomorphs are neither too fat nor too thin.
3 An ectomorph has a frailer skeleton and likes to live in the fast lane. With a rapid metabolic rate, food does not have a lasting effect and with strenuous activity, ectomorphs can suffer from muscle loss. Even with the same blood type, an ectomorph may not be able to thrive on a mesomorph's diet plan or conserve energy like an endomorph.

Is there really an 'average' person?

On the left, I weighed 63kg. After 6 months of Healthy Happy Eating, I now weigh 56kg, yet I look huge in comparison to a 45kg ectomorph.

Antigens and lectins

Antigens are linked to the immune system to identify substances and carry out a positive or a negative response to lectins in food. Antigens are present on blood cells as well as in body fluids like saliva. Lectins are substances in food that tag onto cells and make them stick together. Lectins trigger different reactions in each of the four blood types. Certain antigens you have on your blood cells or the ones you secrete in saliva or digestive juices can deflect the lectins and prevent the agglutinating effect. For example: blood type O and B do not have a wheat-friendly antigen and blood type A and B secretors do not tolerate the lectins in tomatoes.

Polyamines

Polyamines are the basic building blocks of plant and animal cells and are needed for growth, maintenance or development. Harmful polyamines are groups of amino acids that attract bacteria and pathogens and lead to the enlargement of organs like the stomach, liver, spleen and intestines. Meat that has deteriorated due to processing, shock treatment or freezing as well as fermented carbohydrate-laden foods stimulate polyamines to form in the gut. When the lining of the lower bowel has been damaged by grains and incompatible lectins, then large groups of polyamines begin to develop. Symptoms of high levels of gut polyamines are: foul breath, irrespective of good oral hygiene; fetid, odiferous stools; headaches in reaction to eating certain foods; high levels of triglycerides and LDL (bad) cholesterol, abdominal discomfort, flatulence and often chronic constipation.

Methods you can use to be tested for food tolerances

Health foods may not agree with you

So many people are tired, ill or overweight in spite of eating what they think are wholesome or healthy foods. If you battle with your weight or are still suffering from Candida or arthritis, something is wrong with your selection of "health" foods. We regard wheat, wheat germ, soya products, lentils and tomatoes as healthy and beneficial foods but if they are not tolerated by your blood type they will harm you in various ways. Either you react directly to foods with obvious symptoms such as: a headache, itching, unstable blood sugar, a rash or a mucous problem or you may experience the more long term effects like: arthritis, obesity, fatigue, cancer, bowel disorders or immunity problems.

No fixed diet can be 100% accurate

There can never be a perfect food list that suits you exactly as no two people have the same tolerances. Blood-type eating, at best, indicates the major troublemakers in your diet: the lectin containing foods that cause illness and obesity and foods that disrupt polyamine activity. A food allergy exclusion programme takes months of trial and error to identify foods that may harm you. A blood-type diet can easily be modified to suit your needs.

The QX or Quantum Xrroid system

Relax with your head, wrist and ankles strapped to wires that relay impulses from the QX device to a computer. Foods are tested on the sensor panel and an accurate reading of your tolerance to them is recorded. The foods tested usually tally with the blood-type lists you will be using in this book. Intolerances to certain foods that are particular to your constitution or condition can also be detected, regardless of your blood type. (See page 160.)

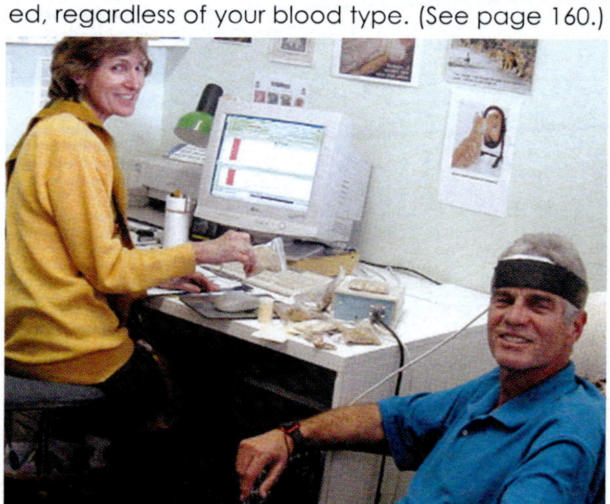

Electronic testing for food allergies

The Acumeasure and similar electronic devices determine the degree of sensitivity a person has to a food or toxin. A specimen is placed into the sensor cup that is attached to the machine. Probes on the patient's fingertips relay the degree of resistance the food or allergen produces on the body's energy fields. The dial on the meter will show your degree of tolerance to the food or offending substance. This is a very accurate indicator and can be used with the blood-type food lists in this book to determine your blood type and sub-type.

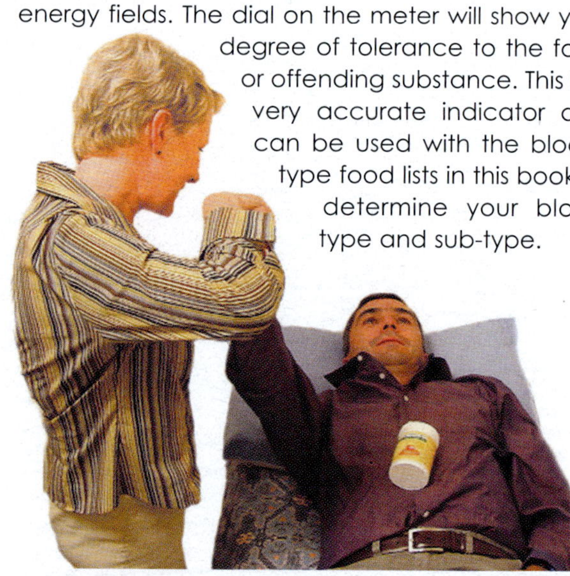

Muscle testing food with kinesiology

The strength of the anterior deltoid muscle is first tested by applying pressure to the patient's outstretched arm to determine the normal resistance. The patient is exposed to a substance and the arm is pushed down with the same pressure. If negative, the arm is weak and gives way easily. If beneficial, the patient's arm will resist the pressure. This technique gives reliable results but it depends on you remaining impartial to the specimen being tested. It is better to blind-test substances to rule out any type of mentally-induced bodily response. Experiment yourself, with an obvious toxin like a mothball in an opaque container versus a similar empty container. Keep these containers and try using the pendulum techniques on page 9.

How to test with a pendulum

Make a pendulum out of a ring or bead on a string or chain, or buy a dowsing pendant from a health shop. Hold the cord between your thumb and index finger and let it swing up and down, for a neutral indication over something inert, like an empty black photo cannister. Put a mothball or some bleach or paraffin into some other cannisters and allow the pendulum to swing over them. An anti-clockwise circular swing indicates it is harmful, even though you hold the cord with a steady hand. Now test over cannisters filled with olive oil, ginger, parsley or almonds for a positive indication. Your pendulum should swing to neutral, then change to a clockwise motion. Test each of the black cannisters until you get the correct results.

Using a pendulum without samples

When you know how to accurately use a pendulum, try the advanced technique of dowsing over pictures or words. Place a finger or pointer on the word with one hand and hold the pendulum with the other hand. The pendulum will give positive or negative indications when you think of having bleach, lemon, rat poison, wheat, apples, etc. Now watch how the pendulum changes when you concentrate on another person at the same time as you point to the word or sample in front of you.

Food tolerance indicates blood type

You can make yourself a test kit with samples of food listed in the four blood-type boxes below. An experienced person can work directly with the words to see if the results tally with those of the blood type. For the sub-type variant of each of the four blood types, use the columns on pages 16 - 21.

Blood type A	Result			
Brazil nuts	no			
sunflower seeds	yes			
beef biltong / jerky	no			
maize / cornflour	yes			
pearl barley	yes			

Blood type B	Result			
rye	no			
pumpkin seeds	no			
cow's milk powder	yes			
lentils	no			
oranges	yes			

Blood type AB	Result			
lentils	yes			
sunflower seeds	no			
beef biltong / jerky	no			
maize / cornflour	no			
pearl barley	yes			

Blood type O	Result			
rye	yes			
sunflower seeds	no			
beef biltong / jerky	yes			
wheat / flour / pasta	no			
pearl barley	no			

How to select suitable foods for your blood type

What blood type are you?

There are four major blood types: A, B, AB and O, regardless of positive or negative. A simple blood test will determine your blood type. Kinesiologists or therapists with electronic testing devices can confirm your blood type by testing your reaction to various foods. Learn how to use the pendulum yourself by following the instructions on page 9.

Are you a secretor or a non-secretor?

According to Peter D'Adamo's classification there is a sub-type or variant of the basic ABO blood typing system based on the secretor status. Our blood cells all have antigens present that modify specific food reactions. Antigens are discussed on page 7. Secretors also have antigens present in their saliva and other body fluids. These four secretor groups are classified as sub-types A^1, B^1, AB^1 and O^1 in the blood tables in this book.

A non-secretor only has antigens present on the blood cells. We refer to these non-secretors as sub-types or variants in the food lists. The four blood types: A^1, B^1, AB^1 and O^1, plus the four non-secretors: A^2, B^2, AB^2 and O^2 make a total of 8 categories.

A saliva test is used to determine your secretor status. Use a pendulum or applied kinesiology, as described on pages 8 and 9, for testing foods yourself. Work up and down the pair of columns for your blood type on pages 16 - 23 and your results should tally with type^1(secretor) or type^2 (non-secretor). If you can't use a pendulum, try kinesiology or consult a practitioner with an allergy-testing synchrometer or QX device to help you. (See page 8).

How to get started

When you have determined your blood type and secretor status, simply select the foods that are recommended in your colour-coded column and avoid those that are crossed out for you. Then combine them with the foods listed in the grey panels that suit everybody. There's plenty for you to eat, so don't give up! Explore the therapeutic and cookery sections in this book for recipes. Try to comply with the food recommendations by at least 80%. For example, cut out the dairy products, but allow yourself a splash of milk in your tea or coffee. If you are dairy- or lactose-intolerant you may need to replenish your intestinal flora from time to time. Take probiotic supplements or a few teaspoons of naturally cultured fresh farm yoghurt.

How to use the blood type tables

☺ Foods that are beneficial to you

😐 Foods that are neutral or tolerated

☒ Foods that are harmful in certain ways

😐☺ Suitable for all blood types

These foods are neutral or beneficial for all of us. They are listed separately in grey panels on each page as well as in the all-type section for foods on page 13. Combine them with the foods that suit your blood type A, B, AB or O and secretor variant (sub-type ^{1} or ^{2}) on the colour-coded lists.

☒ Not suitable for all blood types

These foods are harmful to you. Cut down your consumption to only 20% of your daily intake or avoid them totally if at all possible.

Your blood type is colour coded

Yellow: A^1 (secretor)

Pale yellow: A^2 (non-secretor)

Blue: B^1(secretor)

Pale blue: B^2 (non-secretor)

Green: AB^1 (secretor)

Pale green: AB^2 (non-secretor)

Pink: O^1 (secretor)

Pale pink: O^2 (non-secretor)

Keep up to date with Dr D'Adamo

Information from *Eat Right for your Type, Live Right for your Type* and *The Complete Blood Type Encyclopedia* by Peter D'Adamo was used to compile the blood type food lists in this book. It is a good idea to refer often to the research and updates available at the following website:

www.dadamo.com

This extensive data base interacts with blood type eaters from around the world. Thousands of case histories and scientific studies prove the efficacy of blood type eating, especially for weight control, mental disorders and chronic diseases.

General breakfast foods and baking ingredients

Food Tolerance	A^1	A^2	B^1	B^2	AB^1	AB^2	O^1	O^2
Starch / grains								
wheat flour	😐	☒	☒	☒	😐	😐	☒	☒
wholewheat	😐	☒	☒	☒	☺	☒	☒	☒
spelt flour	😐	😐	😐	😐	😐	😐	😐	☒
wheat germ	☒	☒	☒	☒	😐	☒	☒	☒
wheat bran	☒	☒	☒	☒	😐	😐	☒	☒
barley/flour	😐	😐	😐	😐	😐	😐	☒	☒
oats/flour	☺	😐	☺	😐	☺	☺	😐	☒
oat bran	😐	😐	☺	☺	☺	☺	😐	😐
rye flour	☺	☺	☒	☒	☺	☺	😐	😐
maize/cornflour	☺	☒	☒	☒	☒	☒	☒	☒
mealiemeal	☺	☒	☒	☒	☒	☒	☒	☒
soya beans	☺	😐	😐	☒	😐	😐	😐	☒
soya flour/milk	☺	😐	😐	☒	☺	☺	😐	☒
lentils/flour	☺	☺	☒	☒	😐	😐	☒	😐
sprouted lentils	☺	☺	😐	😐	☺	☺	😐	😐
chick peas/flour	☒	☒	☒	☒	☒	☒	😐	☒
buckwheat/flour	☺	😐	☒	☒	☒	☒	😐	☒
sorghum/flour	😐	😐	☒	😐	☒	☒	☒	☒
tapioca/flour	😐	😐	☒	😐	☒	☒	😐	☒
sago/flour	😐	😐	😐	😐	☒	☒	😐	☺
Seeds and nuts								
sesame seeds	😐	😐	☒	☒	☒	☒	😐	😐
sunflower seeds	😐	😐	☒	☒	☒	☒	☒	☒
pumpkin seeds	☺	☺	☒	☒	☺	☒	☺	☺
peanuts	☺	☺	☒	☒	☒	😐	☒	☒
coconut	☒	😐	☒	☒	☺	☒	☒	☒
walnuts	☺	☺	☺	☺	😐	☺	☺	☺
almonds	😐	😐	😐	😐	☒	😐	😐	😐
hazelnuts	😐	😐	☒	☒	😐	☒	😐	😐
Brazil nuts	☒	☒	😐	😐	😐	☒	☒	☒
cashew nuts	☒	☒	☒	☒	😐	☒	☒	☒
pistachio nuts	☒	☒	☒	☒	😐	☒	☒	☺
Fats / other foods								
dates	😐	😐	😐	😐	😐	😐	😐	☒
prunes	☺	☺	😐	😐	☒	☒	☺	☺
dried banana	☒	😐	☺	😐	😐	☒	☺	☺
dried apricot	☺	☺	😐	😐	😐	😐	😐	☒
sugar	😐	😐	😐	☒	😐	☒	😐	☒
honey	😐	😐	😐	😐	☒	☒	😐	☒
fructose	😐	😐	😐	☒	😐	☒	☒	☒
stevia	😐	😐	☒	😐	☒	😐	😐	☒
aspartame	☒	☒	☒	☒	☒	☒	☒	☒
dextrose	😐	☒	☒	☒	☒	☒	☒	☒
maltodextrin	😐	☒	☒	☒	😐	☒	☒	☒
cinnamon	😐	😐	☒	☒	😐	😐	😐	☒
vanilla	😐	😐	😐	😐	😐	😐	😐	☒
canola oil	😐	😐	☒	☒	☒	😐	😐	☒
sunflower oil	😐	😐	☒	☒	☒	☒	☒	☒
butter	☒	☒	😐	😐	☒	☒	😐	😐
cow's milk	☒	☒	☺	😐	☺	☒	☒	☒
yoghurt	😐	😐	☺	☺	☺	😐	☒	☒

😐☺ Suitable for all blood types

Millet flour or dehusked millet
Spelt flour: special wheat from a health shop
Oat and rice bran
Flaxseeds, especially ground up flaxseeds
Walnuts and almonds, raisins
Molasses: sweet desulphured or blackstrap
Olive oil: cold or for baking and cooking
Lemon juice and grated lemon rind and pith
Ginger: fresh or powdered
All rice products: flour, puffed rice, rice cakes
Rice flour can be used as a wheat substitute
Yellow pea flour: found at Indian spice shops
Liquorice powder: 50x sweeter than sugar
Popular baking flours with minor intolerances:
Oats and oat flour for all types except O^2
Rye flour for all types except B^1 and B^2
Soya flour for all types except B^2 and O^2

Many people have a wheat or gluten allergy.
Gluten is in: wheat, rye, oat and barley products.

☒ Not suitable for all blood types

Margarine: contains trans-fatty acids that are toxic and damage the immune system.
Sunflower oil (except $A^{1=2}$): when heated, it releases harmful trans-fatty acids.
Coconut (except A^2): it contains solid fatty acid chains that aggravate inflammation.
Wheat bran damages the colon.
Aspartame: harmful amino acid derivatives
Saccharine: overstimulates the pancreas
Maltodextrin: metabolic inhibitor (except A^1)
Dextrose: metabolic inhibitor (except A^1)
Baking powder: contains aluminium salts

Make this baking powder substitute:
3ml bicarbonate of soda with 2ml citric acid for every 5ml teaspoon of baking powder you need.
Also try 5ml cream of tartar, known as potassium

Fresh or dried fruits and vegetables and their juices

Food Tolerance	A^1	A^2	B^1	B^2	AB^1	AB^2	O^1	O^2
Fruit: dried / juice								
apple	😐	😐	😐	😐	😐	😐	😐	☒
apricot	☺	☺	😐	😐	😐	😐	😐	☒
pear	😐	😐	😐	😐	😐	😐	😐	☒
avocado	😐	😐	☒	☒	☒	☒	☒	☺
banana	☒	😐	☺	😐	☒	☒	☺	☺
blackberry	☺	☺	😐	☺	😐	☺	☒	☒
sweet melon	😐	☒	😐	☒	😐	☒	😐	😐
coconut	☒	😐	☒	☒	☒	☒	☒	☒
date	😐	😐	😐	😐	😐	😐	😐	☒
guava	😐	😐	😐	☺	☒	☒	☺	☺
kiwi fruit	😐	😐	😐	😐	☺	☺	☒	☒
mango	☒	😐	😐	😐	☒	☒	☺	☺
orange	☒	☒	😐	😐	☒	☒	☒	☒
pawpaw/papaya	☒	☒	☺	☺	😐	😐	😐	😐
pomegranate	😐	😐	☒	☒	☒	☒	😐	☺
prickly pear	😐	😐	☒	☒	☒	☒	😐	☺
quince	😐	😐	😐	😐	☒	☒	😐	😐
persimmon	😐	😐	☒	☒	☒	☒	😐	😐
starfruit	😐	😐	☒	☒	☒	☒	😐	😐
strawberry	😐	😐	😐	😐	😐	😐	😐	☒
naartjie/tangerine	☒	😐	😐	😐	😐	☒	☒	☒
litchi	😐	😐	😐	😐	😐	😐	☒	☒
aloe juice / tea	☺	☺	☒	☒	☒	☒	☒	☒
Vegetables								
cabbage	☒	☒	☺	😐	😐	😐	😐	☒
cauliflower	😐	😐	☺	☺	☺	☺	☒	☒
chilli pepper	☒	😐	😐	😐	☒	😐	😐	😐
Chinese cabbage	☒	☒	☺	😐	😐	😐	😐	☒
cucumber	😐	😐	😐	😐	😐	☺	☒	☒
eggplant	☒	😐	☺	😐	☺	☺	😐	☒
leek	☺	☺	😐	😐	😐	😐	☒	☒
button mushroom	☺	☒	😐	😐	😐	😐	☒	😐
Greek olive	☒	☒	☒	☒	😐	😐	😐	☒
green olive	😐	☒	😐	😐	😐	😐	😐	☒
green pepper	☒	😐	☺	😐	☒	☒	😐	😐
sweet potato	☒	☒	☺	☺	☺	☺	☺	😐
potato	☒	☒	😐	☒	😐	😐	☒	☒
pumpkin	☺	☺	☒	😐	😐	😐	☺	☺
radish	😐	😐	☒	☒	☒	☒	😐	😐
sauerkraut	☒	☒	😐	😐	😐	😐	😐	☒
tomato	☒	😐	☒	😐	😐	☺	😐	😐
yam	☒	☒	☺	☺	☺	☺	😐	😐
maize/sweetcorn	☺	😐	☒	☒	☒	☒	☒	☒
Sprouts / pickles								
alfalfa	☺	😐	😐	😐	☺	☺	☒	☒
mung bean	😐	😐	☒	☒	☒	☒	😐	😐
lentil / wheat	😐	😐	😐	😐	😐	😐	😐	😐
pickles from shop	☒	☒	😐	😐	☒	☒	☒	☒
capers	☒	☒	😐	😐	☒	☒	☒	☒

😐☺ Suitable for all blood types

Fruit

Offer a selection of the following fruits every day :

Grapes, raisins and grape juice
Grapefruit, lemon, lime and their juices
Peach, nectarine, plum
Pineapple and watermelon
Apples, apricots and pears suit all except O^2
Try to find fresh blueberries, loganberries, mulberries, kumquats, cherries, cranberries, red and black currants, figs, prunes, raspberries, youngberries, gooseberries and granadillas.

Choose from these "all type" fruits when you cater for many blood types at the same meal. Combine them with fruit that you buy to suit your own blood type for a delicious variety of beneficial fruit every day.

Vegetables

This group of vegetables is easy to obtain and forms the basis of any meal. Buy a regular supply and learn how to prepare tasty dishes from:

Spinach, onions, broccoli, Brussels sprouts, green beans, butternut, squashes of all types, beetroot (tops as well), carrots, parsnips, turnips, all types of lettuce, endives, celery, parsley, asparagus, green peas, courgettes (baby marrows), lentil sprouts, pimentoes, water chestnuts, oyster mushrooms and portabello mushrooms
Sweet potatoes suit everybody except A^1 and A^2

Look for fresh supplies of:
Ginger, garlic, horseradish, fennel, chives, watercress, basil, thyme, rosemary, majoram and sage for their unique flavours as well as many healing benefits

☒ Not suitable for all blood types

Some foods may adversely affect the formation of polyamines in the gut: they contain lectins or toxins that may be harmful (See page 7.)
Bitter melon (wild calabash)
Black olives that are too ripe or have fermented
Rhubarb can be toxic, even to insects and pests!

Beverages, dairy products and condiments

Food Tolerance	A^1	A^2	B^1	B^2	AB^1	AB^2	O^1	O^2
Beverages								
Ceylon/black tea	☒	😐	😐	☒	☒	☒	☒	☒
coffee	☺	☺	😐	☒	☒	☒	☒	☒
beer	☒	☺	😐	😐	😐	☒	☒	☒
spirits/liquor	☒	☒	☒	😐	☒	😐	☒	☒
soda water	☒	☒	☒	😐	😐	😐	☺	☺
red wine	☺	☺	😐	☺	😐	☺	😐	☺
white wine	😐	☺	😐	☺	😐	😐	☒	☒
apple cider	😐	😐	😐	😐	😐	😐	😐	☒
orange juice	☒	☒	☺	☺	☒	☒	☒	☒
Dairy products								
brie cheese	☒	☒	😐	😐	☒	☒	☒	☒
butter/buttermilk	☒	☒	😐	😐	☒	☒	😐	😐
casein in milk	☒	☒	😐	😐	😐	😐	☒	☒
camembert ch.	☒	☒	😐	☒	☒	☒	☒	☒
cheddar cheese	☒	☒	😐	☒	😐	😐	☒	☒
cottage cheese	☒	😐	☺	😐	☺	☺	☒	☒
edam cheese	☒	☒	😐	😐	😐	😐	☒	☒
emmenthaler ch.	☒	☒	😐	☒	😐	☒	☒	☒
feta cheese	😐	😐	☺	☺	☺	☺	😐	☒
goat's milk ch.	😐	😐	☺	☺	☺	😐	😐	☒
gouda cheese	☒	☒	😐	😐	😐	😐	☒	☒
gruyere cheese	☒	☒	😐	😐	😐	😐	☒	☒
cow's milk	☒	☒	☺	😐	😐	😐	☒	☒
goat's milk	😐	☒	☺	☺	☺	☺	☒	☒
mozzarella/buffalo	😐	😐	☺	☺	☺	☺	😐	☒
parmesan cheese	☒	☒	😐	☒	☒	☒	☒	☒
sour cream	😐	☒	😐	😐	☺	☺	☒	☒
whey powder	☒	☒	😐	☺	😐	😐	☒	☒
yoghurt	😐	😐	☺	☺	☺	😐	☒	☒
milk substitutes:								
soya milk	☺	😐	😐	☒	☺	☺	😐	☒
coffee creamer	☒	😐	☒	☒	😐	☒	☒	☒
Condiments								
miso (soya)	☒	☒	☒	☒	☺	☒	😐	☒
MSG	☒	☒	☒	☒	☒	☒	☒	😐
soya sauce	☺	😐	☒	☒	😐	😐	😐	☒
apple cider vin.	☒	☒	😐	😐	☒	☒	😐	☒
balsamic vinegar	☒	☒	😐	😐	☒	☒	☒	☒
mayonnaise	☒	☒	😐	😐	😐	😐	😐	☒
gelatine	☒	☒	☒	☒	☒	☒	😐	😐
vanilla	😐	😐	😐	😐	😐	😐	😐	☒
nutmeg	😐	😐	😐	😐	😐	😐	☒	😐
mace	😐	😐	😐	😐	😐	😐	☒	☒
cinnamon	😐	😐	☒	☒	😐	😐	😐	☒
chilli powder	☒	😐	😐	😐	😐	😐	😐	😐
aniseed	😐	😐	😐	😐	☒	☒	😐	😐
allspice	😐	😐	☒	☒	☒	☒	😐	😐
tahini/sesame	😐	😐	☒	☒	☒	☒	😐	😐
vinegar pickles	☒	☒	😐	😐	☒	☒	☒	☒

😐☺ Suitable for all blood types

Beverages

Green tea, red wine and red grape juice, rooibos tea, cocoa, carob, lemon juice and juice from suitable fruits and vegetables for all blood types

Dairy products

Feta cheese or goat's milk products except O^2
Substitute dairy milk with rice milk (avoid dextrose or maltodextrin additives and artificial flavours)

Condiments, spices and flavourings

Cocoa, carob, liquorice
Cardamom, cloves, coriander, caraway, bay leaf
Cumin, curry powder, dill, mustard, horseradish
Paprika, fennel, kaloontjie (black cumin or onion seeds are a good substitute for pepper)
Herbs: parsley, celery, mint, bergamot, chives, basil, thyme, sage, rosemary, majoram
Salt, but sea and herb salts are better
Add more potassium to salt with cream of tartar or the salt substitute called potassium chloride.

☒ Not suitable for all blood types

Black and white pepper: 98% of people do not tolerate pepper (For substitutes see pages 29, 60, 141)
2% of us are allergic to MSG (monosodium glutamate); it is found naturally in soya, grapes, potatoes and even breast milk! The Chinese extract MSG from soya beans
Gum acacia: use arrowroot products instead
Gelatine: usually contains pork unless derived from seaweed (agar-agar)
Synthetic colours and known irritants like tartrazine
Ingredients that you are allergic to: gluten, casein, salisylic acid, sodium benzoate, aspartame, etc.

Meat, seafood, fats, oils and popular starch accompaniments

Food Tolerance	A^1	A^2	B^1	B^2	AB^1	AB^2	O^1	O^2
Popular meats								
beef	☒	☒	😐	😐	☒	☒	☺	☺
chicken	😐	😐	☒	☒	☒	☒	😐	😐
duck	😐	☒	☒	☒	☒	☒	😐	😐
lamb	☒	☒	☺	☺	😐	😐	😐	😐
mutton	☒	😐	😐	😐	😐	😐	☺	☺
turkey	😐	☺	😐	😐	☺	☺	😐	😐
veal	☒	☒	😐	😐	☒	☒	☺	☺
venison	☒	☒	☺	☺	☒	😐	☺	☺
Popular seafood								
anchovy	☒	😐	☒	☒	☒	☒	😐	☒
cob/kabeljou	☺	☺	😐	☺	😐	😐	😐	😐
crab	☒	☒	☒	☒	☒	☒	😐	☒
haddock	☒	😐	☺	☺	☒	☒	😐	😐
hake	☒	😐	☺	☺	☒	☒	☺	☺
herring	☒	😐	😐	😐	😐	😐	☺	☺
crayfish/lobster	☒	☒	☒	☒	☒	☒	😐	😐
mussels	☒	😐	☒	☒	😐	😐	😐	😐
octopus	☒	😐	☒	☒	☒	☒	☒	☒
oyster	☒	☒	☒	☒	☒	☒	😐	😐
sole	☒	☒	☺	😐	☒	☒	☺	☺
snails (helix)	☺	☺	☒	😐	☺	☺	😐	😐
calamari	☒	☒	😐	😐	😐	😐	☒	☒
trout	😐	☺	☒	☒	☒	😐	☺	☺
yellowtail	😐	😐	☒	😐	☒	☒	😐	☺
Cooking fat and oil								
canola oil	😐	😐	☒	☒	😐	😐	😐	😐
coconut oil	☒	☒	☒	☒	☒	☒	☒	☒
peanut oil	☒	😐	☒	☒	☒	☒	☒	☒
sunflower oil	😐	😐	☒	☒	☒	☒	☒	☒
soya oil	😐	😐	☒	☒	😐	☒	☒	☒
sesame oil	😐	😐	☒	☒	☒	☒	😐	😐
butter	☒	☒	😐	😐	☒	☒	😐	😐
Starch and pulses								
fava beans	☺	😐	😐	😐	☒	😐	☒	😐
chick peas	☒	☒	☒	☒	☒	☒	😐	☒
kidney beans	☒	😐	☺	😐	☒	☒	☒	☒
lentils	☺	☺	☒	☒	😐	😐	☒	😐
mung beans	😐	😐	☒	☒	☒	☒	😐	😐
soya beans	☺	😐	😐	☒	☺	☺	😐	☒
tofu	☺	😐	☒	☒	☺	☺	😐	☒
yellow dried pea	☺	😐	😐	😐	😐	😐	😐	😐
green dried pea	☺	😐	😐	😐	😐	😐	😐	😐
pearl barley	☺	😐	😐	😐	😐	😐	☒	☒
buckwheat grain	☺	😐	☒	☒	☒	☒	😐	☒
pasta/wheat	😐	☒	☒	☒	😐	😐	☒	☒
potatoes	☒	☒	😐	☒	😐	😐	☒	☒
mealiemeal	☺	☒	☒	☒	☒	☒	☒	☒
couscous	①	☒	☒	☒	😐	😐	☒	☒

😐☺ Suitable for all blood types

Meat and seafood

Turkey is suitable for all blood types
Mutton suits all blood types except A^1
Ostrich meat is super lean and high in iron
Cob (kabeljou), tuna, mackerel, monkfish, mullet, salmon, sardines
Eggs suit everybody but are not eaten by vegans

Oils and fats

Olive oil and clarified butter, known as ghee
Canola oil suits all types except B^1 and B^2

Starches, grains and pulses

White cannellini beans, white broad beans
All rice products: noodles, health rice, puffed rice
Millet grains (dehusked) and millet flour
Dried green and yellow peas and the flour
Barley suits everybody except O^1 and O^2

Fish oil is rich in Omega 3 essential fatty acids.
Flaxseed oil is a plant source of Omega 3 oils.

☒ Not suitable for all blood types

Pork: provokes abnormal blood reactions, inhibits gastric function, increases disease susceptability
Margarine contains harmful trans-fatty acids
Coconut oil, corn oil and cottonseed oil
Peanut oil is only for type A^2
Wheat bran: harms the intestinal lining
Wheat gluten and wheat germ for most people, especially those with allergies or the leaky-gut syndrome. (See page 42 and 43.)

The foods recommended for your blood type are free of lectins

☒ All blood types must avoid lectins

Lectins are blood type specific. Use all the colour coded tables to identify the foods that suit your blood type: ☺ beneficial or 😐 neutral. The major clash is caused by foods containing lectins. The foods marked with ☒ contain lectins as well as substances that upset polyamine development, increase levels of damaged cells or disrupt pH balances in your blood type. Certain antigens you have on your blood cells or the ones you secrete in bodily fluids can deflect these lectins. Some foods even contain beneficial lectins that fight cancer, so it is important to know your blood type and subtype for specific reactions to food-based lectins. See lectins and polyamines on page 7.

☒ A The worst foods for you

Kidney beans, lima beans, chick peas, potatoes, sweet potatoes, pork, lamb, beef, venison, dairy products, crab, calamari, oyster, sole, coconut oil, butter, cabbage, aubergine, tomatoes
A^1 : banana, coconut. A^2 : wheat, maize

☒ B The worst foods for you

Lentils, chicken, duck, maize, peanuts, sesame seeds, rye, chick peas, mung beans, pumpkin & seeds, tomatoes, anchovy, crayfish, trout, mussels, most wheat and soya products, sunflower seeds, canola oil, avocado, coconut products

☒ AB The worst foods for you

Chicken, maize, buckwheat, lima and kidney beans, mung beans, chick peas, sago, coconut, sorghum, sesame seeds, banana, pumpkin seeds, sunflower seeds, orange, green pepper, crayfish, hake, octopus, sole, yellowtail, veal

☒ O The worst foods for you

Wheat, barley, kidney beans, peanuts, maize, cabbage, cauliflower, Brussels sprouts, dairy products
O^1:avocado, lentils, anchovies, button mushrooms
O^2: oats, soya products, chick peas, buckwheat, tapioca, aubergine, sunflower seeds

These lectins cause weight gain, cancer, digestive problems, arthritis, brain fog, mucous or weakened immunity and autoimmune conditions.

😐☺ Lectin-free foods for all types

1 Breakfast and baking ingredients

Rice: puffed, rice cakes and rice flour
Oats for all except O^2, millet flour or dehusked millet, spelt flour
Oat and rice bran, flaxseeds, especially ground-up
Walnuts and almonds, raisins, sweet desulphured or blackstrap molasses
Olive oil and ghee: cold or for baking and cooking
Lemon juice and grated lemon rind and pith
Yellow pea flour found at Indian spice shops
Liquorice powder: 50x sweeter than sugar

2 Fruit

Grapes, raisins and grape juice, grapefruit, peach, nectarine, plum, lemon, lime and their juices
Pineapple and watermelon
Apples, apricots and pears suit all except O^2
Blueberry, loganberry, mulberry, cherry, cranberry, red- and black currant, figs, prunes, raspberry, youngberry, gooseberry, kumquat and granadilla

3 Vegetables

Spinach, onions, broccoli, Brussels sprouts, green beans, butternut, squashes of all types, beetroot (tops as well), carrots, parsnips, turnips, lettuce, endives, parsley, asparagus, green peas, courgettes (baby marrows), celery, water chestnuts, pimentoes, and oyster or portabello mushrooms
Sweet potatoes suit everybody except A^1 and A^2

4 Herbs and spices

Look for fresh supplies of: parsley, celery, ginger, garlic, horseradish, fennel, chives, watercress, basil, thyme, rosemary, majoram and sage for their unique flavours as well as healing benefits

5 Legumes and grains

Small white beans and broad beans, cannellini beans, butter beans, millet, quinoa, kiwicha
Sprouted lentils 4 days old
All rice: noodles, health rice, puffed rice

6 Meat, fish and dairy products

Ostrich, cob / kabeljou, mackerel, monkfish, mullet, salmon, sardines, tuna, eggs and turkey

7 Beverages

Green tea, red wine, rooibos tea, cocoa, carob, lemon juice as well as juice from suitable fruits and vegetables for all blood types
Drink plenty of water every day. (See page 99.)

Blood type A: are you a secretor or a non-secretor?

Food Tolerance	A^1 secretor	A^2 non-secretor
wheat flour	😐	☒
wholewheat	😐	☒
mealies/cornflour	😐	☒
mealie meal	😐	☒
coconut	☒	😐
banana	☒	😐
mango	☒	😐
spanspek	😐	☒
naartjie/tangerine	☒	😐
chilli pepper	☒	😐
aubergine	☒	😐
button mushroom	☺	☒
green olive	😐	☒
green pepper	☒	😐
tomato	☒	😐
mutton	☒	😐
duck	😐	☒
anchovy	☒	😐
haddock	☒	😐
hake	☒	😐
herring	☒	😐
mussels	☒	😐
octopus	☒	😐
peanut oil	☒	😐
kidney beans	☒	😐
pasta	😐	☒
Ceylon tea	☒	😐
beer	☒	😐
cottage cheese	☒	😐
goat's milk	😐	☒

Peanuts are beneficial for blood type A because they help to ward off harmful lectins that cause cancer and weaken the immune system. The peanuts you buy may contain aflatoxins and rancid oils. It is better to roast them yourself. Sunflower seeds are exclusively for type A and are a rich source of vitamin E. Other blood types should not eat too many peanuts or sunflower seeds.

How to find your sub-type A^1 or A^2

Once you know you are blood type A, you can use the list on the left to find out your secretor status. If you are a non-secretor, you only have antigens on the blood cells and do not secrete extra antigens in your saliva or digestive system like a secretor.

Test yourself on each of the foods using a technique that works best for you: either kinesiology, a pendulum or an electronic device. Make a tick next to each result in the appropriate column. The column with the most ticks will determine your sub-type, known as your secretor status. As you can see by the variations on the list, there are two distinct groups of individuals within the A blood type.

Food that makes blood type A fat

Kidney beans, lima beans, chick peas
Sweet potatoes, potatoes, especially potato chips
The above products contain lectins that bind to insulin receptors and stimulate the growth of fat.
Pork, lamb, beef, venison, dairy products
A^1 secretor: banana, coconut products
A^2 non-secretor: wheat and maize products
Cabbage blocks thyroid function and slows down metabolism so foods turn to fat instead of energy.

Avoid foods with harmful lectins for type A^1 and A^2:
Wheat germ and bran, milk (see pages 11-14)
Lectins in these foods can cause metabolic upsets if they are eaten in large amounts every day.

The stressed A gains weight easily

Don't comfort yourself by eating carbohydrates when you feel stressed. Rather eat sensibly.
Eat fruit like grapes, apples, pears, pineapple, etc. instead of cakes, chocolates or chips between meals. Take a deep breath when you get uptight or meditate, go for a walk, do Yoga or T'ai Chi.

Food that makes blood type A thin

All leafy green vegetables like spinach, broccoli, kale, lettuce, bok choy, celery and parsley
A^2 can substitute wheat products with millet and rye. Buy or learn how to make your own bread, cakes, biscuits etc. from grains that suit your type.
Eat lean chicken, ostrich, turkey and oily fish with vegetables and salads instead of starches like rice.
Type A vegetarians can eat lentils, soya and white cannellini beans to substitute for meat. They should also supplement with amino acids or foods high in chlorophyll, like spirulina, spinach or wheat grass.

Blood type A: general characteristics and health advice

Blood type A

Blood type A is best suited to a vegetarian diet and most grains and pulses are well tolerated by them. They were originally cultivators of the land and lived on fruit, vegetables and grains as opposed to the hunter-gatherer type O who thrived on meat and a meagre selection of fruits and vegetables. The type A digestive system is usually delicate and too much milk causes a lot of mucous, sinusitis and asthma. Low hydrochloric acid levels in the stomach make red meats ond fat difficult to digest.

Heart and cholesterol problems

Blood type A's can tolerate eggs, chicken and fish but they cannot cope with rich, fatty meats. These burden the system and lead to heart and cholesterol problems. Ironically, it is not the fat and eggs as much as the protein in red meats that increases levels of homocysteine, a toxic substance that oxidises cholesterol. Vitamin C, B6 and B3 are needed to prevent this from happening. Cholesterol collects around damaged areas on blood vessels to repair and waterproof them. Acidic waste material gets trapped around the weak spots and causes plaque formation. This blocks and narrows the blood vessels. A-type blood clots easily.

Carbohydrates like wheat flour, maize and, of course, sugar are converted to triglycerides (also known as low density cholesterol) when the body does not requiremore glucose for energy. A lack of antioxidants and essential Omega 3 fatty acids inhibits the formation of the good, high density cholesterol. This may explain why type A vegetarians or vegans can have high cholesterol levels even though no meat, fat or eggs are eaten.

Weaker immune systems

The type A immune system is usually very slack. A's are prone to cancer, infectious diseases, anemia and heart disease, as well as skin and fungal infections. Some forms of cancer are tolerated by their systems if there is an antigen present to mask it. In contrast, blood type O's immediately react to any form of cancer, providing the liver is healthy. The immune system can be boosted with olive leaf products, alfalfa, echinachea, vitamin C, B-vitamins, zinc, chrome and selenium. The system should be kept alkaline with calcium and magnesium supplements. Snails, fremented soya products and raw or sprouted peanuts are of specific benefit to the type A immune system.

Stress reactions and cortisol

A's pump out cortisol in reaction to stress. Excess cortisol leads to insulin resistance, causing obesity. Obesity in turn leads to cortisol resistance and hormonal imbalances that lead to an increase in appetite. Strenuous exercise is not a solution for stress as the A-types favour the burning of muscle tissue as opposed to the breakdown of body fat.

Type A's are more vulnerable to stress-related disorders and need to balance their cortisol levels. They should keep to a strict routine of regular meals, small snacks and the old-fashioned habit of "early to bed and early to rise." This helps to maintain the circadian rhythm so cortisol can be released according to day and night conditions.

This group responds emotionally and intellectually to stress and the mind must be calmed down during milder forms of exercises like T'ai Chi, Push Hands, Aikido or Yoga, cycling, hiking, golf or swimming. Highly active competitive sports, strenuous aerobics, muscle-toning circuits or heavy contact fighting should be monitored so that the immune system is not affected and adrenal burnout or muscle wasting do not occur. Green tea and adaptogens like ginseng and don quai (angelica) are recommended for stress. (See pages 83 and 104.)

Prone to cancer because of antigens

A's are more prone to cancer than any of the other blood types. They have blood type antigens that are friendly to cells that have a potential for developing into cancer. Stick to the blood type A diet and stimulate the immune system with supplements. A healthy liver will help to destroy cancerous cells at an early stage, so look after your liver.

Type A secretors

When extra antigens are secreted, more protection is offered to deflect lectins that interfere with your digestion, metabolism and immune system.

Type A non-secretors

All non-secretors are more vulnerable to microbial and immune-related disorders like arthritis, urinary tract infections, gastric ulcers and Candida infections. Auto-immune disorders like multiple sclerosis, Grave's disease, ankylosing spondylitis, rheumatoid arthritis, lupus, fibromyalgia, etc. are more prevalent. A controlled diet is essential to prevent the onset of type 2 diabetes and heart disease.

Blood type B: are you a secretor or a non-secretor?

Food Tolerance	B^1 secretor	B^2 non-secretor
soya beans	☺	☒
soya flour/milk	☺	☒
sorghum/flour	☒	☺
tapioca/flour	☒	☺
sugar	☺	☒
fructose	☺	☒
stevia	☒	☺
sweet melon	☺	☒
potato	☺	☒
pumpkin	☒	☺
tomato	☒	☺
snails	☒	☺
yellowtail	☒	☺
spirits/liquor	☒	☺
soda water	☒	☺
camembert ch.	☺	☒
cheddar cheese	☺	☒
emmenthaler	☺	☒
parmesan ch.	☺	☒

Oranges are good for blood type B. Some people instinctively avoid oranges because they experience acidity. In other blood groups, oranges increase the levels of polyamines in the bowels in response to damage caused by food lectins.

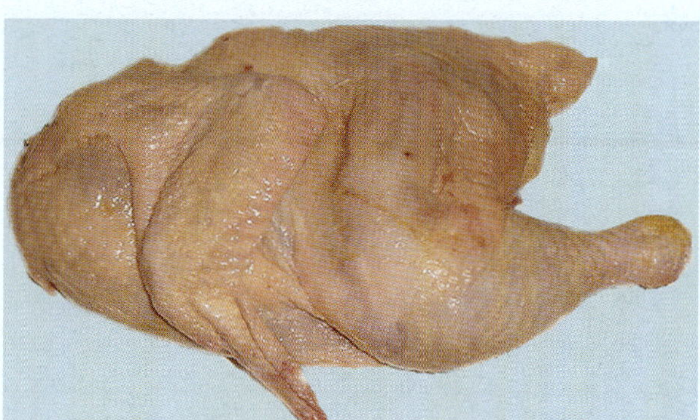

Chicken and duck are bad for blood type B. They contain harmful lectins for B's who do not have any suitable antigens to deflect them. Rather cut out the chicken and settle for turkey, hot or cold!

How to find your sub-type B^1 or B^2

Once you know you are blood type B, you can use the list on the left to find out your secretor status. If you are a non-secretor, you only have antigens on the blood cells and do not secrete extra antigens in your saliva or digestive system like a secretor.

Test yourself on each of the foods using a technique that works best for you: either kinesiology, a pendulum or an electronic device. Make a tick next to each result in the appropriate column. The column with the most ticks will determine your subtype, known as your secretor status. As you can see by the variations on the list, there are two distinct groups of individuals within the B blood type.

Foods that make blood type B fat

These products contain lectins that bind to insulin receptors and stimulate the accumulation of fat:
Lentils (lentil sprouts, 4 days old are beneficial, see page 110), pumpkin seeds, rye, peanuts, wheat products, maize products and sweetcorn, mung beans, sesame seeds, chick peas, buckwheat
Canola oil, sunflower oil, coconut, avocado
Chicken is a particular hazard to blood type B.
B^2: soya products can disrupt hormone activity

B^2 non-secretors gain weight easily

Type B^2, like O^2, does not secrete antigens to deflect the lectins in soya products so they can cause extreme obesity. This is due to the effect of phytoestrogens in soya that disrupt thyroid activities. Vegetarians in this group cannot tolerate soya, wheat and most other starches and sugars. These foods make them more prone to obesity and increase their risk of getting cancer.

Food to make blood type B healthy

Oranges can benefit blood type B the most
Dairy products, especially milk and most cheeses
All leafy green vegetables like kale, spinach, broccoli, lettuce, celery and parsley
Beef, lamb, mutton, turkey, veal and venison
Substitute wheat and soya products with millet and rice or barley. Learn how to make your own breads, cakes, biscuits etc. using the grains best suited to you. See the baking section on pages 144-148. Watch out for sugar and carbohydrate cravings, especially when you feel stressed.
Eat lean meat, fish, vegetables and salads. Have smaller meals more frequently to lose weight.

Blood type B: general characteristics and health advice

Type B is a good all-rounder

Blood type O is a hunter-gatherer and thrives on meat as opposed to the cereal-loving A's who have adapted well to vegetarian diets. The B blood type is a bit of both, with a tolerance to dairy products as a bonus. Under normal circumstances, their constitutions are balanced and tough. When out of balance, B's become very ill.

Sorry, no chicken!

B's have a peculiar intolerance to chicken and duck. Most B's who say they feel OK, just need to look at their waistlines to see what happens when they eat too much chicken, too often. These meats contain lectins for which blood type B does not have an antigen. These lectins, as well as many others, are responsible for diabetes, obesity, arthritis and some of the mysterious age-related diseases like multiple sclerosis or rare viral and autoimmune diseases that affect this blood type. Call it a foul twist of fate but lectins are blood-specific.

Blood type B is advised cut out chicken or replace it with ostrich or turkey if they want to experience an improvement in their health. Next, they must cut out the offending foods, especially the carbohydrates for their blood type and find substitutes.

Syndrome X strikes hardest at the B's

Blood type B produces more cortisol in response to stress than the other blood types and unlike the O's, who work it off with heavy exercise, cortisol affects blood type B adversely as they are prone to developing cortisol resistance. Excess cortisol then shuts down thyroid activity, slows down the metabolism and encourages insulin resistance. This in turn plays havoc with the waistline,causing Syndrome X, well known for the collective symptoms of diabetes, obesity, high blood pressure, heart and cholesterol problems, arthritis, asthma and Alzheimer's.

Stress is not as much to blame as the excessive consumption of food-based lectins, especially from carbohydrates. When you comfort-eat in response to stress and sit around munching endless sweet starchy goodies, you become a physician's best friend!. At all times, blood type B has to monitor stress levels and keep the output of cortisol to a minimum to avoid cortisol resistance. Cortisone therapy is not the best option when one is cortisol-resistant. Take adaptogens (see page 83) and try the cleansing diet on page 31.

Blood type B has a herding instinct

Believe it or not, most of the best club leaders and successful networkers have type-B blood coursing in their veins. They have an easy-going nature and are usually well-balanced, providing they are not provoked and start to pump out too many adrenal hormones, especially cortisol! Originally, the B blood group adapted to a nomadic style of life, tending to their herds, living off dairy products and having no fixed abode. Their tolerance to dairy products is the widest of all the blood types and they can enjoy milk, yoghurt and most of our favourite cheeses with impunity. It is rare to find these people with a lactose or a casein intolerance but some type B's do have this problem, so it is best to always test for food intolerances first.

Supplements for stress and digestion

Cortisol activity makes the body acidic, so supplement with calcium and magnesium. Take lecithin, digestive enzymes and herbal bitters to aid digestion. For stress, herbal adaptogens like ginseng, don quai (angelica) and St John's wort are very beneficial to blood type B. The amino acid DPLA (DL phenylalanine) and vitamin B5 can also help. To improve insulin sensitivity, boost your levels of antioxidants like vitamin C and E. The organic form of sulphur called MSM (methylsulphonylmethane) lowers blood sugar when combined with vitamin C. Also take zinc and chrome supplements.

Lifestyle and exercise

Cortisol release is affected by one's attitude to life. Remain calm, easy-going, happy and balanced in your daily activities to avoid cortisol-related problems. Unfortunately we live in a modern world full of strife, territorial issues and materialistically-based ideals. The competitive edge is well-embedded in blood type B and this is what most of the stress is about for these people. Blood type A or AB have a natural aptitude for meditation and spiritual development and this is their best way of coping with stress. Blood type B needs to handle stress in a different way: creative visualisation, positve planning and activities that centre and balance the mind and body work best for them. Try Qi Gong, T'ai Chi, meditaiton, yoga and breathing exercises, hiking, cycling or swimming. However, for a good fat-burning workout, B's can also excel at Karate, aerobics, Kickboxing, Kung Fu, rowing and any hard or competitive physical activities.

Blood type AB: are you a secretor or a non-secretor?

Food Tolerance	AB[1] secretor	AB[2] non-secretor
wholewheat	☺	☒
wheat germ	😐	☒
Brazil nuts	😐	☒
cashew nuts	😐	☒
pistachio nuts	😐	☒
prunes	😐	☒
sugar	😐	☒
honey	😐	☒
sweet melon	😐	☒
naartjie/tangerine	😐	☒
chilli pepper	☒	😐
cayenne pepper	☒	😐
venison	☒	😐
trout	☒	😐
soya oil	😐	☒
fava beans	☒	😐
spirits/liquor	☒	😐
beer	😐	☒
emmenthaler	😐	☒
coffee creamer	😐	☒
miso(soya)	☺	☒

AB secretors and non-secretors

The difference between secretors and non-secretors is not so well-defined in this blood group. This is because AB is a combination of A and B and shares many common antigens. AB shares blood type A's vulnerability to attacks on the digestive, cardiovascular and immune systems. The AB cancer risk is more severe than type A but the type B inclination to suffer from slow-growing bacterial infections is far less. AB is a hybrid blood type and the blood type diet has to be strictly adhered to in order to lessen the disease risks that are caused by lectins in food.

AB's with Celiac disease are prone to gluten intolerances, regardless of blood type recommendations. Wheat is a major source of gluten. Gluten is also found in rye, barley and oats. Test with a practitioner for individual sensitivities.

How to find your sub-type AB[1] or AB[2]

Once you know you are blood type AB, you can use the list on the left to find out your secretor status. If you are a non-secretor, you only have antigens on the blood cells and don't secrete antigens in your saliva or digestive system like a secretor.

Test yourself on each of the foods using a technique that works best for you: either kinesiology, a pendulum or an electronic device. Make a tick next to each result in the appropriate column. The column with the most ticks will determine your subtype, known as your secretor status. As you can see by the variations on the list, there are two distinct groups of individuals within the AB blood type.

AB foods to strictly avoid

Chicken and duck, maize, buckwheat, lima beans and kidney beans, chick peas, coconut, sago, sesame, sunflower and pumpkin seeds
These foods contain lectins that bind to insulin receptors and stimulate the accumulation of fat or aggravate cell agglutination.

AB eating habits to reduce stress

Have a good breakfast and a few small meals eaten at regular intervals. Red meat is not your main source of protein so eat more soya and fish. Don't drink coffee, undereat or skip a meal when you feel upset or threatened. Caffeine or fasting triggers the release of adrenalin and noradrenaline. AB's tend to oversecrete these hormones.
Eat foods rich in potassium or take supplements to increase the alkalinity of your digestive tract.

AB needs to increase NK activity

The NK (natural killer) cells of the immune system have to keep functioning and their numbers should be replenished as one gets older. Rather maintain them than run out and succumb to pathogenic invasions. AB's immune systems are very vulnerable because of the extra antigens they have inherited from blood type A as well as B.

Boost natural killer cell activity with herbs like olive leaf, echinachea, the amino acid L-lysine, anti-oxidants and soya products, especially the fermented varieties that are rich in natural enzymes.
Take adequate multi-vitamin supplements with plenty of minerals, especially zinc. A diet rich in fresh fruit and vegetables and the avoidance of lectin-laden foods will get you off to a good start.

Blood type AB: general characteristics and health advice

The AB enigma

People with blood type AB comprise only 2% - 5% of the population and are unique in their make-up. They share the O-type response to stress. They have an A-type digestive profile with a tolerance to most grains, yet they share the meat preferences of type B but without all of the dairy-friendly antigens. When it comes to genetically inherited tendencies to diseases, they take on some of the weaknesses as well as the strengths of blood type A and B.

The AB blood type is accommodating and easy-going by nature and is well-liked. With the balancing effect of blood type B and the sensitive nature of A, many alternative therapists and spiritual healers are blood type AB. They adapt well to vegetarian diets and simple eating habits, often as a result of a spiritual path. By nature they are helpful, non-materialistic and seldom violent yet they have a fixed mindset and can be stubborn. They often take themselves too seriously, however, due to a low self-esteem that can result from lower dopamine levels. People with low dopamine levels are usually introverted and prone to depression, manic or bipolar disorders. Their movements can become clumsy and unco-ordinated and children can suffer from ADD, whilst adults are vulnerable to Parkinson's disease. Supplements like guarana and other dopamine boosters may be helpful.

Low stomach acid triggers disease

Low stomach acid causes problems with the digestion of fatty foods and meat, regardless of being tolerant to beef and lamb. This makes them prone to heart disease and high levels of LDL (low density, called "bad" cholesterol). Digestive upsets make the liver vulnerable to the formation of gallstones or jaundice. Both the colon as well as the stomach are prone to cancer.

Another problem with low stomach acid is a vulnerability to parasitses that are not wiped out by high-intensity hydrochloric acid prior to entering the digestive tract. As a result, E-coli and Shighella bacteria can get the upper hand. E-coli can cause stomach ulcers. Bacteria often erodes the top stomach valve, allowing acid to leak upwards.

Diseases like osteoporosis take their toll when calcium cannot be ionised by the correct pH of gastric acid and thus the bones do not receive enough calcium to achieve their maximum density.

Problems with immunity and cancer

AB shares an A-type immune-friendly disorder in that cancer cells and other pathogens are often tagged with a body-friendly antigen that escapes the watchful eye of the immune system. Whereas type O would immediately squelch the offenders, type AB tolerates and often welcomes them as a part of its own constitution. In a system that has become acidic and is plugged up with lectins that cause cell agglutination, cancerous cells are not easily detected or eliminated.

Rheumatic heart disease, kidney disease, leaky gut and Celiac disease are prevalent in this group. Celiac disease is a gluten intolerance and even if foods may suit blood type AB, gluten has to be eliminated. Gluten is found in wheat, rye, barley and oats. (See page 42.) Leaky gut can also result from a gluten intolerance as well as a sensitivity to casein, the protein found in milk and yoghurt.

Chronic viral and bacterial infections

Viral infections and even a simple cold or flu can linger with AB's for many weeks and never seem to clear up. A weakened immune system increases the risk of low-grade infections from attacking the system. When chronically ill, AB's tend to introspect and get depressed or even become manic. They are more vulnerable to drug addiction and substance abuse when they are ill or upset.

The AB formula for stress

Adapt to situations in your own time and try to become more outgoing. Increase your dopamine status as this will make you more confident and self-assured. Do a lot of strenuous aerobic exercise at least twice a week and be wary of competitive sports if they make you feel self-conscious or uncomfortable in front of large groups of people.

The AB group reacts spiritually to stress and needs an outlet for creative energy. They require time alone and activities to do by themselves on a regular basis to keep up a balanced lifestyle. Recommended exercises are: T'ai Chi and Aikido, Hatha Yoga, swimming, cycling, dancing, aerobics, hiking and brisk walking.

Supplement with antioxidants, immune boosters, adaptogens for stress plus calcium and magnesium for alkalinity. Take digestive enzymes, vitamin B5 and betaine HCL to strengthen stomach acid.

Blood type O: are you a secretor or a non-secretor?

Food Tolerance	O^1 secretor	O^2 non-secretor
oats/flour	😐	☒
spelt flour	😐	☒
soya beans	😐	☒
soya flour/milk	😐	☒
tofu	😐	☒
lentils/flour	☒	😐
chick peas/flour	😐	☒
buckwheat/flour	😐	☒
tapioca/flour	😐	☒
sesame seeds	😐	☒
pistachio nuts	☒	😐
dates	😐	☒
sugar	😐	☒
honey	😐	☒
stevia	😐	☒
cinnamon	😐	☒
vanilla	😐	☒
canola oil	😐	☒
apple	😐	☒
apricot	😐	☒
pear	😐	☒
avocado	☒	☺
strawberry	😐	☒
cabbage	☒	☺
aubergine	😐	☒
button mushroom	☒	😐
green olive	😐	☒
sauerkraut	☒	😐
anchovy	😐	☒
crab	😐	☒
apple cider	😐	☒
feta cheese	😐	☒
goat's milk ch.	😐	☒
buffalo mozzarella	😐	☒
miso (soya)	😐	☒
MSG	☒	😐
soya sauce	😐	☒
cider vinegar	😐	☒

Wheat products are not suitable for blood type O. They cause mucous problems and weight gain.

How to find your sub-type O^1 or O^2

Once you know you are blood type O, you can use the list on the left to find out your secretor status. If you are a non-secretor, you only have antigens on blood cells and do not secrete other antigens in the saliva or digestive system like a secretor.

Test yourself on each of the foods using a technique that works best for you: either kinesiology, a pendulum or an electronic device. Make a tick next to each result in the appropriate column. The column with the most ticks will determine your subtype, known as your secretor status. As you can see by the variations on the list, there are two distinct groups of individuals within the O blood type.

Food that makes blood type O fat

All wheat products: bread, pasta, flour, wheat germ and wheat bran, sweetcorn and maize products, kidney beans, barley and peanuts
Lentils, especially for O^1 (lentil sprouts are OK)
These foods contain lectins that bind to insulin receptors and stimulate the accumulation of fat.

Cabbage blocks thyroid function in O^1 but the fresh juice is good, especially for gastric ulcers. Brussels sprouts and cauliflower block the thyroid function and this slows down the metabolic rate so that food turns to fat instead of energy.

O^2 non-secretors gain weight easily

In addition to the above foods, the O^2 group must avoid oats, spelt flour, soya products, chick peas, buckwheat, tapioca, sesame seeds, dates, honey and sugar. They are to be avoided because type O^2 does not secrete antigens to deflect the lectins these foods contain. Soya products can cause extreme obesity due to the anabolic effect of the phytoestrogens in them. Vegetarians in this group who do not eat meat, fish or eggs cannot tolerate soya, wheat and most of the starches and sugars. These carbohydrates can be very fattening.

Food that makes blood type O thin

Kelp, seafood, iodised salt
Liver, red meat and biltong/jerky without the fat
All leafy green vegetables like kale, spinach, lettuce, broccoli and parsley. Substitute wheat and soya products with millet and rye. Learn how to make your own breads, cakes, biscuits etc. Eat lean meat, vegetables and salads to lose weight.

Blood type O: general characteristics and health advice

Type O is a lean mean machine

The O blood type originated as a hunter-gatherer, designed to endure long days of trekking about combined with heavy physical activity in spite of small or infrequent meals. A strong immune system and very active adrenal glands enable this type of person to easily feed on bodily reserves of fat should the need arise. With high stomach acid levels, the hunter lived on fresh meat and the fruit or vegetables that grew in his territory.

Type O^2, the non-secretor, was originally a lean mean machine that was well adapted to eating meat and very few carbohydrates. Blood type O^1 secretes antigens in saliva and other bodily fluids and can cope with more items on the O-type list of modern foods containing starch or sugar. It is important to determine your secretor status.

Causes of type O illness and obesity

Today it is evident that most blood type O's have not adapted well to a modern diet of sugar, wheat and other grains. When exercise is neglected and these foods are eaten, they begin to suffer from mucous problems. They become prone to obesity, thyroid disorders and gastric or digestive upsets. They suffer from stomach ulcers, Celiac's disease, irritable bowel syndrome and Chronn's disease.

Type O wheat addiction

On the wrong diet, O's suffer from mucous problems, especially post-nasal drip, hay fever, asthma and snoring. As soon as wheat is removed from the diet, these symptoms vanish! Bread contains a lot of the amino acid tyrosine and this makes them feel well emotionally, so they crave wheat. Tyrosine supplements and meat alleviate a wheat craving.

Thyroid and autoimmune disorders

Leaky gut or permeable membranes usually result from eating wheat products. When undigested protein escapes into the bloodstream from a damaged gut lining, it carries codes that alert the ever-suspicious O-type immune system. Some of these codes resemble thyroid, adrenal or pancreatic tissue. The result? A wipeout of thyroid, pancreatic and adrenal function. Autoimmune diseases like lupus, fibromyalgia or rheumatoid arthritis whereby the body begins to attack its own tissue, are common. Foods containing a lot of lectins and estrogenic substances such as are found in lentils for O^1 and in soya for O^2 can disrupt thyroid function.

Gastro-oesphagal reflux disease

Type O's with strong gastric acid can suffer severely from eating the wrong foods and get burning sensations in the upper abdomen and chest. There is no point in taking an antacid and still eating wheat, especially bread and pasta. Eat right for your blood type and these acidity problems can clear up without the need for surgery or medicines.

Syndrome X in blood type O

This is a combination of obesity, high triglycerides and insulin resistance, all stemming from eating lectin-containing foods like wheat, lentils, maize, etc. Unchecked, this condition leads to diabetes.

The vegetarian O^2 non-secretor

Being a type O vegan goes against the grain, but not quite so badly as eating the wrong grains! Vegetarians of this blood type who eat a lot of soya, lentils, barley, wheat, cheese and other foods to compensate for not eating meat have to face a more serious challenge. They are prone to allergies, mucous problems, fatigue, water retention and obesity. Avoiding cow's milk and other offending lectins in food would alleviate many of these ailments. With sufficient discipline, O^2 vegans and vegetarians, can be healthy, happy eaters, remaining lean and mean, despite obstacles they face with a limited choice of starches and grains.

Protein is made by the body and there is sufficient raw material provided by legumes, fresh fruit and vegetables to maintain tissues. Spirulina and amino acid supplementation is beneficial to make up for any anticipated need for protein. Soya is not suitable for O^2. Quinoa grain contains all the essential amino acids and is a complete protein. Vitamin B12 supplements are recommended and they have to be taken in the form of injections or sublingual lozenges. For iron deficiencies, take blackstrap molasses or Ferrum Phos. (See page 75.)

Exercise is a top priority

Hard physical exercise is recommended for keeping the body in tone and for mood and stress control. Blood type O thrives on hard, competive sports like squash, watersports, martial arts and the cardio, spinning, tough-stepping or aerobic routines at the gym. Endorphins are released after 1 hour of strenuous exercise. The muscles are toned, fat is converted to energy and O's emerge both physically and mentally fulfilled.

Get to grips with making the right choices for your blood type

Begin with your worst enemy! All those sugar cravings have to go. Sugar robs you of chrome, zinc and antioxidants. Every teaspoon weakens the immune system for an hour. Find alternative sweeteners and healthy substitutes for sweets that suit you

Blood type A has a problem with this group of vegetables, known as the deadly nightshades: potatoes, tomatoes, green peppers, aubergines and chillies. Type O thrives on everything in this group except the potatoes. Types B[1] and AB are neutral to potatoes.

Many people get upset if they cannot eat bread. Allergies to grain and bean lectins cause over 80% of our health and digestive problems, yet people are addicted to wheat products. Change to rye bread, providing you are not blood type B. Eat rice cakes.

Fatty fries in wheat batter, saturated in sunflower oil that has been heated up time and again? Forget it! All blood types get trans-fatty acid poisoning from this type of fried food, especially if it lies around and is served cold and half rotten. (See page 51.)

Breakfast cereals can cause a lot of mucous and allergy problems as well as heartburn, blood sugar imbalances and a morning slump in energy. Test to find the ideal grains that suit each person in the family and watch out for all that milk and sugar!

Blood type B is more tolerant to milk products but they, too, can suffer from lactose intolerance as individuals. Casein in milk is a serious irritant to many people, regardless of whether milk products like yoghurt and cream cheese are free of lactose.

Smart food to enjoy throughout the day

Prepare food in advance before you leave home to avoid having to buy junk food. Use the lists on pages 11-14 to select the food that will suit you best.

No margarine or white bread

Margarine is universally bad, regardless of any claims we hear. When oil is heated to high temperatures and altered with chemicals so the fat hardens into solids, it certainly is not a health food. If you prefer a soft spread to keep in the fridge, try softened butter mixed with olive oil as a healthier alternative. (See page 50.)Use avocado on bread or make nut butters. (See pages 114, 115.)

Forget the white bread, laden with gluten and a variety of chemicals to make it fluffy and white. It is addictive and causes heartburn, mucous and colon disorders. Wheat germ and bran can even do more harm than white flour. Wholewheat "health" bread is not healthy for most of us. (See page 43.)

Gluten may be a problem

Special health bread and rice cakes or crackers are better for most blood types. Gluten-free products like allergy bread are available, but like some brands of gluten-free pasta, contain maize, sago, potato flour and other ingredients that may be unsuitable for your blood type.

This selection is for a vegetarian or vegan blood type O^2 (non-secretor) who needs to lose weight.

Special food for blood type O^2 (non-secretor)

Blood type O^2, (the non-secretors) have a particular problem with lectins in wheat and sugars that cause insulin resistance with resultant obesity, mucous problems, heartburn, blood sugar imbalances and constipation. The food pictured above was prepared for a day at work for type O^2 vegans and vegetarians who don't eat meat, although it is highly recommended for blood type O. Here are healthy alternatives to junk food, take-aways, soft drinks, cakes, sweets and chocolate bars. All it takes is a little planning and some disciplined shopping to have a good stash of munchies at hand, lest you be tempted to eat rubbish.

Working from blood-type lists, I left put in grapes, pineapple and banana. The puffed rice is nice to have as a snack with the walnuts and raisins. For lunch there's a fresh salad with lettuce and an avocado and rye crackers or rice cakes with a bean dip. (See page 114.) Lemon juice and ground-up flaxseeds can go on the salad with some herb salt. Drink herb tea, juice or fresh water instead of all the coffee and sugary drinks.

Aircraft meals do not cater for blood type eating. If you want gluten-free meals, they can be ordered in advance. Vegetarian meals that are gluten-free as well as suitable for your blood type are unheard of!

If you are at work or are unable to buy healthy snacks and lunches, then take your own supply of food along. Don't fall for junk food just because everybody else does! A light and nutritious lunch provides far more energy than a heavy stodgy meal that makes you drowsy because it is so hard to digest. Make yourself smart desktop food!

Ten easy ways to change your foods into delicious medicines

1 Grind up flaxseeds for extra fibre and Omega 3

Flaxseeds are also known as linseeds, the small brown shiny seeds from the linen plant. They are not expensive to buy at the health shop. It is only the inner part that contains the essential fatty acids. Merely soaking seeds in water and swallowing them will only release the mucilage that surrounds them. For a better cure for constipation, invest in an electric coffee grinder and make yourself some flaxmeal. Keep it in the fridge and have a few teaspoons with cereals, salads, vegetables and juices. Grind up other seeds and nuts with flax for a delicious blend.

2 Grow fresh sprouts and eat loads of them

Use the information on pages 110-112 to produce a variety of sprouts. Lentil sprouts are suitable for all blood types because sprouting destroys the starch-bound lectin that is harmful to blood type B and O^1. A tablespoon of sprouts made from cheap soup lentils supplies all the vitamins and minerals the average person needs for the day. Sprouts can be eaten in salads, soups, stews or curries but preferably raw to release all the heat-sensitive nutrients like vitamins and enzymes.

3 Make healthy and sustaining breakfast cereals

This sustaining cereal mix can include breakfast ingredients that suit your blood type. Bake a mixture of oats, a little olive oil, brown sugar (if permitted) and other ingredients like soya flour or soya mince (not for O^2 or B^2) or barley flakes (not for O^1 or O^2). All can enjoy oats, except O^2 or those with a severe gluten allergy. Use the same oven as for roasting or baking at medium to low temperatures or leave in a hot oven that has been turned off. Mix in some ground-up flaxseeds and your choice of seeds, nuts and chopped dried fruit. For breakfast, moisten with boiling water, then add a tiny splash of milk or juice and sweeten to taste.

4 Bake your own health cookies and muffins

Use the recipes in the baking section on pages 144-149. These delicious home bakes are easy to adapt to all blood types and contain so many beneficial nutrients that you can use them to replace meals (even breakfast cereals when you are in a hurry). Ground-up flaxseeds are just one of the ingredients you can add and nobody will ever be constipated again! The recipes do not contain any eggs, dairy products, baking powder, wheat, aspartame, saccharine or margarine. Natural alternatives to brown sugar are: honey, molasses, fructose or stevia. Liquorice powder is 50x sweeter than sugar.

5 Healthy beverages to replace the "baddies"

Coffee suits blood type A, but more than two cups a day is looking for trouble. Pure cocoa contains less caffeine than Chinese green tea! See pages 99-105 for more about these beverages. Don't forget about plain old water and rooibos tea, but make them more interesting and therapeutic by adding lemon juice, herbs, cream of tartar, etc. Cut out the soft drinks, especially if you have a blood sugar problem, as there are up to 8 teaspoons of sugar in a 350ml can. Try to avoid caffeine, guarana, aspartame and saccharine in diet or energy drinks.

6 Grow your own wheat and barley grass

Wheat and barley grass supplements are expensive and claim to cure all ailments. Spend a few cents on some wheat and barley grains at the health shop and unleash fresh natural phytochemicals such as enzymes, chlorophyll and trace elements into your own power juices. See page 113 for instructions. Each pot of grass will grow again to the same height after cutting. You can also grow alfalfa seeds and clip off their tops once they are big enough. Alfalfa is not recommended for blood type O but it is a great immune booster for other blood types.

7 Make fresh therapeutic juices and herbal tinctures

Fresh juice is the ultimate energy drink. Recipes and combinations are on pages 89-91. These extracts yield fresh enzymes as well as chlorophyll, the substance that traps sunlight energy into plant cells. No supplement can equal the natural nutrients and phytochemicals that fresh juice has to offer, because these enzymes are alive. Buying a simple electric blender is all you need. To make herbal tinctures, see pages 106-107. They can be made with fresh or dried herbs. Powdered spices like fenugreek, cinnamon, ginger, etc. can be added. See pages 57-62 for more about herbs and spices.

8 Unleash the healing qualities of citrus fruits

Grapefruit is perfect for slimming and curbing the appetite. Learn how to make grapefruit and lemon pith for adding to any of the baking mixtures for extra cancer-fighting nutrients, fibre and to reduce the Glycaemic Index for diabetics (See page 146.) Lemons are beneficial to all of us in so many ways (See page 32.) Oranges are very good for blood type B, but what about the rest of us? This does not mean they contain harmful lectins but they can aggravate polyamine growth in the digestive system if you eat too many at a time.

9 Pack up healthy food boxes for the day

Don't fall for the fast food trade and undo your blood type diet. Always take suitable meals and snacks with you, as junk foods will never suit any blood type! Buy rye bread and rice cakes or do your own baking, to make sure that the ingredients have your approval. Pack up fruit and salad ingredients like lettuce, carrots, cucumber and tomato. Make savoury dips to go with them. Soup can be taken in a flask or heated up at work. Keep a stash of dried fruit and nuts as well as juice or water in the car to control blood sugar blues and dehydration. Make healthy sweet treats using the recipes on pages 150-151. Never skip meals when you are feeling stressed out.

10 Make delicious herb salts and seasonings

Cutting out salt can be a bore, especially when most people have a potassium deficiency that causes the sodium imbalance. When you add potassium chloride or cream of tartar to your salt, the balance is restored. Rev up the mixtures by grinding up dried herbs, spices and seeds with a little sea salt. Black pepper does not suit all blood types and 98% of the population cannot digest it. It can cause intestinal cramps, gas, bloating and abdominal pains. Change over to black cumin (kaloontjie) seeds as they are universal healers. (See pages 60 and 141.)

Healing vegetables we can enjoy every day as medicine

Try to eat at least 1 or 2 raw or cooked onions every day, especially if you have high cholesterol. Parsley helps to boost natural enzymes and is rich in chlorophyll, minerals and trace elements.

Broccoli is rich in special cancer-busting enzymes. According to new research, broccoli is more effective if eaten raw. Try broccoi lightly steamed or juice it.

Beta carotene is the vegetable precursor to vitamin A. It is found in yellow as well as leafy green vegetables. A daily helping protects against most forms of cancer and helps to alkalise the bowels.

Lycopene is a cancer-fighting chemical in tomatoes. Beetroot, guavas, black grapes, grapefruit and other red fruits also contain lycopene, for those not suited to tomatoes. Eat them with flaxseed and lecithin oil to activate the lycopene.

These vegetables are free of harmful lectins and can help to heal polyamine damage in the gut

Prevent organ damage and enlargement

It is important to maintain a balanced activity of the building blocks known as polyamines. When the intestines or the liver and pancreas are damaged by food lectins, parasites, toxins or pathogens, then polyamine activity increases in an attempt to repair the damage. (See page 7.) The result is a profusion of scar tissue that can lead to organ enlargement or deformities. Most of the leafy green vegetables recommended for all blood types, as well as the dark purple fruits like plums and grapes, can prevent this from happening and even reverse the silting-up of organs. A diet of beneficial foods for your blood type is essential for a healthy colon. Green tea, ground-up flaxseeds, fish oil, turnips and walnuts also help to modify polyamine reactions. We need to control polyamines to keep levels of indicans (the damaged cell material) as low as possible. See page 7 for more about lectins and polyamines.

Turnips are the best

Turnips have a profound effect on lowering gut polyamines. This often-neglected vegetable should be eaten in substantial quantities during times of illness, especially when cancer rears its ugly head. When your colon is giving you trouble, give turnips a chance. Try to cook turnips as well as their green tops in unusual and exciting ways. For instance, grated turnips can be added to just about any salad, stirfry or soup or add them to vegetable dishes. Work with your blood type lists and cut out foods that contain harmful lectins. Avoid the starches, pulses and grains that are not suited to your blood type. Keep large quantities of healing vegetables on hand and eat plenty of the fruits that help to cleanse and detoxify your system. (See pages 86,87 and 93-96.)

Natural solutions to a load of gas

Why do dried peas and beans cause gas?

Dried pulses and legumes are full of lectins (proteins that cause cell agglutination). Lectins latch onto sugars and bacteria, causing cells and food particles to stick together. These little clumps interfere with normal digestion and cannot be digested themselves, so they ferment in the gut and generate gas.

It is best to select the peas and beans that agree with your blood type. Sprout them before cooking and you will not have a problem with the lectins thickening your blood, interfering with your digestion and wrecking your immune system. Cooked peas and beans (dried pulses) are best eaten on their own if you have digestive problems or you suffer from cramps, bloating and gas. Do not drink water with the meal. Start by eating a little at a time. Taking digestive enzymes and activated charcoal tablets also helps to combat gas.

Day 1 day 2 day 3 day 4 and ready to cook

Soak beans or sprout them before cooking

Dried lentils are unsuitable for blood type O and B, but sprouted lentils benefit all blood types because they are free of lectins. (See pages 110-112.) Even large beans can be soaked and left to sprout for a day or two prior to cooking, to make the beans lectin-free, reduced in starch and more nutritious. They are both much tastier and free from the evil gas effects. Don't cook beans with salt because they will not get soft. Season them after cooking. (See page 118.)

Black pepper can cause cramps and gas

Black pepper can be replaced with black cumin seeds

Black pepper cannot be digested by 98% of the population and may lodge in the intestines for over seven years. Many people experience colicky pains or gas after meals. When no other cause for this discomfort can be found, it usually relates to the amount of black pepper you ate! Grind up black cumin seeds (kaloontjie)and use them instead. The taste is pleasant and the seeds relieve gas and flatulence. Make your own delicious herb salt and pepper. (See page 141.)

Nature's special gas busters

Cinnamon kills E-coli in food. (See pages 57-62.)

Cloves for Shigella and gut parasites

Fennel for gas, cramps and bad breath

Mint to freshen breath and stimulate digestion

Cardamom seeds can be chewed for digestion

Coriander seeds help to break wind

Some other causesof gas, cramps and flatulence

1 Eating pasta or doughy starch without chewing it properly.

2 Drinking water, juice, beer, wine or cold liquids with meals.

3 Eating acidic fruit with starches or nuts at one sitting, as they can cause fermentation a few hours later and the gas has to escape.

4 Eating too many raw or fibrous foods together in a meal. Often green beans, celery, cauliflower or broccoli cause gas if they are not lightly cooked to break down the cellulose.

5 Infected milk or meat products that contain bacteria like Shigella. (See pages 71-72 for more remedies.) Read about more problems with digestion on page 63.

Preventing colds and flu

Garlic is one of the oldest and best known kitchen medicines. Eating one or two cloves of garlic every day helps some people ward off colds and flu. Chew a lot of parsley afterwards to freshen breath. Eat according to your blood type because lectins can cause mucous in the system. Infected mucous causes secondary infections like bronchitis.

Give your immunity an extra boost

We need to maintain our immunity at all times and this is why we should eat plenty of fresh fruits and vegetables every day. Herbs like olive leaf and echinacea help to boost the immune system. Olive leaves attack the cold and flu virus head-on and can even prevent a cold from developing. If you don't have olive leaf tablets or drops, chew one or two fresh olive leaves or add them to the fruit juice you make. (See page 34.) Zinc and vitamin C help to eliminate many pathogens like moulds that encourage cold and flu viruses.

Onions are a remedy for mucous

A combination of onions and honey is a folk remedy for a tight chest and a bad cough. Grate up two onions and place them in a jam jar. Mix in a pinch of salt and a tablespoon of honey. Allow the juice to accumulate at the bottom of the jar and take a few teaspoons of this instead of a cough mixture. Eat the grated onions with your food when the juice has been used up.

Easing blocked noses and sinuses

To a pot of gently boiling water, add 1 teaspoon of bicarbonate of soda and 1 tablespoon of hydrogen peroxide. Lean over the pot and inhale the fumes with a towel over your head for 10 minutes. Repeat a few hours later. This is an effective decongestant and boosts your oxygen levels. Add a few drops of thyme, mint or eucalyptus oil.

Kitchen cures for coughs, colds, sore throats and flu

Sore throat and cough remedy

1 tablespoon honey
1 tablespoon lemon juice
1 teaspoon powdered ginger
Mix together and take a teaspoon at a time.

Liquorice sweets are soothing to the throat and help to loosen a tight cough. Liquorice drops like Borsdruppels can be added to the mixture above. (See page 59.) You can sip a glass of hot water to which a teaspoon of the mixture has been added. Also chew fresh sage or nasturtium leaves; they taste better with a little honey. The leaves contain natural antibiotics that kill germs. Chewing a lot of parsley or soup celery leaves is good for a sore throat as they contain chlorophyll which works as an antiseptic.

Mouth and throat gargle

Stir a teaspoon of the honey mixture into half a glass of warm water and add a pinch of salt. Gargle well and spit out. Use this mixture for sniffing up into the nostrils as well.

Chillies loosen and expel mucous

Make a drink using hot water, lemon juice and honey and add a little fresh chilli. Chillies help to release thick sticky mucous deposits from the lungs, throat and chest. Chillies contain guaiphenesin, the same chemical used in cough mixtures to expel mucous. Try adding chilli powder or a few fresh chilli slices to your food and gradually build up your tolerance. Eat yoghurt if you feel on fire!

When your eyes stream and your nose runs, you know it is working! There are many hot and spicy sauces you can make or buy. Avoid the very hot little orange gabanero chillies as they can burn the eyes, nose and throat quite badly. Keep chillies away from the eyes and also from small children and babies.

The natural liver and gall bladder flushing technique

This traditional liver and gall bladder cleansing technique has been used for thousands of years to remove gallstones and to cleanse the bowels of age-old debris. Olive oil with lemon, lime or grapefruit juice is the key to the success of this method.

Using Epsom Salts as part of the cure produces more rapid and thorough results as it opens up all the bile ducts. In hundreds of cases, nobody experienced any pain or went to hospital and gallstones were expelled without the need for surgery. This cleanse works well for parasite elimination and should be done twice a year. (See page 35.)

Epsom salts and olive oil mixtures

Take this mixture four times during the treatment:
1- 2 teaspoons Epsom Salts, dissolved in ½ cup boiling water. Let it cool down before drinking.
Non-acidic fruit juice to drink after the Epsom Salts.
Take this mixture once at bedtime: ½ cup olive oil mixed with ½ cup grapefruit juice or lemon juice.

Day one: cut out all oil and fat

It is best to do this over a weekend or when you can be at home. For two days prior to the liver cleanse, eat simple food without oil or fat. Bile in the gall bladder needs to build up some pressure.

Day two: only fruit and vegetables

Eat only fruit and vegetables, and no fat to ensure a good evening flush-out. Drink a lot of water.

Day two: late afternoon

Take 1 or 2 teaspoons of Epsom Salts and dissolve them in ½ cup of boiling water. When cool, drink it quickly and have some fruit juice to get rid of the taste. Homemade juice is best.

Day two: 2 hours after a light supper

Have a fat-free evening meal of lightly steamed vegetables. Two hours later take more Epsom Salts followed by some fruit juice that is not acidic.

Day two: bedtime cocktail

At bedtime, drink the ½ cup of olive oil mixed with lemon or grapefruit juice. Then lie down, flat on your back with your head on a pillow and go to sleep. During the night, the gallstones begin to loosen and move down the ducts and into the intestines. Epsom Salts open up the valves and ducts in the gallbladder and olive oil activates the pumping action. Your system begins to gurgle!

Day three: out they come!

Take another dose of Epsom Salts and juice the following morning and one more two hours later. Take it easy and stay in bed for a while as you will be going to the toilet frequently and all the gallstones will come out, along with a lot of old muck. Do not be alarmed at the smell of sulphur from the Epsom Salts. Later on you can have some fruit for breakfast and then go back to normal healthy, happy food. You will feel light and energetic like never before!

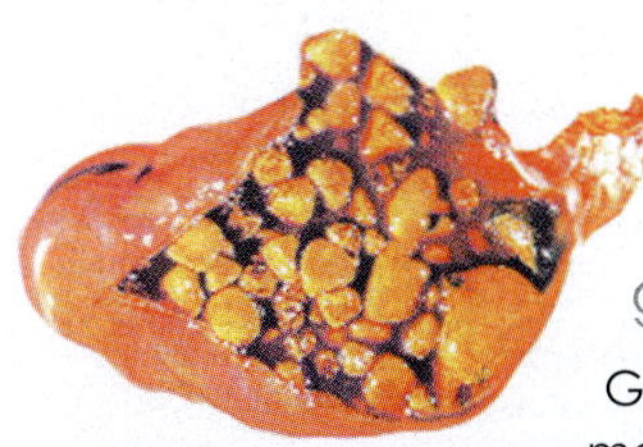

Thousands of gory green gallstones!

Gallstones are composed mainly of cholesterol. They will float in the toilet and show up as bright green when you shine a torch on them. Other than gallstones, some of the cholesterol appears as tan coloured crystals of floating "chaff". You should see this often in any bowel movement when you eat enough ground-up flaxseeds and your liver is purging out these waste products.

Control constipation on a daily basis

Most people feel rejuvenated, light and wonderfully clean the next day. If you feel a little ill for a few days, you may need to attend to parasites. (See page 35.) Eat ground-up flaxseeds every day to control constipation, or try 1 teaspoon of bicarbonate of soda in a little water, followed by a glass of water. Take this two or three times a day.

Lemons and limes are the ultimate health remedy for all blood types

Lemon juice

Warm up the lemons in hot water or in the sun before squeezing them as they will yield far more juice. Dilute lemon juice with water and drink a few glasses a day. Lemon juice alkalises the body and has profound medicinal effects. When the juice of one lemon is taken with a few tablespoons of olive oil, it cleanses the liver and flushes out the gall - bladder. (See page 31.) The citric acid in lemon juice helps to slow down insulin reactions that cause a drop in blood sugar after sweet substances like honey are consumed. (See page 33.) Use lemon juice to help treat sore throats or arthritis. It can be mixed with herbs, honey and spices. Use lemon juice instead of vinegar for salad dressings. Baking powder is toxic, so use the following alternative: two teaspoons of lemon juice added to the cake mixture, then stir in a teaspoon of bicarbonate of soda. Slices of apple or banana will not go brown if you sprinkle them with lemon juice.

First aid and nausea

For upset tummies, add lemon juice to mashed banana or grated apple and add a pinch of cinnamon. Lemon juice and honey ease a sore throat or a nagging cough. For nausea, drink a glass of hot water with a squeeze of lemon juice and a few slices of fresh bruised ginger or half a teaspoon of powdered ginger. Add in a spoon of honey to sweeten, if you so desire.

Beauty treatments

Mix a few drops of lemon juice into a teaspoon of almond oil and rub the mixture onto your skin. For a vaginal rinse, add a teaspoon of lemon juice and a tablespoon of table salt to a litre of warm water. Normal soap makes this area too alkaline and is a common cause of odours and irritations. If you cannot find a specially pH-balanced vaginal cleanser, use this lemon juice rinse. Use an old lemon rind as a heel and elbow rub to soften rough skin. Add lemon juice to the rinsing water after washing your hair to get rid of soapy residues.

Lemon or lime pickle

Slice up a few lemons and coat them with a layer of coarse salt. Pack the slices into a jam jar and keep in the fridge. After a few days, this delicious lemon relish can be used in sambals and side dishes. We are advised by naturopaths to eat a few slices of lemon pickle every day as a cure for arthritis or skin disorders. The white pith of lemons and grapefruit is rich in natural bioflavonoids.

Quest for zest

Grate off the lemon rind to make zest. It adds a lovely flavour to cakes and even meat dishes, curries and casseroles. This zest can be dried and added to herb salt. Thicker strips of lemon peel can be dried and used when you make special blends of herb or fruit teas. Add a slice of fresh lemon to hot and cold drinks. If you have a lot of lemons, freeze some lemon slices in layers between sheets of plastic. This makes a very convenient and tasty addition to water or juices and doubles up as an attractive ice cube.

Lemons in the home

To clean brassware, cut a lemon in half and rub it over the tarnished brass. After a few minutes, you will see a shiny metallic glow return. Rinse the brassware with soapy water and dry off. You may need a few more treatments to remove stubborn marks. A bowl of lemons is a thing of beauty and deserves a place in your living area. It is said that lemons raise the vibrations of a room. Small lemons can be studded with whole cloves and dried out to make decorative pomanders to keep moths away from clothes.

Honey is our oldest and most natural remedy

Honey, a delicious combination of bee enzymes and flower nectar, is one of the oldest medicinal substances known to man. Honey is extremely nutritious and is an excellent natural sweetener, although diabetics and blood types O[2] and AB[2] should not use it too freely, especially when taken separately from meals. Honey is rich in vitamins, minerals, enzymes and trace elements as well as natural anti-microbial agents. The amino acid content of honey is 35%. Don't cook honey, or these vital heat-sensitive nutrients will be destroyed.

Honey as a wound healer

Honey is an excellent wound healer; being effective against germs and infections. Staphylococcus aureus and Escherichia infections were cleared up by using honey in trial cases where antibiotics had failed. Honey keeps a wound sterile and hastens the healing process. Eczema patients can use honey to wash their skin . Pure honey is good for mouth and gum infections. Believe it or not, honey helps to prevent tooth decay but only if it is not taken with foods containing starches that set off a fermentation process when combined with saliva. Use pure honey with water, salt and lemon juice for a mouthwash or throat gargle.

Honey for depression and low energy

Honey has sedating and calming properties and works like sugar in enhancing serotonin levels as an anti-depressant. Honey and apple cider vinegar or lemon juice with water is a well-known folk medicine, used for sore throats, arthritis and convalescence. My favourite energy shot before taking a long run on an empty stomach is a little water, a teaspoon of honey and a teaspoon of apple cider vinegar. I prefer it to commercial "energy" drinks.

Honey can be added to many herbal medicines. In China medicinal herbs, teas and spices are often sold on the street.

Bee careful with honey

Honey can be used for sweetening foods but it does contain a percentage of simple sugars that behave like glucose. Diabetics or those with blood sugar problems such as hypoglycaemia or glucose intolerance should not take honey in large quantities because of an insulin reaction. This effect can be modified by using a little honey with foods that contain fibre, fats, protein or acids. It is better to take honey for medicinal purposes with apple cider vinegar or lemon juice as these acids lower the Glycaemic Index. (See page 43.)

When honey is combined with a starch such as bread, it ferments in the mouth, causing tooth decay, so clean your teeth afterwards. Honey must not be given to very young infants as it may contain botulism spores which the baby's immature intestine cannot yet eliminate like adults can. Never give babies honey by itself because it overstimulates the pancreas in the same way that sweets or concentrated grape or apple juice does.

Honey as a natural medicine

According to folk medicine from around the world, honey can be used to treat coughs, muscle cramps, burns, stuffy noses, sinusitis, hay fever, bedwetting, insomnia, and on wounds, ulcers, infections, stings and rashes. Honey is good for gut infections such as Salmonella, Shigella, E. coli, and Cholera. When mixed with cinnamon, turmeric, fennel or cloves, the results are even more effective. See pages 57-62 for herbs and spices you can combine with honey. Some doctors give honey before surgery to prevent infections.

Diarrhoea, vomiting or dehydration

Combine a teaspoon of honey with a cup of water and a pinch of salt. Controlled medical studies have proven this recipe to be more effective than electrolyte mixtures due to the anti-microbial effects of the honey. A cup of warm water with honey and a pinch of ginger and cream of tartar helps nausea and vomiting.

Olive leaves are a potent alternative to many common drugs

How to use olive leaves in the home

In South Africa the wild olive tree, known as Olienhout, grows in many regions. The organically grown leaves have superior medicinal properties to the cultivated ones. You can buy Olienhout or the normal olive trees from your nursery. Having an olive tree growing in your garden or in a flower pot is like owning a natural medicine chest, providing you know how to use the leaves to treat ailments.

Fresh olive leaves are the best to use

One or two fresh olive leaves can be chewed every day but they do not taste very nice. You can put a few of the leaves in an electric blender with the fruit juices you make. (See pages 89, 106, 107.) Strain the juice through a stocking or cloth and drink it fresh. A glass of this potion will deliver the freshest and most potent extract of olive leaves to your system along with fresh enzymes and phytochemicals that are not available in supplements containing only extracts of oleacin and oleuropin.

Make yourself an olive leaf tincture

Pour a cup of vodka or cane spirits into the blender goblet with two cups of fresh green olive leaves. Add the leaves a few at a time and process this mixture into a smooth pulp. Keep it in a glass jar for at least two weeks and then strain it through a fine cloth. You now have a very potent olive leaf tincture to keep in dark glass bottles. Take 5 - 10 drops daily as a tonic or every 2 hours for bad conditions, like the onset of flu.

Using dried olive leaves

If you do not have an olive tree, buy dried olive leaves from the health shop. Add the crushed leaves to rooibos tea. Olive leaf tea is used to treat high blood pressure in Spain. As heat destroys most of the other healing properties, buying pure natural olive leaf tablets or tinctures made from whole, fresh leaves is a better option. These products are more convenient, especially when travelling or to use for emergencies like the onset of colds and flu.

The medicinal effects of olive leaves

According to Dr. Morton Walker's reports based on research from 1985 on olive leaves, adequate clinical evidence proves that olive leaves can:

1 Boost your immune system and give you a chance to fight off the effects of chronic as well as acute health conditions without antibiotics.

2 Lower blood pressure and boost the micro-circulation, especially that of blood capillaries in the brain, fingers, toes and penis.

3 Olive leaves combat many viral, fungal and bacterial infections including malaria, colds, flu, kidney or bladder infections and organisms causing the leaky-gut syndrome and food poisoning.

4 Help to improve memory, circulation and sexual prowess. Olive leaves are mainly indicated as a natural alternative to modern drugs like antibiotics, cold and flu remedies, anti-coagulants, diuretics and antihypertensives.

5 For diabetics, olive leaves help to lower blood sugar levels as well as improving their heart function, peripheral circulation and sexual ability.

6 Persistent cases of Candida albicans have cleared up permanently by using olive leaf tablets at daily doses of 4 - 6. They destroy the organisms Giardia lambellus and Gardenerella. These two parasites thrive on yoghurt! They cause leaky-gut (permeable membrane) syndrome and Candida.

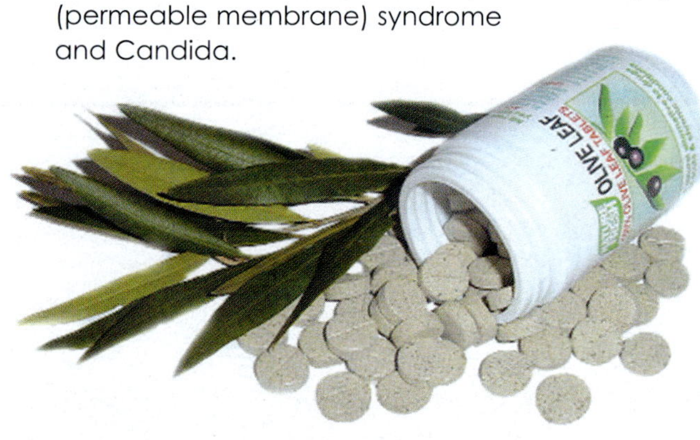

Olive leaves are totally non-toxic, coming from a tree that provides both food and medicine. Oil from the leaves is nourishing, improves fatty acid levels and protects the delicate lining of the intestines.

Natural parasite remedies for the whole family

Parasites have to be eliminated

Detoxification programmes or health regimens are not complete without regular parasite cleansing sessions. Large parasites range from the helminths like tapeworm, hookworm and roundworm to the slug-like flukes that invade the pancreas and liver. There is also a teeming host of microbial organisms like bacteria, fungi and viruses living inside us. They breed continuously and can do a lot of damage to the body regardless of eating correctly, drinking water or taking supplements. (See pages 71-72.)

Symptoms of parasite infestations

Symptoms include: irritability, mental disturbances, aching muscles, strange cravings or eating habits, weight loss or gain, constant hunger or spells of nausea, fatigue, genital and anal itching, colicky pains, upset tummy, poor concentration, seizures, insomnia and tooth grinding, especially at night. If there are tapeworm cysts in the brain, epileptic seizures can occur. Parasites upset normal levels of friendly bacteria and cause acidity, Candida albicans or yeast overgrowth in mucous linings.

Parasites, worms and flukes can invade just about every part of the body and interfere with the absorption and assimilation of nutrients in the body. Some forms of amoebae and protozoa cause the linings of the respiratory tract and the gut to become permeable, allowing foreign matter such as pollen, protein, gluten or casein particles to invade the tissues and trigger off autoimmune diseases. When a Candida patient has not responded to anti-fungal treatment or a special diet, the problem may be: Entamoeba histolytica, Gardenerella or Giardia lambila infestations. These microparasites thrive on friendly bacteria, especially probiotics, yoghurt or lactobacillus! Olive leaves help to eradicate these parasites. (Page 34)

Eliminate and prevent large worms

The most common cause of anemia is parasites especially roundworm, hookworm and tapeworm. Over 25% of the population suffers from this type of anemia. The pips of pumpkin, butternut or squash seeds made into a juice should be given every second day for a week. (See juices on pages 89-91.) They contain an amino acid that gets rid of these parasites. Ground-up flaxseeds and black cumin help to keep large parasites at bay if a few teaspoons are taken daily with food. Take a worm remedy like mebendazole or piperazine from your pharmacist every six months as an alternative.

Herbs to control microbials and flukes

Most of the parasites, especially amoebae and the protozoa like malaria, can be safely eradicated with herbal remedies such as olive leaf tablets, cloves, cinnamon, artemesia or black cumin. QX, Rife or electronic zappers can also kill parasites.

Make a tincture from olive leaves as described on page 34, then add an extra cup of water with 1 tablespoon of cloves and ½ cup of artemesia, known as wormwood or wilde als, available from health shops. Take a teaspoon of this mixture every day to get rid sof most parasites, including malaria and cold and flu viruses. To discourage liver and pancreatic flukes, chew sprigs of watercress or nasturtium leaves with lunch and dinner. Have them with foods like beef and lamb, especially if you prefer your meat underdone. Add a few drops of Lugol's iodine to the water when you grow sprouts, to kill parasites that may be present.

Cod liver oil capsules, salmon oil, vitamin E and flaxseed oil help to restore the selective permeability of the mucous lining of the gut and respiratory tract.

Help yourself to hormone therapy from the kitchen!

Plants like fennel, sage, alfalfa, flaxseeds, liquorice and even spinach can help to boost estrogen levels. Seaweed such as bladderwrack and kelp contain natural iodine to stimulate a sluggish thyroid gland. Cabbage and cauliflower can inhibit thyroid function, especially in blood type O.

Ground-up flaxseeds help flagging estrogen levels and provide essential Omega 3 fatty acids to reduce PMS symptoms. Walnuts and avocados also contain omega 3. Release your own progesterone by chewing a piece of raw red sweet potato every day. For more information, refer to my website, listed on page 160.

There's a cure for everything, but where is it?

If you really believe that food is your medicine, then take it seriously. Even our hormones are influenced by the common foods and spices we eat. Eating the wrong food has a lot to do with thyroid problems, bloating, weight gain, premenstrual tension and menopausal mayhem. (See pages 18, 22, 47, 55.)

Hot flushes do not always need HRT drugs

When you eat according to your blood type and clean out your liver , most of your hormonal imbalances have a chance to correct themselves. Even hot flushes can indicate that the liver is not processing and eliminating estrogen. A signal to the endocrine system shuts down the release of estrogen. This is why women with low estrogen begin to feel panicky. First attend to the liver if you have estrogen problems. (See pages 31 and 70.)

Hot flushes due to low blood sugar occur 2-3 hours after eating! Don't eat sugar as this just makes them worse. Try small, nourishing meals and snacks every two hours. Night sweats can often indicate the presence of parasites and pathogens or slow growing bacterial or viral infections, especially in blood types A and B.

Fennel, alfalfa and soya boost estrogen

Fennel seeds deliver estrogen to the body almost immediately. Emergency doses of estrogen are given to women who suffer from profuse uterine bleeding, but fennel is a safer alternative. Take ½ teaspoon of fennel powder, known as barishap, with a spoon of honey. Repeat every 2 hours if the bleeding is still profuse. The estrogenic effect of fennel can help the blood to clot, but in larger doses it causes bloating and weight gain. Both natural and synthetic estrogenic hormones displace thyroid hormones and raise cholesterol levels. They promote the formation of ovarian cysts and stimulate the development of tumours and breast cancer if the levels remain too high, for too long, in the bloodstream. Do you really want more estrogen? The isoflavones in alfalfa, known as lucerne (not for O^1 or O^2) also boost estrogen levels. Soya promotes a milder estrogenic activity, but it is not recommended for blood type O^2 or B^2. Estrogen is proving to be a risky option; that's why levels drop naturally after menopause.

The safest way to regulate estrogen without cancer threats or circulatory disorders associated with HRT is to use selective estrogen receptor modulators (SERMS) made from red clover or black cohosh tinctures. Take them as sublingual drops for rapid results.

How much progesterone do you want?

Natural progesterone supplements contain extracts of Mexican yam, but there is a better solution in your very own kitchen! Phytochemicals in the red sweet potato can activate the pituitary gland to stimulate the release of progesterone. Chew a small chunk of raw sweet potato for about ten minutes every day. This helps to expel hot flushes within half an hour. Avoid larger doses as too much progesterone inhibits menstruation.

2 Happy Foods

Please note that this information should not be used to diagnose, treat or cure a condition. Consult your doctor or an experienced practitioner, especially if you are pregnant, breast-feeding, epileptic, diabetic or have blood pressure or heart complaints. (See page 2.)

Fruit and vegetables

Fresh fruit and vegetables and foods that are free from harmful lectins form the basis of Happy Eating.

Carbohydrates

Most people gain weight or become ill from eating carbohydrates that contain harmful or fattening lectins that are blood-type specific.

Eggs and dairy

Eggs suit everybody, but what about milk?

Fats and oils

Good fats, bad fats and essential fatty acids.

Meat and fish

Select those that suit you. Vegans and protein.

Soya products

Soya is called meat from the ground, but is it good for everybody?

Herbs and spices

Herbs and spices add flavour and aroma to food and also have medicinal uses.

Buy more fruit and vegetables and use them for all your meals

Let's go shopping

Fresh fruit and vegetables are all we really need for nourishment and to keep healthy. There is no point in eating anything that makes you sick, tired or fat. Most of the health problems we have today come from eating food that does not suit us.

Let us start with a selection of fruit and vegetables that are known to be allergy-free and good for all the four major blood types. We can learn to use them to heal ourselves of many common ailments while we enjoy the lovely soups, salads and vege - table platters. Become acquainted with nature's special medicine which is so versatile, tasty and affordable. All you need is a basket of fresh fruit and vegetables and you can heal and entertain your family and friends at the same time.

Most fruits are beneficial to all blood types. People on a cleansing diet will be having just fruit for breakfast and during the morning. (See pages 93-97.) For healthy eating, buy more fruit than you usually do. Use bowls of fruit to decorate your home and enjoy looking at that lovely fruit as well as eating it. Refer to the blood type lists for specific fruits to suit your family and make sure everybody has plenty of fruit to choose from every day.

Fruit is easy to digest and you immediately benefit from all the vitamins, minerals and life-giving enzymes. It is best not to combine fruit with starches and other foods that will interfere with its rapid digestion. For the price of a packet of greasy rancid potato chips, you can buy a large bag of fresh, juicy sweet apples!

Eat fruit instead of carbo-loading

Consuming a lot of starches, fats, sugar and protein to the exclusion of fruit and vegetables leads to major health problems. We actually need far less food than you may think. The reason we feel we need more energy is because most of the food we eat has not been properly digested or put to good use. It stagnates inside us, turns to fat or becomes putrid and toxic. This is why we get so hungry; we eat more and more stodgy "foodless" foods and get tired from trying to digest it!

Learn to love your veggies

Vegetables are one of the best natural medicines you can get. They are full of antioxidants, phytochemicals, immune boosters and miraculous enzymes, vitamins and trace elements. Never overcook your vegetables. It is best to eat as many of them as you can in a natural raw state either as snacks or with dips and salads.

We can use vegetables as well as some of the pips, peels and offcuts in juices, so nothing is wasted. The unique medicinal qualities of vegetables can then be released; valuable nutrients with healing qualities that usually end up in the dustbin.

Fruit to enjoy every day

The fruit you see here is suitable for all blood types, but O^2 should not eat too many apples and pears.

☺☺ Fruit for all blood types

Grapes, raisins and grape juice

Grapefruit, lemon, lime and their juices

Peach, nectarine, plum

Pineapple and watermelon

Blueberry, loganberry, mulberry

Cherry, cranberry, red- and blackcurrant

Fig, prune, raspberry, youngberry

Gooseberry, kumquat and granadilla

The following suit all except O^2:

Apple, pear, apricot, strawberry

These fruits only suit some of us

If this fruit does not suit your blood type, rather cut it out or limit your intake. Oranges are best for blood type B whereas they cause acidity in a lot of people of other blood types. Pawpaw should not be consumed by blood type A in large amounts on an empty stomach.

☺☺A All -type fruit plus

Avocado, guava, kiwifruit, pomegranate, prickly pear, quince, starfruit, litchi
A^1: sweet melon, naartjie. A^2: banana, mango

☒A Fruit to avoid

Orange, pawpaw
A^1: banana , mango. A^2: naartjie/tangerine

☺☺B All-type fruit plus

Orange, banana, guava, kiwifruit, mango, pawpaw, quince, tangerine, litchi. B^1: sweetmelon

☒B Fruit to avoid

Avocado, pomegranate, prickly pear, starfruit
B^2: sweet melon

☺☺AB All-type fruit plus

Kiwifruit, pawpaw, litchi. AB^1: sweetmelon, naartjie/tangerine

☒AB Fruit to avoid

Avocado, banana, mango, orange, pomegranate, prickly pear, quince, starfruit
AB^2: sweet melon, naartjie/tangerine

☺☺O All-type fruit plus

Banana, sweetmelon, mango, prickly pear, guava, pawpaw, pomegranate, quince, starfruit
O^2: avocado

☒O Fruit to avoid

Blackberry, kiwifruit/tangerine, naartjie, litchi
O^1: avocado. O^2: apple,apricot, pear, strawberry

A tasty selection of vegetables that are very easy to prepare

Cook up a storm with vegetables. Vegetarians and vegans can enjoy them as they are for a hearty meal. Eat them raw, stir fried, steamed, roasted or grilled. Serve them with sauces, dips and salad dressings. Eat vegetables to suit your blood type. They can be combined with salads, fish, eggs and meat. For beginners, start on page 116. See pages 108, 109, 114, 115, 140 and 141 for more ways to jazz up your veggies.

Stir fried root vegetables
Fry sliced onions in a little olive oil. Add chopped vegetables with a splash of water. Season and cook for a few minutes more.

Browned and steamed
Fry chopped vegetables like carrots, courgettes or parsnips in a little olive oil. And a splash of water, cover with a lid and turn on low.

Oven baked with herbs
Chop up a mixture of vegetables. Mix in a little olive oil and season with herbs. Bake in a medium oven whilst you bake or cook rice, etc.

Boiled or steamed squash
Cook squash or butternut and top with yoghurt and a salad dressing with herbs, onion, parsley or celery.

Broccoli combinations
Lightly steam broccoli and combine it with fried onions, apples or pears and creamy yoghurt sauces.

Stir fried semi-raw greens
Fry onions in olive oil. Add spinach and apple. Chop while it cooks for a few minutes, Then serve.

Eat plenty of fresh vegetables

These vegetables suit all blood types; except the sweet potatoes that are not so good for blood type A.

Vegetables for all blood types

Spinach, onions, broccoli, Brussels sprouts

Green beans, green peas, courgettes

Butternut, squashes of all types

Beetroot (tops as well), carrots, parsnips

Turnips, lettuce, endives, asparagus,

Lentil sprouts, pimentoe, water chestnut

Oyster and portabello mushrooms

Sweet potatoes suit everybody except

A[1] and A[2]

Fresh herbs for all blood types

Parsley, celery, chives, garlic, watercress
Bay leaves, fennel, thyme, majoram

These vegetables only suit some of us

The nightshade vegetable family of tomatoes, aubergines, green peppers, potatoes and chillies do not suit blood type A[1]. Blood type O does not tolerate cucumbers.

A All-type vegetables plus

Cauliflower, cucumber, leek, radish, sweetcorn, pumpkin
A[1]: button mushrooms, green oilves
A[2]: aubergine, tomato, green pepper

A Vegetables to avoid

Cabbage, sweet potato, potato, yam
A[1]aubergine, tomato. A[2]: mushrooms, green olives

B All-type vegetables plus

Cabbage, leek, button mushrooms, cauliflower, cucumber, aubergine, green olives, green pepper, sweet potato, yam. B[1]: potato. B[2]: tomato

B Vegetables to avoid

Sweetcorn, radish, Greek olives
B[1]: pumpkin , tomato. B[2] potato

AB All-type vegetables plus

Cabbage, cauliflower, potato, Greek olives, green olives, cucumber, aubergine, button mushrooms, yam, sweet potato, pumpkin, tomato

AB Vegetables to avoid

Green pepper, radish, sweetcorn

O All-type vegetables plus

Tomato, radish, pumpkin, green pepper, sweet potato, yam.
O[1]: cabbage, aubergine, olives

O Vegetables to avoid

Cauliflower, leek, cucumber, potato, sweetcorn

Gluten intolerance is a serious issue

Wheat, the No. 1 cereal killer!

Wheat products and wheat bran don't suit everybody, especially blood type B and O. Wheat bran is totally indigestible and very harmful, but many doctors recommend it. The phytic acid in wheat bran robs the body of calcium. Bran can scour and strip away the delicate velvet-like lining of the small intestine, causing it to bleed in places.

Essene bread made from sprouted wholewheat can also damage the gut lining, if the wheat is rich in bran. Regardless of being highly recommended for all blood types, it caused three days of painful gut inflammation for me when I tested some I made out of sprouted wholewheat kernels.

How wheat bran still finds its way onto the breakfast table and into "health" muffins to keep people regular, is a mystery to me. In the old days, the wheat was separated from the chaff and the chaff was blown away by the wind. Bran abrasion makes the gut membrane permeable to larger particles of food and especially to undigested proteins from wheat germ and gluten. Once these particles escape into the bloodstream, the immune system is alerted and inflammation sets in. These protein structures can mimic the tissue of adrenal or thyroid glands or similar tissue. The immune system then attacks the whole group of proteins, including those that belong to you!

Some of the food particles that escape through the damaged gut membrane also get trapped around the joints and causes a painful type of inflammation, commonly mistaken for arthritis, especially in people who get mucous, post-nasal drip or heartburn from eating wheat products as they contain the most harmful type of gluten.

Contrary to popular belief, wheat germ is not really beneficial to anybody. According to the blood type lists, only AB[1] (secretors) can tolerate it. Have sensitivity tests done to make sure you are not wheat- or gluten-intolerant. (See pages 8 and 9)

Celiac Disease is widespread

From a ratio of 1 : 5000 historically, Celiac Disease is now as common as 1 : 33. Celiac Disease is an autoimmune condition arising from not being able to digest gluten, especially wheat gluten. It results in severe damage to the intestines, the immune system as well as the nervous system.

Symptoms of Celiac Disease

Abdominal pains, chronic diarrhoea with alternating constipation, weight problems, stunted or delayed growth, anemia, fatigue, numbness or tingling in the legs, joint pain, seizures, irritability and depression, learning disorders in children (ADD and ADHD), gall bladder and thyroid problems.

Today we feed on denatured white flour and use the bran to scour it out of our bodies. How sad it is that many patients with Celiac Disease, Chronn's Disease or irritable bowel syndrome, especially the blood type O individuals, are never advised to stop eating wheat. Some patients are instructed to eat wholewheat bread and bran every day as part of their "treatment" without knowing how harmful it is.

The cure is obvious: symptoms abate shortly after gluten from rye, barley, oats and mainly wheat is removed from the diet. The blood type diet can make a big difference by eliminating other harmful foods and within weeks the patient is miraculously free of many of the symptoms of Celiac Disease. Prior to the days of man growing grains and baking bread, people relied totally on fresh fruit, roots, nuts, herbs and vegetables for sustenance. Even when they ate raw meat, there is adequate proof that these foods kept them very healthy.

Rice and maize cereals are gluten-free. Cereals contain mainly starch so they need to be thoroughly chewed and pre-digested by salivary enzymes prior to being swallowed. Most people eat their breakfast cereals with milk so the starches are not digested. It is better to chew dry cereal. Try roasting these cereals in a little olive oil and herb salt for a delicious snack.

Carbohydrates and the Glycaemic Index

How does the Glycaemic Index work?

The GI system gives every food a rating from 1 to 100 in terms of the amount of insulin that is immediately required to process the carbohydrates and sugars it contains. The top value is based on glucose, at 100. When foods contain fats and different fibres, it slows down the rate of insulin release as these foods take longer to digest in the stomach. Foods like soya beans contain fat and fibre with very little, if any, carbohydrates, so the Glycaemic Index is only 18 out of 100.

Carbohydrates to suit you

All types

Oat bran, millet flour and dehusked granules, , dried green or yellow peas, dried white beans, all rice products including rice flour and noodles

Suit only very few

Maize products (only A^1), wheat flour (only AB and A^1), wheat bran (only AB), wheat germ (only AB^1), chick peas (only O^1), potatoes (only AB, B^1)

A

A^1: wheat flour, wholewheat, barley, oats, rye, maize products, cornflour, soya, lentils, buckwheat, sorghum, sago, mung beans, tapioca, sugar, honey, fructose

A^2: barley, oats, rye, soya, lentils, buckwheat, sorghum, tapioca, sago, mung beans, sugar, honey, fructose

B

B^1: barley, oats, soya flour, potato, sweet potato, sago flour, kidney beans, sugar, honey, fructose

B^2: barley, oats, sorghum, tapioca, sago, sweet potato, honey

AB

AB^1: wheat flour, wholewheat, wheat germ and bran, barley, oats, rye, soya and lentil flour, potato, sweet potato, sugar, honey

AB^2: wheat flour,wheat and oat bran, barley, oats, rye, soya, lentils, potato, sweet potato

O

O^1: oats, rye, soya flour, tapioca, buckwheat, chikpeas, , sago, sweet potato, mung beans, sugar, honey

O^2: rye, lentil flour, sago flour, mung beans, sweet potato

Foods with high GI scores of 70 - 100

These foods cause a flood of insulin, which can cause blood sugar fluctuations and attacks of hypoglycaemia. Examples are: Sugar, honey, grapes, carrots or refined rice and wheat grains.

Foods with low GI scores of 20 - 50

Eat more of these foods: whole grains, unrefined natural foods rich in fats, fibre and protein like dried beans, nuts, seeds, lean meat, eggs, dairy products, fish and all leafy green vegetables.
To lower the Glycaemic Index of rice, potatoes and plain white starches, add fibre like oat bran, flaxseeds, etc. and olive oil to slow down digestion. Acidify anything sweet, like honey, with lemon juice or citric acid to slow down insulin responses.

Diabetics and carbohydrate junkies

You probably consume ten times the amount of carbohydrates you need every day. Even worse, is the fallacy that carbohydrates should form the major part of your food intake. Your worst health problems are caused by lectins that are harmful to you. You can see where the fattening lectins are hanging out! They are usually in morning cereals, pasta, pizza, bread, rolls, potatoes and chips. Carbohydrates and sugar deplete your levels of chromium and zinc that are used to make insulin.

Select and modify your carbohydrates to suit the whole family

No cheating: learn to substitute!

By now you will have a list of suitable grains, legumes and carbohydrates for your blood type. With a bit of practice and perseverance you can still enjoy a large variety of your family favourites. I hope you have already discovered many new foods and dishes that are making your meals more interesting and enjoyable. There are plenty of ideas in the cookery section for using beans, grains, etc. It starts on page 108.

Reduce the starch content and GI of meals

To eat less rice, millet, pasta or potatoes, simply add more lovely vegetables, nuts and herbs to your dishes. To reduce the GI, known as the Glycaemic Index (page 42), we add a little olive or flax oil to the rice, some ground-up flax- and sesame seeds, oat bran and chopped walnuts to the foods. This slows down the insulin reaction. Cook only brown health rice and combine it with non-fattening ingredients like lettuce and parsley to make healthy snacks or starters. For more easy ways to cook and serve rice, see page 127.

Millet replaces couscous

Cook dehusked millet grains the same way as you cook rice; either steamed in a pot or baked in the oven as a casserole. Try a blend of rice and millet. Millet is high in protein, low in fat and is very good for all blood types.

Low GI meals for slimmers with brown rice, vegetables and salads need not be boring!

A Chinese rice hotpot. When you are using a hot oven for a long time, casserole the rice. Use the same ratio of 1 rice to 2 water, add olive oil, sesame seeds, leeks or tofu.

Make delicious risotto with leftover rice. Stir fry onions, celery, mushrooms and other chopped vegetables and then the rice. Add a little stock and simmer.Also add seeds.

Use lettuce leaves and a rice mix for a quick salad, starter or side dish. Dolmades are made from vine leaves wrapped around a small portion of rice and then casseroled.

A big thank you to Mr Bean!

Beans have it all, and more

Fibre, protein, low Glycaemic Index and a delicous base for hummus and beanie dips.

Hummus only for O[1]: so substitute

Chick peas are only for blood type O[1]. Make your own "hummus" with white broad beans, to suit everybody.

Finely chop up onions and garlic and mash them with cooked white beans. Add lashings of olive oil, garlic, herb salt, lemon juice and the essential hummus spice, ground-up cumin seeds. If you have an electric food processor or hand-held blender, work the mixture into a smooth, creamy pulp and enjoy your "hummus".

See pages 29 and 110-112 for good ways to soak, sprout and cook beans to prevent gas, bloating or indigestion.

Dry beans are a rich source of protein

Either canned or home-cooked beans are an economical standby for stretching meals and providing more nourishment to vegetarians. All you need to remember is that not all beans suit all blood types. By now you will be familiar with your permitted selection. Most of your dishes can be prepared with the big white butter beans or the little white beans. The cans of common baked beans also suit all blood types, but rinse off that tomato sauce!

Rice tortilla with bean topping

A tortilla is a flat round cake. You can make them out of rice, stir fried veggies, mashed potato, etc. Pour a few beaten eggs into a pan over any fried bits and pieces and cook till the base sets. Then flip it over and you have a tortilla. Top with fried onions mixed with celery, parsley and whatever else your blood type fancies. Top up with cooked beans, chopped chillies, parsley, tomatoes or grated cheese. Cooked soya mince can be served instead of beef mince. See pages 54-56 for more exciting information about soya beans.

Refried kidney beans or pinto beans contain lectins that only suit blood type B. When dry beans are soaked and sprouted for a few days, the lectins and toxins diminish.

A delicious mixture of fried onions and bits and pieces prepares the way for a can of white broad beans. This is a quick meal, served with salads, toast or tortillas.

Noodles from beans? Mung bean noodles become transparent when cooked. Try a clear soup with lashings of snippered green vegetables (not for B & AB).

Solving the pizza and pasta dilemma!

Alternative pasta: No wheat, tomatoes, meat, or dairy products?

When you crave your favourite Italian foods, don't give in to temptation. These foods revolve around forbidden foods that affect the blood types: harmful lectins that lurk in tomatoes, aubergines, green peppers, pork products, cheeses and especially wheat.

On a strict blood type diet, this means that blood type A[1] and B[1] have to find a substitute for all that tomato.

A delicious alternative to cooked tomatoes

Substitute cooked tomatoes with stirfried onions and grated carrots. Add a few teaspoons of paprika powder, lemon juice, garlic and your own blend of delicious herbs and spices. By the way, the dishes in these pictures do not contain any tomatoes or wheat!

Pasta does not have to be made out of wheat or gluten. Rice noodles are an alternative for people who cannot tolerate the delicious rye pasta that is now available. A gluten-free pasta is also available but check the label as the ingredients often include potato and maize flour. Mung bean noodles are fun to use as they cook up as clear noodles but they are not for B's and AB's . Cheese is a big problem, so select the best you can from page 47. Reduce carbohydrates by cooking green beans with your pasta.

A pizza base to suit your type

If you are not a wheat-eater or have a gluten intolerance, then make your own pizza bases with a combination of suitable flours for your blood type. With a bit of practice you can toss out a tasty pizza. Mix up rice and rye or soya flour in equal quantities. Rub in a little olive oil and herb salt and a pinch of bicarbonate of soda. Moisten with hot water and a splash of lemon juice and mix up the dough till it is like soft putty. Separate into balls, rub with flour and flatten into discs. These can be rubbed with olive oil and pre-baked or just add your topping and place under a hot grill to enjoy your lectin-free pizza!

Dairy, dairy, quite contrary

Milk used to be a health drink?

Our parents drank milk and were encouraged to enjoy lots of wholesome dairy products like cheese, yoghurt and of course, ice cream and milkshakes. In those days, people accepted milk as a major tooth and bone builder and a natural source of calcium and vitamins A and D. Even bone scans from 1945 show bone density improving in direct response to drinking milk. What has changed?

The hazards of milk today

The worst thing that has happened to milk is intervention by modern agricultural science. Floods of antibiotics and bovine growth hormones are injected into cattle and they gush into the cow's milk. As a result, scientists have noticed a direct increase in prostate cancer in men. When it comes to osteoporosis, women who consume large quantities of milk seem to be worse off, with lower bone densities.

Many people have a lactose intolerance but allergies to the milk protein casein are on the increase, although they are seldom diagnosed as such. The leaky-gut syndrome causes casein to escape into bodily tissues where it sets off autoimmune disorders in the same way that gluten, found in grains like wheat, does. See page 42 for the gory story.

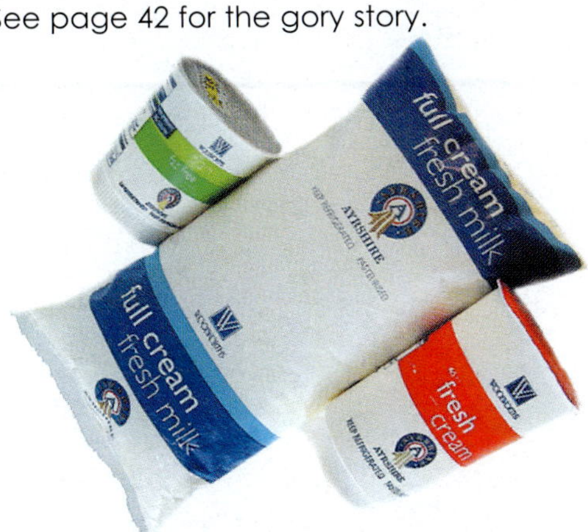

Look out for milk products that are free of bovine hormones and antibiotics. This milk comes from specially reared Ayrshire cows that feed on fresh open pastures, just like they used to! Organically produced eggs, meat, fish and chicken are also available.

Our society revolves around dairy products

Imagine a life without milk, cheese, butter, yoghurt and ice cream? Sadly, these products do not suit all of us and can cause annoying mucous problems like post-nasal drips, hay fever and wheezy chests. Even though blood types B and AB are suited to cow's milk and most of the delicious cheeses, they too, can be allergic to lactose or casein. It is best to first test people for individual intolerances. (See page 8.)

Blood types O and A need alternatives to cow's milk. Try rice, soya or goat's milk. Lactose intolerance means yoghurt and cheeses made from cultured milk are OK, but avoid whey as it is rich in casein that A's and O's do not tolerate . Buttermilk and butter are fine for types O and B, but they are not ideal for blood types A and AB. Vegans know one better and avoid the lot, with no ill effects!

Alternatives to milk and milk products

Goat's milk and cheese suit all blood types except O². although available at most of the better supermarkets, you pay more. Infants who are fed baby formulations and cereals that contain cow's milk, whey, wheat or other prime blood type trouble-makers usually thrive on goat's milk. Soya milk is also good as an alternative, especially for vegans, but not O² and B². Genuine Mozzarella cheese is made out of buffalo milk. That tiny ball of buffalo Mozzarella cheese in the blue packet costs the same as 7 litres of milk!

Make your own nut butters and cheeses

Get nifty with a hand-held blender, some seeds and nuts and a little olive oil, spices, etc. Make healthy nut butters and even a type of "cheese", like the sunflower seed cheese, pictured above. Recipes and techniques are on page 115.

Eggs suit all blood types and do not raise cholesterol

The cholesterol enigma: should we eat eggs?

People react with fear and suspicion when eggs are mentioned, because of the assumed cholesterol problem. One automatically reasons that because an egg contains cholesterol, you are going to suffer an increase in your blood cholesterol if you eat eggs. "Egged" on by their misinformed doctors, heart patients deny themselves the health-giving nutrients contained in eggs. Lecithin, a cholesterol-busting substance that emulsifies fats is part of the miraculous structure of the egg yolk. Choline and inositol are nutrients provided by eggs that control fat metabolism in the liver. Slating eggs is truly an "eggnigma" to me!

Lecithin granules and liquid are made from extracts of soya beans as well as eggs.

The proof of the problem is in the eating

The Townsend magazine reports on egg-eating trials which really prove that human cholesterol levels are not raised by eating eggs. Over a period of two years, 8 000 individuals from a cross section of the population were allowed to eat one or two eggs every day, along with their usual food intake. Their cholesterol levels were monitored on a regular basis. No rise in blood cholesterol could be measured in relation to egg consumption .

Steam an egg in a hollow of stir fried spinach in a pan. Add some feta cheese.

The sinister side of eggs

Raw eggs are often contaminated with bacteria like Salmonella. Make sure you buy fresh, free range eggs and eat them lightly cooked: either boiled or poached. Raw egg white destroys biotin, a B-vitamin, so take vitamin B complex if you consume raw eggs or albumen frequently. Vegans do not eat eggs.

Microwave a whole egg, but the yolk will burst unless it is pierced. To keep the hole open, use a toothpick or a twig of rosemary. Line the dish with leftover rice, etc.

Now enjoy your eggs and try these new ideas

1 Line a bowl with leftover rice and vegetables. Pop in an egg and microwave for a minute. First prick in the yolk with a skewer.
2 As a variation, add cheese and mushrooms to the bowl of rice, cheese, etc. Pour on a beaten egg. Microwave for 1 minute or place into a steamer for a few minutes.
3 Pour a beaten egg over vegetables stir fried in a bit of olive oil. Top with cheese, grill and enjoy as a crustless quiche.
4 Stir fry a pan of spinach and onion. Crack an egg into a hollow, made in the middle of the spinach and cover with a lid for one minute. Crumble some feta cheese on top.

Make a sensational egg pie. Line the dish with rice and vegetables, add chopped mushrooms and cheese. Pour over a beaten egg. Microwave for a minute or place in a steamer.

Oils, fats and dairy products to suit your blood type

We all need fats and oils, but...

We need more of the essential fatty acids that suit our blood type, especially more of the Omega 3's. (See page 50.) Some fats may suit your blood type but lashings of them can still do you harm, especially the trans-fatty acids that form when you overheat any fat. It is best to only use a little olive oil or ghee for cooking. A fat-free diet is not benefical because we need essential fatty acids. Weight gain and heart problems may also have other causes.

All blood types

Olive oil, walnuts, eggs, flaxseeds, salmon oil, cod liver oil capsules, clarified butter (ghee), oily fish: salmon, mackerel, tuna, sardines and pilchards

Not for all blood types

Coconut oil (except A^2), corn and cottonseed oil, pork fat, margarine, foods cooked at a high heat, rancid oils or nuts. No commercial ice cream
Peanuts only for A^1, sunflower products only A, butter only B and O

A

Peanuts, canola oil, soya oil, sesame and sunflower seeds and oil, feta cheese, goat's, sheep and buffalo cheese, yoghurt, soya milk
A^2: peanut oil, coconut

B

Butter, casein (whey), most cheeses eg: cottage, feta, edam, gouda, goat, gruyere, buffalo, goat's and sheep cheeses, etc.
Cows' milk, cream, yoghurt
B^2: No camembert, cheddar, emmenthaler, parmesan cheeses, no soya milk or soya products

AB

Casein (whey), most cheeses eg: cheddar, edam, cottage cheese, feta, gouda, goat's, gruyere, etc., milk, cream, yoghurt, soya milk, canola oil
AB^2: no soya oil

O

Butter, canola oil, sesame seeds and oil.
O^1: Feta, buffalo and goat cheese, soya milk
O^2: No feta cheese, no cow's, goat's or buffalo milk products or soya milk or soya products

Why no ice cream for any of us?

What a blow! Chocolate and red wine suit all blood types but the ice cream we eat today is not exactly nutritious. First of all, we have milk, lactose and casein allergies to consider. Some sorbets as well as ice cream contain mainly whey and milk solids. To make them extra creamy, coconut oil and indigestible hydrogenated vegetable oils that cause inflammation are often added to the "ice cream".

Read the label: ice cream contains sugar, chemical emulsifiers, whiteners, stabilizers and the like. Tofu (soya) ice cream is a better choice and so is frozen yoghurt, but they do not suit all blood types. Make your own healthy frozen delights out of fruit. (See pages 152 and 153.)

Cut out the fatty fries and greasy goo

Watch those harmful fats! Frying is not the best option, neither is pork.

This Malaysian roti made from white dough, filled with old mince and drenched in palm oil leads to diabetes and heart attacks!

Are you getting enough Omega 3 oil?

Omega 3 oils are scarce

Essential fatty acids are those we cannot make in our own bodies, so we need to add them to our diet. We get plenty of the Omega 6 fatty acids from common oils like olive oil, canola and sunflower oil. Although they are essential, the ratio to the Omega 3 group is usually way off, being 90% Omega 6 and only 10% omega 3. This causes inflammatory reactions in the body, especially when levels of trans-fatty acids from margarine and fried foods as well as too many saturated fats from animal products, are eaten.

The margarine myth

Spread a little poison! South Africans consume margarine in preference to butter and battle with high blood pressure, blocked arteries and heart attacks, despite the promotion of "healthy margarine" laden with trans-fatty acids as a way to prevent these conditions. If you want an easy spreading butter, simply blend softened butter with an equal quantity of olive, grapeseed or canola oil. Keep it in the fridge for a convenient and economical spread.

Blend softened butter with olive oil. Keep it in the fridge for a handy alternative to margarine.

How to include more Omega 3 oil in your daily diet

Cod liver oil and salmon oil provide the best form of Omega 3 oil available to the body. We can also eat foods that are naturally high in omega 3 oils every day.

1 Flaxseeds (linseeds) are very cheap and 1kg costs far less than the cold pressed oil. You get all the extra nutrients like lignans, fibre and a cure for chronic constipation or estrogen deficiencies as well. The secret is to grind them up fresh every day in an electric coffee grinder. Make delicious combinations with the nuts and seeds that suit you best. Take at least a tablespoon of the mixture every day. Use it as a sprinkle on cereal, salads, on open sandwiches, on vegetables or in dips.

2 Walnuts are very rich in Omega 3 oils. They also suit all blood types and are healing to the body in many ways, as well as being a delicious treat.

3 Eggs are a good source of Omega 3, as are fish oil and oily fish like tuna, pilchards and mackerel.

4 Avocados contain a perfect ratio of all the essential fatty acids (not for B, AB & O[1]). The fleshy green leaves of the herb purslane are rich in vitamin E, Omega 3 and 6 oils as well as vitamin C.

Prostaglandins control inflammation

Prostaglandins, like hormones, relay information to our cells. We react to an excess of prostaglandin PGE2 by producing symptoms : sore joints, redness, itching, swelling, asthma, PMS, water retention, bloating, headaches, mood swings and depression. To switch to a dominance of the anti-inflammatory prostaglandins known as PGE1 and PGE3, we need to reduce the intake of saturated fats from cream, coconut, peanuts and animal fats. They have to be replaced with the anti-inflammatory group of Omega 3 oils plus we need anti-oxidants and more alkaline minerals. (See page 82.)

Fish is nutritious and affordable, but...

Fish spoils rapidly and it gets infected

Fish should be eaten within 24 hours of leaving the water and be kept refridgereated. Fish like mackerel, tuna, sardines, anchovies and herring are subject to rapid microbial decomposition. All these fish contain high levels of the amino acid histidine that converts to histamine once a bacterial infection develops in the polyamines and putrescene contained in fish flesh. This begins once the fish dies, often prior to any bad taste or odour forming. Parasites that live inside the fish gut and flesh add to the toxic levels and tapeworm cysts can be released into your body if you eat raw or undercooked fish. After a few days of lying around the fish counters, fish lets off a characteristic ammonia-like smell: a sure sign that the fish is decomposing.

Fish often leaves the boat and hangs around all day in the heat. We all know about fish markets and fish jokes. Sometimes large worms ooze out from the heads of decapitated fish such as snoek. Try to buy fresh fish straight out of the water and eat it soon.

Nothing could be fresher than these mackerel, being cooked on the boat that is moored in a Turkish harbour. Straight from the sea but fried in sunflower oil that has seen better days. The chef simply tops up the pan of old black oil with his can.

Eat your fish fresh and free from toxins

Pregnant women are warned not to eat too many cans of tuna per week as the mercury contamination accumulates in the unborn child. As more toxins are dumped into the ocean, fish begin to die from chemical poisoning. Most of the toxins accumulate in their livers. There is no guarantee that the fish in your sushi was not already dying in the sea.

Unless fish is eaten fresh, it releases high levels of infected polyamines (amino acids), putrescene and histadine that trigger the formation of histamine. Some people react and get ill within 10 minutes of eating tainted fish. Cooking and freezing do not help to destroy histamine and putrescene.

Symptoms of seafood poisoning

Severe allergic reactions occur within 10 minutes to 2 hours after ingestion of contaminated fish or toxic shellfish: facial flushing or swelling, a tightness in the chest, sweating, nausea, vomiting, itching, severe headaches, thirst, red body rashes, dizziness and diarrhoea. Get medical help fast!

Getting the most out of fish

Eat the fish recommended for your blood type on page 53. Be wary of eating fish out, unless you can be sure it will be fresh and served grilled, steamed, stir fried or cooked in olive oil. Canned fish like tuna, sardines, mackerel and salmon make a quick and delicious meal. See page 134 for some quick and practical ways to prepare canned fish.

Fish oil and the Omega 3 contribution

Salmon oil is rich in Omega 3 essential fatty acids. These supplements are very expensive, so try cod liver oil capsules or eat more oily fish. Cod liver oil is rich in vitamins A and D and is good for arthritis and skin disorders. Do not overdose as it accumulates in the liver. Flaxseed oil or walnut oil are alternative but inferior sources of Omega 3 oil for vegetarians.

The hazards of eating meat

Why meat is not always safe to eat

The original blood type O hunter-gatherer thrived on a diet of fresh, organically grown free-range meat. His high intensity gastric acids and digestive juices were designed to break down meat fats and protein. This is why many pathogens like bacteria and parasites could be destroyed prior to entering the rest of the digestive tract.

Today we scoff down meat with starches and fatty fries. Our stomach acid has weakened and we unleash a host of potential hazards and diseases into our bodies: E-coli bacteria, Salmonella, tapeworm and liver flukes. Furthermore, the animals have been dosed with anabolic hormones such as estrogen, steroids, growth hormones, antibiotics and the like. These animals no longer have clean open fields to graze in. They are often pumped full of fattening grains, fishmeal and animal waste products that cause degenerative or genetic disruptions in their constitutions. Eating "unclean" or unsuitable meat can be downright dangerous. Remember mad cow's disease and SARS?

Beef is not for blood type A

Blood type A does not have strong stomach acid and at best should only eat small amounts of well-cooked turkey, chicken, mutton or ostrich meat. Beef eaters should try to obtain free-range organic meat that is free from hormones or antibiotics. Cook it well to destroy tapeworm cysts and other pathogens. Eat meat on an empty stomach so that it can be properly digested. Starch is best eaten separately. Don't drink cold beverages as stomach acid works best at higher temperatures.

Lamb is the home of liver flukes

Lamb and mutton that is not well-cooked can harbour liver and pancreatic flukes, plus their eggs or cysts. Many common diseases such as diabetes, cancer, liver toxicity and even endometriosis are linked to the way these flukes travel inside your body and set up new breeding sites.

Why pork is bad for us

Jewish and Muslim people are instructed to stay away from pork for a very good reason. Pork and ostrich meat are regarded as unclean meats because these animals are scavengers and are not designed to be eaten, according to their laws.

Pseudo-vegetarians also avoid pork, even if some of them eat fish or eggs. Pigs harbour many diseases because of their diet: rotten fermented food, offal, animal dung, dead animals and human excreta. You are what you eat! Smoked or cured pork products like bacon and salami or kasseler ribs offer no protection from parasites, bacteria and even viral infections. Meat that lies around at room temperature for weeks on end is by no means hygienic or safe to eat.

Raw pork meat is infested with bacteria and parasites, especially tapeworm and liver flukes. Vast amounts of fatty tissue absorb toxins but this slows down the pig's blood circulation to such an extent that it cannot be slaughtered or bled according to religious custom. Swine flesh is thus regarded as unclean. It is infused with higher levels of toxins and bacteria than other types of meat. Pigs do not eliminate toxins via the skin because they have no sweat glands. Instead, the waste material exudes from an outlet under their feet, as you can see in the picture below.

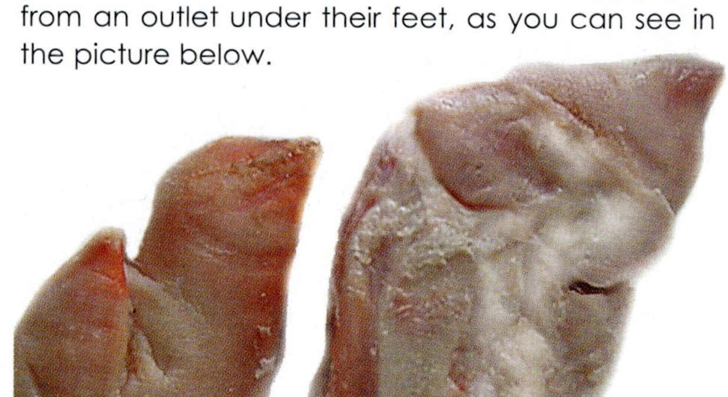

Meat, fish, game and poultry for your blood type

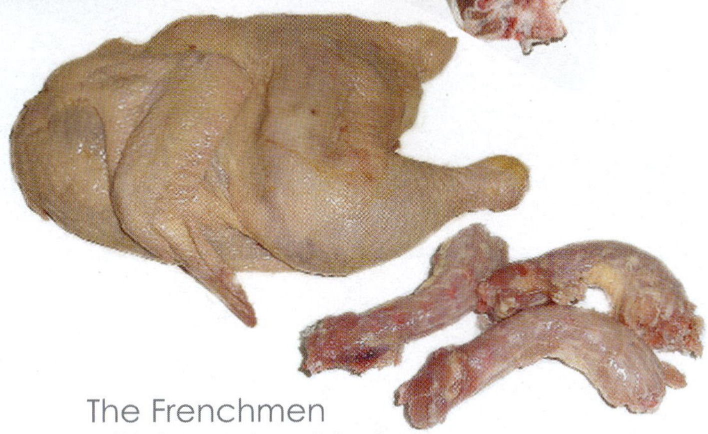

All types

Turkey and ostrich meat, mutton except A^1, cob (kabeljou), mackerel, monkfish, mullet, salmon, tuna, sardines and pilchards

Not for anybody

Pork in any form, especially pork fat.
Octopus only suits A^2 and oysters are only for O.
Vegetarians: watch out for foods containing animal products as in liver, hormone and arthritis supplements or glandular extracts and gelatine. in

A

Chicken, turkey, carp, snails, trout, yellowtail. A^1: Duck, mutton. A^2: haddock, hake, herring, mussels, octopus

Both A's avoid: beef, lamb, veal, venison, crab, crayfish, oyster, sole, and calamari

B

Beef, lamb, mutton, turkey, veal, venison, carp, haddock, hake, herring, sole, calamari. B^2: snails, yellowtail

Both B's avoid: chicken, duck, anchovy, crab, crayfish, mussels, octopus, oysters and trout

AB

Beef, lamb, mutton, turkey, carp, herring, mussels, snails,calamari

AB^2: venison & trout
Both AB's avoid: chicken, duck, veal, anchovy, crab, haddock, hake, crayfish, octopus, oysters, sole, yellowtail

O

Beef, chicken, duck, lamb, mutton, turkey, veal, venison, carp, haddock, hake, herring, crayfish, mussels, oysters, sole, snails, trout, yellowtail. O^1: anchovy, crab

Both O's avoid octopus and calamari

The Frenchmen with large boobies!

In France, unwanted chicken necks were often given to the labourers in meat-processing plants. After a steady diet of this discarded delicacy, they really got it in the neck, as voluptuous breast tissue began to develop. Their wives objected to this form of competition, especially when some of them complained of moodiness, bloating and shall we say, symptoms of "a-menstrual stress"!

Chickens are injected in the neck with anabolic steroid hormones like growth hormones and especially estrogen. As we know, estrogen is a notorious weight-enhancing hormone and this produces chickens with more fat and plump breasts and thighs. Oh dear! Fortunately the men returned to normal once the fault in their diet was detected and the chicken necks were made into pet food.

Blood type B and chicken

Telling blood type B that chicken is unsuitable for them can make me as a blood-type eating enthusiast very unpopular! Muslims and Jews with health problems are usually blood type B chicken-eaters. They argue that chickens are Halaal or Kosher and therefore bled and blessed, but what about those lectins, growth hormones and antibiotics?

The soya bean is full of surprises!

Soya substitutes just about everything

The Chinese people call soya beans "meat from the ground". Not only can they mimic meat and especially mince, they act as fillers and binders for many of the processed meats you eat. Soya beans are not considered to be starches, due to their unique composition of fibres, fats and protein. Soya milk can be made out of boiled soya beans as a substitute for milk. When soya milk is coagulated, it becomes a white curd known as tofu or beancurd. Fried or steamed tofu is an alternative to fish or scrambled eggs. Ice cream made out of soya milk is dairy-free, nutritious and high in protein.

Soya products are very versatile

Dried beancurd is as enjoyable to eat as biltong or jerky, the dried meat that so many people love. Plain green soya beans, lightly boiled are as compulsively delicious to eat as peanuts and are far lower in toxins and kilojoules. The dried and salted black soya bean is an essential flavourant for Oriental foods, as in soya sauce. Miso paste makes a good substitute for stock cubes. Fermented soya products where cultures have been introduced into bean extracts provide cancer-fighting enzymes that are beneficial to blood type A and help to strengthen their immune systems.

Soya textured vegetable protein, soya flour, fermented beans, dried beans, fresh green soya beans

Soya beans are rich in lecithin

Soya beans contain a lot of lecithin. Although fatty in appearance and texture, lecithin is an emulsifying agent and helps to break up fatty deposits in the blood vessels. It disperses fats into water so they can be expelled by the body. Lecithin helps prevent arteriosclerosis, protects against cardiovascular disease and increases brain function. Lecithin promotes energy and helps to alleviate liver congestion as well as ailments. It is being used successfully in health regimens for immune problems, brain and nervous disorders, herpes viruses and diseases associated with ageing. Lecithin surrounds all the cell membranes, preventing oxidation and making them flexibile and more waterproof. It protects the brain and all nerve cells. Lecithin is composed of choline, inositol and linoleic acid. Lecithin granules can be added to foods like cereals and chocolate drinks. (See page 150.)

Soya meat substitutes often contain wheat, so read the labels. Try making your own soya protein foods.

Soya flour for body-building or baking

Soya flour is available in a raw as well as a cooked form. De-fatted soya flour and soya protein isolates are also for sale, but are usually incorporated into expensive health drinks and body-building formulations. Make sure that you can tolerate soya products before you eat them in large quantities. Check up on pages 11 and 13. Use soya flour as a substitute for white flour and even eggs when baking. Soya flour works well for thickening soups and stews.

Textured vegetable protein (TVP)

The brown granules and chunks in the picture above are made out of soya textured vegetable protein. When well-prepared, it can be used as a meat substitute in most of our favourite dishes. Being very cheap, it provides excellent nourishment to the family and is good for binding meat balls, stews, etc. instead of using flour or breadcrumbs. Grinding the soya mince in an electric coffee grinder makes a nice coating for frying meat or fish or it can be used in baking as a substitute for biscuit crumbs.

There are soya meat substitutes, but...

Read the labels of the products carefully. You may be able to escape from meat, but not from wheat. Health shops sell a selection of soya sausages and burgers but I am still looking for some without wheat or any form of gluten. See page 56 for more ways to enjoy soya protein.

Soya is the "meat from the ground"

Soya as a protein

Soya contains all eight essential amino acids. It is free of cholesterol and lactose and is high in fibre, essential fatty acids and lecithin. Soya digests easily and is one of the cheapest forms of protein to produce in agriculture as compared to milk, meat or eggs. Symptoms of protein deficiency are said to be: water retention, a weak immune system, impaired muscle development, hair loss, poor concentration and a lack of energy. Amino acids are required for the development of bones, muscles, blood and body tissues. Many modern illnesses arise from a classic protein deficiency.

Soya for leaky gut and heart disease

Soya reduces plaque formation in arteries. The high content of lecithin and essential fatty acids plays an important role in maintiaining the strength and elasticity of blood vessels. It helps to keep them selectively permeable, thus preventing the escape of undigested food particles into body tissues, a condition known as leaky-gut syndrome.

Soya for diabetics and slimmers

Soya increases insulin sensitivity by making the receptor sites more responsive, so food is immediately available as a source of energy. Soya scores a low 18 on the glycaemic index as opposed to over 80 for sweets, bread, potatoes and fruit juice. It has a slower passage through the digestive system and helps to stave off hunger pangs for longer and prevent hypoglycemia, or low blood sugar spells. Soya contains oliglysaccharides which encourage the production of bifido micro-organisms, helping to promote the growth of friendly gut microflora to control yeast overgrowth and maintain a healthy gut. The high fibre content speeds up the elimination of toxins and cholesterol.

CAUTION: soya, cancer & estrogen

Non secretors: O^2 and B^2 should not eat all of the soya products as they do not secrete the antigen that favours soya. First test your tolerance to each one or get a practitioner to advise you.

Do not fall for claims that soya cures or prevents hormonally-affected cancers, because it can also do just the opposite! Soya can be of benefit in providing antioxidant compounds, protease inhibitors and other nutrients to help modify lung and colon cancer, but so can many other foods.

Soya is rich in the isoflavones genistein and daidsein. Some remedies for the menopause contain these extracts, but they occur naturally in soya. Phyto-oestrogens contained in soya attach to the body's oestrogen receptors and act like estrogen. Herbs like red clover and black cohosh also contain these two isoflavones, plus two more, called biochanin and formonometin. This makes them safer remedies with a weaker estrogenic effect. Both these herbs have been well-researched in terms of cancer and cardiovascular safety.

Soya can cause weight gain

Soya boosts estrogen levels and this can cause weight gain. When excess oestrogen is not effectively broken down by the liver and removed from the body, it accumulates and may cause breast cancer, heart disease, blood clotting and high blood pressure. Eating too much soya can be harmful in this way because it triggers estrogen dominance and this blocks thyroid activity. In turn, this produces a sluggish metabolism and weight gain. If you gain weight when you eat a lot of soya, this may be your problem.

New ways to cook and prepare soya textured vegetable protein (TVP)

Make TVP taste good and everybody will enjoy it

Soya textured vegetable protein (TVP) is available in two colours. The dark chunks and mince best resemble meat when making stews, etc. The lighter variety is nicer for chicken dishes, baking and to add to granola-type cereals or for making toasted soya snacks. Large soya protein chunks are very cheap, but we need to make them more palatable. When soaked in hot vegetable stock, they swell up to twice their size. Tear these chunks into smaller pieces and they almost look like pieces of meat. Add them to meat dishes, or transform them into vegetarian dishes. Begin by browning your onions, then add them to the pot.

Toasted soya mince for cereals and snacks

Mix a few cups of soya granules with a little olive or canola oil and a few tablespoons of brown sugar or sweet molasses. Spread them in a baking dish or flat tray and bake at a moderate heat for about twenty minutes. Alternatively, mix into raw oats and then bake them. Stir every ten minutes as the edges begin to brown. You can also do this in a heavy frying pan on low heat. Remove when crispy and allow to cool. Keep in containers and mix with nuts and seeds.Add these to the morning granola or enjoy as snacks. Instead of sugar, you can flavour the granules with herb salt and spices for delicious spicy Indian curry snacks.

A mince base for pasta, bobotie, samoosas, etc.

Although you can buy flavoured soya mince granules, there is no guarantee of them being free of nasty chemicals and artificial flavours. To make your own dishes, soak the plain dark soya mince in hot stock. Add herb salt and an exciting blend of herbs and spices. Then fry up onions, celery, etc. in olive oil in a pan. Stir in the soaked soya granules, add more liquid, tomato paste or curry sauce. Place a lid on the pot or pan and allow to simmer gently for about twenty minutes. The mixture must be quite moist. Just before serving, sprinkle in a little rice flour to instantly thicken the mixture. Add sprouts and fresh herbs like coriander, etc.

Soya burgers and meatballs

Grind the soya mince in a coffee grinder to use instead of flour or breadcrumbs when making meat balls or fish cakes. Fried soya patties can be made out of cooked soya beans that are mashed up or use soya mince, soaked in stock. Drain off the water and squeeze out excess moisture before combining with a binder like soya or rye flour or oats. Season with herb salt, spices and chopped onions, celery, parsley, garlic, etc. The mixture must be firm and sticky so you can form it into balls. Roll them in the ground-up soya crumbs and fry gently in a shallow smear of olive oil till golden brown and crispy.

Everyday herbs to use for healthy happy eating

Parsley

Parsley for iron, chlorophyll and fresher breath

Fresh parsley only costs a few rand a bunch. By eating a generous handful daily you can effectively flush out toxins whilst you gain extra vitality. Parsley helps to cure anaemia, bad breath, body odours, water retention, kidney disorders, arthritis, gallstones, poor circulation and menstrual problems. Parsley is rich in iron, chlorophyll, vitamins A, B2, B6 and C as well as potassium. Parsley can be eaten with crude black molasses to increase iron absorption. Add lots of freshly chopped parsley to soups, salads, and other meals. Serve sprigs of parsley after meals, to freshen breath, especially after eating garlic.

Sage for boosting estrogen

Sage cleanses and stimulates the liver and aids the digestion of fats. It helps to increase the circulation of blood to the brain. Sage is a powerful antiseptic for wounds. Make a strong tea from fresh or dried sage leaves to apply to cuts and grazes. Gargle sage tea with salt, honey and lemon juice for sore throats or use as a mouthwash after surgery or for mouth ulcers. Sage tea is used for fevers, night sweats and menopausal hot flushes as it can mimic the action of estrogen.

Sage

Rosemary

Rosemary to eat with fatty foods

Rosemary remedies have been used to effectively treat flatulence, coughs, dizziness, colds, nervousness, cramps, poor circulation, sore throats, headaches, nausea, gout and especially hangovers! It also aids the digestion of fats and rich food. Use dry or fresh rosemary in teas or mixed with food; especially lamb and rich, fatty dishes. It grows easily from sprigs. Use a bunch of sprigs as a basting brush. The older twigs can be stripped of leaves to use as kebab skewers. A few rosemary leaves burning on the stove, hotplate or open fire will burn like fragrant incense. CAUTION: not for pregnancy, high blood pressure or epilepsy.

Thyme for coughs, tight chests, asthma and parasites

Thyme is a very powerful healer of many ailments including high cholesterol, nasal and chest congestion, poor circulation, asthma, headaches, depression, fatigue, aches and pains and weakened immunity. Thyme is one of the best known herbs in the kitchen for its delicious aroma when added to omelettes, salads, fish and stews. Thyme eaten regularly in large amounts will help eliminate body parasites. Inhale thyme infusions to clear congested sinuses and chests or add it to a baby's bath. Use fresh thyme when you can get it or grow it yourself.

Thyme

Fresh peppermint

Mint for stimulating the brain

Mint oil is a powerful brain stimulant. Chew fresh mint leaves and include it in teas and juices. Mint tea is good for nausea, chills, colic, indigestion and rheumatism. For a minty spray, fill a spray bottle with water, add a few drops of peppermint oil and spray around you for drowsiness, nausea, as an appetite suppressant and to help keep flies and mosquitoes away. Mint oil can be used to get rid of hair lice and nits so use a few drops in shampoo, conditioners and hair gel as well as the rinsing water. Mint is excellent for colic and flatulence. The dried leaves can be rubbed through a sieve and sprinkled onto food, or use fresh mint.

Fennel seeds are good for cramps and low estrogen

Fennel is one of the best cures for cramps, bloating, gas and colic as it is a powerful antispasmodic. It is a component of gripe water (Behoedmiddel). If you are breastfeeding, chew a few fennel seeds with every meal to help your baby's colic. For severe bloating, flatulence and abdominal pain , mix 1 teaspoon of fennel powder (barishap) in a little honey. Fennel can help stop copious menstrual bleeding because it mimics the action of estrogen. Chew fennel seeds after a meal to aid digestion, prevent hot flushes, flatulence and to freshen breath.

Fennel leaves, flowers and seeds

Common garden dandelion

Dandelions for water retention and extra potassium

To herbalists, the dandelion is the safest diuretic to use, as its high potassium content prevents minerals from being lost via the urine. Dandelions relieve water retention and bloating and they strengthen the liver. They help both the pancreas and the liver to detoxify and release more digestive enzymes and hormones like insulin. Pick a few fresh dandelion leaves every day and add them to the juices, soups, stir fries and salads you make. The yellow flowers and their stems can be eaten. They also make an attractive garnish for salads and snacks.

Bay leaves help diabetics with their insulin

Bay leaves assist in the digestion and absorption of food. They stimulate the release of digestive secretions, especially fat-digesting enzymes and insulin. After recent trials it was found that bay leaves helped to increase the effect of insulin. Diabetics can try taking a pinch of bay leaf powder with their meals. Modern uses: for warming the stomach and bladder, to relieve wasp and bee stings, for liver and gallbladder complaints, digesting rich foods and breaking up fats. Bay leaves stimulate the onset of menstrual periods.

Dried and fresh bay leaves

Soup celery. Eat the leaves for a lovely golden tan.

Celery eases water retention and improves your tan!

Bergapten is a herbal compound contained in celery leaves that stimulates suntanning. Crunching fresh green celery stalks is said to be a powerful aphrodisiac. Celery seeds have been used medicinally for over 3000 years, especially in Egypt and China. They help kidneys dispose of uric acid, mucous and toxic wastes to reduce acidity. Uses: for arthritis, gout, sore muscles and joints, to improve blood circulation, kidney and bladder infections, asthma, bronchitis, water retention and high blood pressure. Take half a teaspoon of ground-up celery seeds in a little honey once or twice a day for the best benefits. Add celery leaf and seed powder to table salt.

Fresh garlic cloves

Garlic cures all, including high cholesterol

How many of us take antibiotics, decongestants, blood thinners, cholesterol drugs, heart medicine and immunity boosters on a continuous basis without looking for safe, cheap and effective alternatives? Garlic is all of the above. It is one of the most extensively used and researched substances ever known to man. It has antibacterial, antifungal, antiparasitic, antiprotozoan and antiviral properties. Trials based on people eating one to three whole garlic cloves per day have produced remarkable results in terms of preventing colds and flu, keeping the blood thin without a daily aspirin and bringing down their cholesterol levels.

Nasturtiums and watercress to expel liver flukes

The leaves of these plants have a strong mustard-like flavour and are delicious chopped up in salads. Nasturtiums have antibiotic properties and can even shake off colds, chest infections or sore throats. The juice is excellent for skin infections. Nasturtium leaves can be eaten every day in salads or in sandwiches. Chewing a lot of watercress a few times a week will rid the gut, liver and pancreas of flukes, the miniature slug-like parasites that breed there. They usually come from infected meat, especially undercooked mutton. (See page 71.) Watercress is good for digestion and to detoxify the blood.

Watercress

Nasturtium leaves and flowers

Alfalfa, called the Father of all foods

Alfalfa leaves and seeds

Alfalfa and its sprouts are not good for blood type O. The isoflavones in alfalfa leaves are highly estrogenic in activity. Alfalfa stimulates the immune system, is rich in nutrients, especially minerals, vitamins, alkaloids and trace elements. A tablespoon of the sprouts contains all the vitamins, enzymes and minerals we require for a day. The seeds were eaten by the Persians and Greeks for thousands of years. Alfalfa is not recommended for those with autoimmune diseases like lupus. Estrogenic effects may lower thyroid activity or interfere with conception.

Flaxseeds/linseeds help to protect against malaria

Ground-up flaxseeds provide a host of nutrients and phytochemicals like fibres, lignans, essential Omega 3 fatty acids and even a type of estrogen. (See page 36.) They also help to expel tapeworm. The green flax plants are a valuable source of many of these nutrients, plus a few more. Plant yourself a patch of flaxseeds. Within a few weeks the young shoots can be eaten. Taking capsules made from the shoots is a mosquito deterrent as they do not like the way you smell when your blood is impregnated with these phytocemicals. Pregnant women can try flax shoots, combined with olive leaves against malaria. (See page 34.)

Flaxseeds and fresh flaxseed sprigs

Salted liquorice, Borsdruppels, Sen-Sen

Liquorice to balance sodium and potassium

Liquorice contains aldosterone, a hormone that balances sodium and potassium to prevent dehydration. Liquorice encourages the flow of saliva and improves the fluidity of mucous, to ease dry and sore throats. It soothes gastric ulcers. Liquorice is used for treating low blood pressure, chronic fatigue, hypoglycemia, estrogen deficiencies and adrenal dysfunction. It is available as a powder from health shops, as the Dutch remedy Borsdruppels, as black liquorice sweets or Dutch salted liquorice. The breath freshener called Sen-Sen is made out of liquorice. Deglycyrrhised liquorice (DGL) is the best form to take.

Kitchen spices come from Mother Nature's medicine chest

The aromatic curry spices we use today all have medicinal uses. Spices like ginger, chillies, cloves, coriander and turmeric have served as medicines to mankind for thousands of years. Using spices to flavour our food and make it taste delicious is proof indeed that medicine does not have to be such a bitter pill to swallow.

Fresh ginger root

Kaloontjie seeds/black cumin

Ginger for nausea, motion sickness and blood thinning

Ginger stimulates the circulation, thins blood, lowers cholesterol and helps to relieve motion sickness and morning sickness. Instead of taking a daily aspirin or rat poison to thin the blood, ginger can be just as effective. It does not irritate the stomach lining, cause gastric bleeding, or destroy capillary tissue, either! A few slices of fresh ginger can be added to food or to herb teas every day. Ginger has a warming action and is good for cold hands and feet. Jamaica Ginger tincture is sold at supermarkets and pharmacies. Use ginger every day in your food to prevent blood-clotting.

Black cumin, known as kaloontjie or onion seeds

To the Islamic people, kaloontjie seeds are regarded as a panacea, to cure all ailments except death. They benefit the digestive system, soothe stomach pain, ease wind, bloating and colic. They have antiseptic properties and help to expel intestinal worms. People chew a few seeds to relieve headaches, nasal catarrh and toothache. Taken in larger quantities of about a quarter of a teaspoon twice a day, kaloontjie is traditionally used as a diuretic, a cure for diabetes or arthritis, to promote menstruation and to increase breast milk production. These seeds can be ground up and used as a substitute for black pepper. (See page 29.)

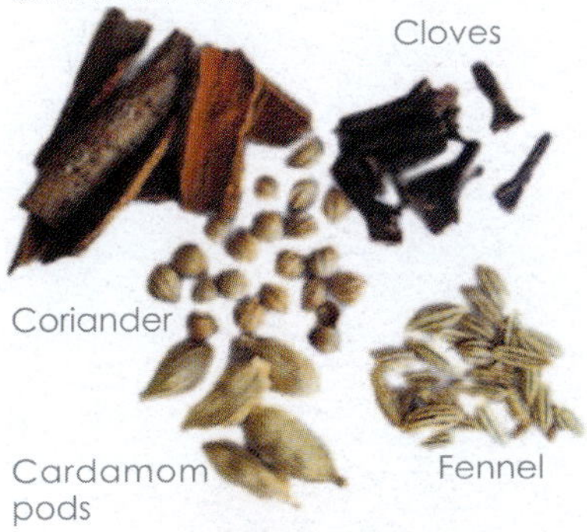

Mix powdered spices with honey to take as a medicine.

Learn how to use your spices to treat common family ailments.

Cloves for toothache and eliminating parasites

Cloves are one of most effective and safest remedies we have for intestinal parasites like worms, protozoa and gut flukes. Add a quarter of a teaspoon of clove powder to a teaspoon of honey or molasses and take it at lunch, supper and bedtime for a few days. Reduce this dose to a tiny pinch for small children. Taking a few teaspoons of ground-up flaxseeds in your daily cereal will speed up the process. Medicinally, clove oil or whole cloves are a reliable standby for toothache and some people suck them to freshen breath. Clove oil keeps most insects away and ants will not come near a line of clove oil that has been painted across a doorway. Use cloves in potpourri and in herbal sachets.

Cinnamon for gut infections and diabetes

Cinnamon is a valuable remedy for diabetics, but not for blood type B or O[2] . Research based on taking 1ml of cinnamon daily at meals containing carbohydrates and sugars showed its effectiveness in lowering levels of glucose in the blood. Cinnamon can kill the E-coli bacteria contained in food and helps to relieve diarrhoea and colic. Properties: warming, stimulating, antiviral, antiseptic, and carminative (for expelling wind, like burping and colic). It improves circulation to hands and feet, helps digestive problems, nausea and vomiting, colds, flu, diarrhoea and aching muscles. Also used as a general tonic and for menstrual disorders.

Cardamom for incontinence, menopause, etc.

Cardamom promotes digestion and reduces gas formation in the bowel and bloating. It is acure for vomiting. Urinary incontinence, menstrual problems, headaches, water retention, depression and nausea can be helped by chewing a few cardamom seeds. Many women suffer from urinary incontinence after childbirth when they sneeze, so chewing cardamom seeds is the answer! They add a distinctive flavour to sweetmeats like nougat, cakes, milk desserts and biscuits. Cardamom can be ground up as a powder and is popular in coffee and tea, especially in the Middle East, where cardamom is considered to be an aphrodisiac.

Chilli, the best cure for tight chests, coughs or asthma

Chilli is one of the best cures we have for chronic asthma, bronchitis and an overload of mucous that makes breathing difficult. The active ingredient is a natural decongestant similar to Guaiphenesin, a common ingredient in cold and cough remedies. It expels mucous, opens the airways and facilitates breathing. (See page 30.)The burning stimulates the respiratory system. Capsaicin, the hot component of the chilli, does not irritate the stomach lining so it is safe for stomach ulcers. Build up your pain threshold by eating a tiny piece of chilli with something fatty like meat or cheese and increase this amount every day. You will notice a vast improvement in your breathing. Avoid the eyes and keep chillies away from small children who may play with them by accident.

Properties: warming and stimulating, a good tonic, antiseptic, relieves muscle cramps, increases sweating and blood flow to the skin, reduces inflammation, stimulates the immune system and expels mucous.

Uses: for poor circulation, blood clotting and heart problems, for diabetics; for cold, rheumatic and arthritic conditions, for removal of waste and mucus from the tissues; asthma, bronchitis and coughs, sore throats, colic and wind, ulcers (it is anti-inflammatory) and digestive complaints due to microbial or mucous infections.

Black and yellow mustard seeds

Mustard is hot and fiery; yet soothing to muscles

Mustard may irritate the nasal and mouth linings but it is extremely soothing to tired muscles, creaking joints and worn out, aching feet. A detoxifying bath can be made by adding mustard powder and Epsom Salts to warm water. This mixture helps to draw toxins out of the body whilst it soothes and relaxes you. Mustard has warming and decongestant properties. Grind up mustard seeds with other spices and use it on meat and fish. Wasabi mustard is not mustard; it is related to the horseradish family and is a white root to which the Japanese add green colouring.

Chill out with nutmeg and mace

Caution: not for O[1]. Eating a whole nutmeg frequently can be fatally toxic! Nutmeg has a dulling effect on the nervous system and should not be taken in large quantities. Mace is a popular aromatic curry spice. It is the yellow stringy fruit that grows around the pip or dark brown seed we know as nutmeg. Mace is a component of some self-defence sprays. Nutmeg is a folk remedy for diarrhoea, especially for children. A pinch of powder can be mixed with honey and given with mint or cardamom tea, three times a day. Consult a doctor if a fever is present. Grated nutmeg is delicious in a white fish sauce or on cauliflower. Most people grate their nutmeg freshly, to capture the full aroma.

Strips of mace, used in self defence sprays, and whole nutmeg

Oblong caraway seeds and rounded aniseed are from the same family and have similar properties.

Aniseed and caraway seeds

These tasty seeds all have antispasmodic, relaxing effects on the smooth muscles of the intestinal walls. They are excellent for digestion and help to break winds and expel colicky gas. They should be included in rich meals or chewed separately or drunk in tea and coffee. They are both used medicinally for water retention, excessive heat, to expel mucous in bronchitis and to relieve heavy congested coughs. Ajowan seeds, of the same family, have a profound anti-histamine effect in the body, helping to reduce itching and swelling. (See fish, on page 51.)

Coriander is an aphrodisiac and preserves meat

Coriander was traditionally added to love potions, due to its legendary properties as an aphrodisiac or a tonic and stimulant to the reproductive system. This spice is used for poor circulation, water retention, colic, diarrhoea, nausea, spasms, headaches, nervous tension, exhaustion and neuralgia. In the old days, a mixture of coriander, cumin and vinegar was used to preserve meats. Coriander seeds add a refreshing and pungent flavour to herb tea, curries, chutney, pickles, bread, fish and soups. Coriander powder is called koljana.

Coriander seeds (koljana)and fresh leaves (dhania).

Ground up turmeric (borrie) powder and a piece or turmeric root. Make a paste of turmeric powder and olive oil to apply to skin problems.

Turmeric is one of the best all-round medicines

Turmeric or borrie is a liver remedy, especially for jaundice, dyspepsia, or weakness and fatigue. People also take it for coughs, colds and fevers. It stimulates bile secretion, eases stomach pain, is antioxidant, antifungal and antibacterial, it thins blood and is an anticoagulant. Anti-inflammatory research from 1971-1991 indicates an action similar to hydrocortisone. It Lowers cholesterol levels (Chinese research 1987.) Uses: As an antioxidant it is stronger than vitamin E; protects the stomach lining and liver, increases the flow of bile; for jaundice, nausea; thins the blood, prevents clotting and reduces the risk of strokes and heart attacks. Take a few doses of ½ teaspoon of turmeric powder with honey every day. Mix turmeric with a little olive oil and apply to psoriasis, fungal infections like ringworm eczema and athlete's foot, scabies, eczema and itchy rashes.

3 Happy Digestion

Golden rules for happy digestion

A good understanding of how each food is digested is essential and is explained to you in terms that are easy to understand.

Following the basic rules for easy digestion is as important as selecting foods that suit you. Food combining can improve the digestion and assimilation of foods.

Digestive stimulants like herbal tinctures and teas can be taken before the main meal.

Supplements and remedies

We like to believe that our diets contain all the nutrients we need but although some foods score high on the list of vitamins and minerals, we cannot assimilate them to the same level. Many foods that contain a lot of calcium, like sesame seeds, ice cream and whole wheat actually rob us of calcium.

It is true that supplementation can be kept to a minimum when you eat more fresh, natural foods but everybody is different and some of us need more micronutrients than others.

The diet is restricted once wheat, meat or dairy products are excluded so a few supplements are required, especially when your food is not organically grown.

Please note that this information should not be used to diagnose, treat or cure a condition. Consult your doctor or an experienced practitioner, especially if you are pregnant, breastfeeding, epileptic, diabetic or have blood pressure or heart complaints. (See page 2.)

Happy Digestion means eating what suits you best

What a load!

Autopsies show that our digestive tracts contain 9kg-22kg of waste material. Lots of garbage in, but food should only stay in the gut for 16 - 24 hours before being expelled. Symptoms of a sluggish digestive system are fatigue, headaches, sore muscles and joints, bad breath, a clogged-up lymphatic system and a sallow skin. Ironically, carbohydrate and sugar cravings go hand in hand with constipation and poor digestion.

Auto-toxicity from the rotting and fermenting contents of congested bowels is becoming serious in the light of the newly recognised 'leaky-gut " syndrome. Formerly benign or dormant bacteria, parasites, viruses, fungi, moulds and other pathogens proliferate in this acidic environment starved of oxygen; just right for a takeover! As a good host, you have provided them with plenty of food: weeks of fermenting sugars, undigested starches, putrefying protein and solidified chains of fatty acids all churned up with supplements and medicines.

Opportunistic flukes, roundworms, tapeworms and larger parasites thrive and breed in the colon and can deprive you of most of your nutrients. See page 35 for natural forms of parasite control. Colonic irrigation to clear out stubborn deposits of old waste and toxins is often advisable. After that, it's up to you to get yourself regular once the last bit of muck has been flushed away. Too many people turn to fibre supplements, bulking agents, stool softeners and purgatives instead of changing what they eat. A "greener" more natural approach to your eating habits helps to liberate your constitution without any damage to your gut.

Avoid lectins, even in vegetables

Even the vegetables on this page do not suit all blood types. Use the comprehensive blood type lists on pages 11-14 to identify foods that suit you best. Lectins (see page 7) in food not recommended for your blood type can have disruptive effects on your digestion, so cutting them out is advisable.

Look at the food you eat every day

Something is wrong with the food you eat if it makes you uncomfortable and you need to forcefully remove it from your body. We spend a lot of money on food, yet it can cost even more to get it out again. As you learn to select foods that suit you best, you will feel more comfortable.

Many health regimens make sweeping claims but they do not suit everybody's constitution. The best indication is how they make you you feel. The wrong food causes belching, heartburn, gas, stomach or abdominal cramps and bad breath. If food lodges in your bowels for longer than 24 hours it can cause weight gain, water retention, bloating, fermentation, rectal bleeding or flatulence. Food forms hard impacted lumps and even calcified bowel stones; then you are not eating correctly for your blood type.

Indigestion and heartburn

Ptyalin is the only enzyme that can digest starch. It is contained in saliva in the mouth so starches must be thoroughly chewed and mixed with this enzyme before being swallowed. No wonder you get heartburn from wolfing down all that pasta and bread, especially if you drink whilst you eat. It is better to eat starch separately and chew it well. One can still also get heartburn from eating wheat in any form, should you be intolerant to it. The problem is worse with gluten intolerance as wheat, oats, rye and barley all contain gluten.

Most people who cut out the wheat or offending glutens find they are free of heartburn for good. (See page 42.) Heartburn is also linked to low stomach acid. (See page 69.) We blame meat and fatty or spicy foods for causing heartburn but they are usually eaten with starch that then swirls around the stomach undigested and interferes with the digestion of fats and protein.

Natural ways to treat sluggish bowels and constipation

Eating foods that contain disruptive lectins that affect your blood type can lead to the enlargement of organs like the liver, spleen, pancreas and intestines.

Why food causes us discomfort

The reason most people have heartburn, gas and abdominal cramps or are chronically constipated is simply that they do not understand the digestive process, let alone the need to eat the right food at the right time for the right reason. Eating foods that contain harmful lectins for your blood type will aggravate any condition, especially weight gain, arthritis, diabetes, immunity disorders, hormonal upsets and heart problems.

Constipation is a big problem

People gobble up any old garbage during the day then they wonder why they are constantly hungry, tired or constipated. This in turn results in booming sales of energy foods, antacids, purgatives, bulking agents, fibre supplements and laxatives that help them to alleviate the effects of poor eating habits. Dependence on these products makes you incapable of gaining any benefit from your food, let alone making you able to empty your bowels by yourself. In the good old days when we ate only fresh, natural if not raw foods, the waste would leave our bodies regularly within 18 - 24 hours.

Today people have impacted stools and even calcified stones lodged in their bowels that are sometimes a few years old. The general complaint people seem to have is that they cannot go to the toilet every day or even once a week without the use of some form of purgative or medication. This is a far cry from the twice a day routine of a healthy individual on a natural diet.

How water affects constipation

The purpose of the large intestine is to conserve water. When the mobility is impaired by eating the wrong foods or the unnatural use of laxatives, too much water is absorbed back into the body and the stools become hard and dry. Drinking large amounts of water is no instant cure for constipation as the water does not reach the dried-out stool. The kidneys have to work harder instead and a lot more urine is passed, much to the frustration of the constipated individual. It is far easier to convey water and bulk to the colon in the form of fresh fruit and vegetables that contain natural fibre. Omit denatured, white starch and sugar as they cause gas and fermentation.

Colonic cleansing is very beneficial

Water acts as an instant cure for constipation when it is directed up into the colon via tubing inserted into the anus. Known as colonic irrigation, this method really works in extreme and debilitating cases. Afterwards, it is up to the individual to eat in such a way that it does not have to happen again! Watch out for the frequent use of enemas that contain strong solvents and alkaline chemicals as they destroy the friendly gut flora. Some therapists enthuse about coffee enemas, made famous by Gerson, who claims it stimulates the liver!

It is best to have a colonic irrigation done professionally. Do-it-yourself enthusiasts can try the following method, recommended by a famous naturopath: use a one metre length of tubing about 10ml thick with a smoothed off tip attached to a two litre bottle of purified water or a tap opening. Squat down in the bath, carefully insert the tip of the tube and gently squeeze the bottle or open the tap on low pressure for a few seconds. Then relax, lie on the floor, feet up and massage the tummy until you are ready to go the toilet.

Eat plenty of spinach, lettuce, apples and raw onion every day. Add them to salads, soups and stir fries.

Diabetics and slimmers need extra discipline

A perfect lunch for diabetics.

Natural foods to control insulin

Large servings of cooked green beans promote insulin activity. Better still is to eat fresh leafy greens instead of starches or sugars. Pineapple contains digestive enzymes and suits all blood types. Fenugreek (methee) helps to lower blood sugar. Make fenugreek sprouts (see page 110) and add the powder to your food or take half a teaspoon in a little water before meals. Cinnamon and bay leaves also improve insulin sensitivity.

A supplement of MSM (methylsulphonylmethane) with vitamin C lowers blood sugar effectively when it is taken at mealtimes. (See page 83.) Take chrome supplements or the GTF combination of zinc, chrome and manganese to control blood sugar fluctuations. The herb gymnemia sylvestra helps to restore pancreatic function and lower blood sugar. Eat only fresh, natural foods that suit your blood type. Clean out your liver and digestive system regularly by using the methods on pages 31 and 65. Eat foods that are low on the GI (Glycaemic Index) to reduce the need for insulin. Make yourself a list according to your blood type of suitable foods that don't contain sugars and refined carbohydrates. (See page 43.)

Why eat according to blood type?

If you do not have antigens (see page 7) to process lectins in a particular food, it means you cannot digest it properly. It is of no benefit to you and thus has to be expelled from your system. Lectins from food cause cells to agglutinate and weaken your immunity. Along the way they interfere with your insulin mechanism and can cause weight gain. They impair hormone secretion, block digestive enzymes, interfere with absorption, cause gut permeability, damage the intestinal lining and cause inflammation.

What about cutting out all fat?

A diet that severely restricts the intake of fats and oils will cause constipation. This is because the gall bladder shuts down in reaction to having too little fat, so a lack of bile causes undigested fats to react with calcium. Hard insoluble soaps are then formed. These become rocky structures in the intestines and they can remain there for many years. Food and debris gets stuck in-between the stones and causes uncomfortable obstructions in your gut. Blocked ducts in the liver and gall bladder can cause gallstones to form. When you suffer from constipation alternating with diarrhoea, this is ususally the case. Refer to the gallbladder flush on page 31 to get rid of them. Diabetics need to have a sufficient intake of essential fatty acids and vitamin E to prevent these problems.

Restrict refined sugar and starches

No more white flour or sugar! Eating complex carbohydrates like whole grains and legumes that suit your blood type slows down the digestion of simple sugars, creating a fuller feeling for longer. The soluble and insoluble fibres help to lower cholesterol and promote natural bowel movements. Eating sensible food combinations can modify your insulin demands. Honey will trigger an instant demand for insulin if taken on an empty stomach, but honey with complex carbohydrates, acids or olive oil will digest very slowly. If you take a little honey with a natural remedy you can lower the Glycaemic Index by adding lemon juice or olive oil.

If you drink fruit juice or herb tea that is high in natural sugar or you have used honey, always add a quarter of a teaspoon of citric acid or vitamin C to each glass to slow down the insulin reaction. A pinch of cream of tartar is also beneficial. (See page 81 for more about salt and potassium.)

Diabetics can have fresh fruit and vegetable juices but should acidify them; add a quarter of a teaspoon of citric acid or some lemon juice to each serving.

Fasting to improve body and mind

A health fast is usually recommended for patients to rest their bodies and speed up the elimination of toxins and impurities. A lot of water should be drunk to keep the kidneys functioning and to help flush out the waste material.

This form of fasting is very beneficial and during the time taken to rest, pray or meditate one is once again rejuvenated and strengthened. Many people opt for fruit fasting and some individuals live only on fruit , water or fruit juices for the rest of their lives. Proof indeed, that we take our carbohydrate, fat and protein intake far too seriously!

Fasting on religious occasions

Religious fasts usually exclude the intake of water. This causes levels of uric acid, toxins and waste products to build up during the day if the body is not purified beforehand with fruit fasting. When the fast ends , people tend to eat vast and sudden amounts of starch, sugar, meat and fat. This in turn will immediately affect insulin levels and cause blood sugar upsets.

When rich, fatty festive foods are eaten with wads of starchy rice and potatoes, the digestion will take strain. I receive a lot of complaints from people who undergo this type of fasting. Some admit to spending most of the day in a weakened state, feeling terrible. During the evening, the onslaught of rich eating when the body is accustomed to resting and digesting does not help one gain strength or vitality. People who step down their food intake and live mainly on fresh fruit, herb tea and lightly cooked fresh foods would be better off.

Healthy Happy fasting

Ramedaan Mubarak!

Those who suffer from diabetes, high blood pressure, heart complaints and digestive disorders are advised to have a thorough detox of the bowels and liver well in advance to embarking on a month's fasting and feasting during Ramedaan. All parasites should be eliminated beforehand to ease the burden of detoxification during the day when no food or water is taken. Diabetics should consult their doctors, should they wish to fast. They must strictly avoid any offending foods at night. Insulin doses have to be reduced if less is eaten.

After a day without food or water, many complain of fatigue, constipation, gout and debility. These conditions arise from intense dehydration in hotter climates, neglect of antioxidants, alkalising minerals and a build up of toxins. As soon as the sun sets, the body receives an onslaught of tempting delights: sugars, white flour, fried foods and cooked food. During the day, after an early "breakfast" of starchy bread, cereals, milk and sugar, people soon complain of intense hunger, fatigue and irritability. Drinking a teaspoon of blackstrap molasses in hot water at night with a quarter teaspoon of cream of tartar helps to prevent dehydration during the day. (See page 81.)

Health-conscious Muslims sail through the Fast because they stick to natural foods and strictly limit their intake of festive foods during the evening. If you visit friends who have no regard for healthy eating, offer to bring fresh fruit and salads along.

When away from home, prepare fresh healthy foods to eat when it is time to break the fast. Try to avoid the sweetmeats and greasy junk food and you will feel much better. Happy Fasting!

Natural ways to improve your digestion

Make your own digestive bitters. See page 107.

Herbal remedies for digestion

Many herbal remedies for the liver are availalble. They help to stimulate bile production and detox the liver. Milk thistle is a great liver rejuvenator. Vitamin B deficiencies are also responsible for some types of constipation. Often it is the vitamin B content of whole grain foods and not the fibre and roughage content that is needed to prevent constipation. Vitamin B5 helps with the digestion of fats, proteins and carbohydrates and is a cure for gout. Hydrochloric acid supplements and digestive enzymes are good to take before a large meal, especially for older people.

Digestive bitters are popular and you can make your own, using the recipes on page 107. Include herbs like sage, rosemary, thyme, mint, basil or bay leaves with powdered spices such as cinnamon, cloves, ginger, fennel, kaloontjie seeds or turmeric. Aloe leaf powder is good for arthritis and constipation. Dutch remedies like "Lewensessens" are popular as are specially blended herb teas. The folk remedy of a teaspoon of apple cider vinegar and a teaspoon of honey taken in water before meals works well for those who suffer from arthritis.

Large quantities of vitamin C are sometimes used to clear the bowels in an emergency. Tolerance to vitamin C varies in individuals so begin with 1 or 2 grams. Some people swear by taking a teaspoon of bicarbonate of soda mixed in some water if they have overindulged. Add a half a teaspoon of citric acid to make it into a fizzy antacid drink.

Why we need to look after the liver

The liver is responsible for expelling waste from your system as well as making many of the hormones, enzymes and metabolites that keep you fit, energetic and able to utilise your food. It detects and expels excess estrogen from the bloodstream and destroys potential cancer-forming cells.

People with high cholesterol have liver problems. Cholesterol-lowering drugs are harmful to the liver and can cause impotence. A liver and gall bladder cleanse can help to lower cholesterol. Women with hot flushes and estrogen imbalances are also showing symptoms of liver congestion. Hormone replacement therapy has a disastrous effect on a the liver that struggles to keep up with the breaking-down and excretion of unwanted hormones, let alone more hormones! Most of us are overloaded with unnatural forms of estrogens that increase our potential to develop cancer. The liver has to constantly detoxify our system but cannot do so if it is congested or diseased.

Symptoms of a liver overload

If bile ducts become blocked and gallstones develop, you become sluggish, depressed, constipated, full of headaches, allergies and sore joints. You gain weight because you feel tired and hungry all the time, yet you cannot digest your food properly! You are also unable to assimilate amino acids to restore protein to worn out body tissues. You suffer from vitamin, hormone and enzyme deficiencies. The tongue has a white to yellow furry coating, the eyes are not clear and bright and the breath begins to smell. Once you have sorted out the liver and gallbladder, it's easy to control cholesterol with flaxseeds and special foods by using the dietary guidelines in this book. (See page 31.)

Help yourself to digestive remedies that come from your own kitchen.

Heartburn and osteoporosis are linked to low stomach acid

Stomach acid has a pH of minus two

The hydrochloric acid in a healthy stomach is so strong it can dissolve razor blades. This acid usually has a pH of about minus two but if we do not eat correctly and we take too many antacids, the pH becomes slightly more alkaline, this is when many illnesses occur. Stomach ulcers, arthritis weakened immunity and even osteoporosis can arise from a condition of weakened stomach acid.

We often eat a lot of bacteria and bugs with our food and usually they are immediately destroyed by stomach acid. Helicobacter pylori, a strain of bacteria, causes stomach ulcers if the acid level is too weak. The stomach begins to produce a lot more of this diluted acid and this rises in the oesophagus. When Salmonella is not destroyed this bacteria can damage the valve that keeps acid inside the stomach so it escapes and gives the sensation of heartburn. Taking antacids for these conditons will not correct the initial cause. Restoring the strength of the stomach acid pH with Betaine HCL supplements most certainly will.

Arthritis, your stomach and protein

We need stomach acid to digest protein completely so that the amino acids can reach the bloodstream and be transported to the tissues. Undigested protein particles from the stomach escape through weak spots in small blood vessels around the joints. When this happens it causes inflammation and arthritis. This is why a raw diet and fruit-cleansing can ease symptoms of arthritis as these foods are free of protein. Improving the strength of stomach acid and taking more vitamins and essential fatty acids to help repair the damaged or leaky blood vessels miraculously alleviates arthritic symptoms. Eliminate parasites because they also cause pain and acidity around joints.

Is osteoporosis a calcium deficiency?

The stomach is the place where minerals from food and supplements are split up, ionised and bound to food molecules so they can perform their required functions. When the stomach acid is too low, as it is in many women over 40, a calcium deficiency develops regardless of how much calcium they take. Vitamin B12 deficiencies also develop at this age and are also associated with having low stomach acid. Boost stomach acid with Betaine HCL and digestive enzymes. Low stomach acid can also occur when there is a bismuth deficiency.

This combination of bread, meat, cheese, fruit, nuts, tomatoes, orange juice and watermelon is not easy to digest all at once.

Does food combining make sense?

Eat foods high in protein first and by themselves. Why? Stomach acid at the right temperature and without any interference from other foods enables protein-rich foods like meat and cheese to be easily and rapidly digested. In food combining, proteins are never eaten with starchy foods for this reason. Starch has to be mixed with a lot of saliva whereby the starch-busting enzyme called ptyalin can convert starch to glucose. Starch is not digested anywhere else, so any bread, pasta, etc. that you wolf down without sufficient chewing is going to ferment in the gut as soon as it combines with the acids and sugar from the fruit salad you just ate. Meat takes about 3 hours to digest, but when it is combined with unsuitable foods, its passage through the digestive tract is slowed down to over 24 hours. This is how putrefaction of the bowel sets in and paves the way for cancer.

Is it wrong to drink with meals?

Don't drink water, wine, beer or juice with food. Avoid cold drinks at the table as they lower the temperature of stomach acid and this reduces its efficacy. They gush in and dilute your precious hydrochloric acid. Drinking water or wine before meals will benefit you more. Water enhances the effect of stomach acid, especially when herbal bitters or a few grains of salt are added to it.

A quick guide to a HEALTHY HAPPY digestive system

Stimulate the digestion

Drink plenty of fresh water and fruit juices or herbal tea between meals. Eat digestive and fat-emulsifying herbs like rosemay and sage with your food. Take herbal liver remedies to stimulate the flow of bile. Herbal bitters in a little water before meals is very beneficial. Eat a lot of fresh parsley and celery every day as the chlorophyll helps to cleanse the digestive system and prevents the build-up of old mucous that causes bad breath, an indication of an unhealthy intestinal tract. Drinking lemon juice every day, as well as eating slices of fresh or salted lemons is good for the liver as well as the whole digestive system.

Fennel, mint, dandelions and fenugreek

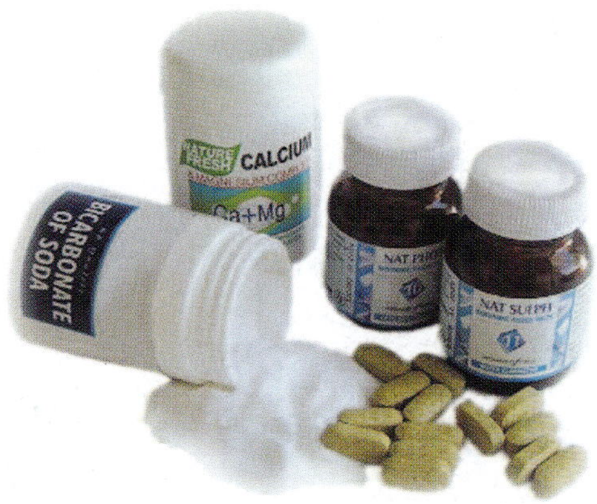

Herbs, vitamins and minerals

Milk thistle supplements are excellent for maintaing and restoring a weak and diseased liver. If you are going out to a party, take lots of it with vitamin C beforehand. This combination helps to prevent hangovers. Vitamin B complex is very important, especially with high doses of Choline and Inositol. Antioxidants are essential for the liver, so load up on Vitamin A, C, D and E. Alkalise with calcium and magnesium supplements every night. A teaspoon of bicarbonate of soda in water helps to neutralise acidity after eating fatty foods or something disagreeable.

Keep tabs on cholesterol and parasites

Stay away from simple carbohydrates as they raise cholesterol, believe it or not. They form triglycerides in your blood, known as LDH lipids and this is the oxidised form of cholesterol that is bad for you. Eggs do not raise cholesterol as they contain a lot of lecithin. Keep away from greasy fried food. Eat more onions, garlic, spinach and apples, both cooked and raw as they are prime cholesterol-busters. Eat foods rich in natural edible fibre, especially ground-up flaxseeds to break up cholesterol deposits and stimulate the bile action. Eat more cooked, dried and sprouted peas and beans as they contain cholesterol-binding and cholesterol-eliminating chemicals. Eliminate liver flukes. (See page 71.)

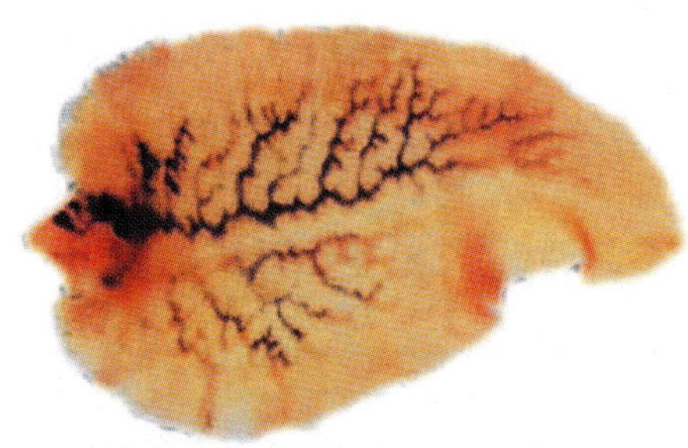

Liver flukes can block ducts in the liver and pancreas. How many liver flukes do you have inside your body?

Take salmon oil or Cod liver oil supplements. Grind up flaxseeds with nuts and other seeds.

Essential fatty acids instead of animal fats

Omega 3 and 6 oils are provided by foods like walnuts, olive oil and flaxseeds. Salmon or Cod liver oil capsules need to be taken as supplements. Grind up flaxseeds every day for your family. They help to prevent constipation. Combine them with sesame seeds, pumpkin pips and other nuts. Use the mixture on cereals, in smoothies and especially when you bake. Increase your intake of foods high in potassium, especially blackstrap molasses and fresh green leafy vegetables. Lecithin is a potent fat emulsifier. Soya beans and eggs are a good source. Lecithin granules from health shops can be mixed with food. If you soak these granules in water, the suspension can be added to fruit smoothies, desserts, sauces or chocolate recipes. (See page 150.)

Dinner time: parasites live inside us and swim in our blood!

A single drop of blood tells all

Live blood analysis gives a magnified view of the microbial parasites that inhabit your blood. This test can reveal food sensitivities, toxic substances and nutritional deficiencies. (See page 160.)

Roundworms and hookworms

Hook worms

These larger worms, called ascarids, hatch in the gut and bite onto the intestinal walls, where they sap you of vital nutrients every time you eat. Their eggs are transmitted to other hosts for procreation once they leave your body.

Round worms

Liver flukes and your digestion

Liver flukes

Flukes are classified as flatworms and can laying thousands of eggs inside your body. Fluke and tapeworm eggs come from uncooked meats and raw vegetables. Flukes live in tiny ducts inside the liver and pancreas, where they block the output of bile or pancreatic juices. Most insulin-dependent diabetics test positive for fluke infestations.

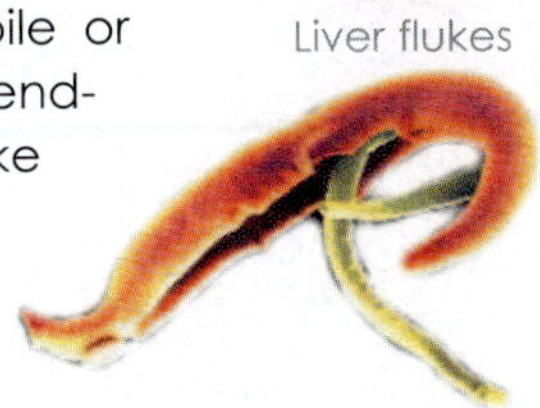

Metres of tapeworm

Tapeworms grow to a length of nine metres and live for up to ten years. Tiny hooks attach to your intestines. They lay thousands of eggs every day, so take Mebendazole or natural worm remedies regularly.

Left: hookworm and right, tapeworm head

Parasites dine with you, like it or not!

We are marvellous hosts to our uninvited guests, the teeming droves of parasites. Today exposure to chemicals and solvents makes it easy for the egg, cyst and larval stages of many parasites to hatch inside our bodies. This never happened until the extensive use of solvents like benzine, propylene alcohol, etc. The hard cyst around a liver fluke could withstand the digestive system and be expelled to find a new host, but now the coating is dissolved by the chemicals we expose ourselves to.

The occurrence of cancer, endometriosis, diabetes and liver diseases has increased in direct proportion to the amount of common alcohols and solvents we encounter daily. In all cases of these conditions studied by Dr Hulda Regher Clark and her team, it was discovered that parasites cause many of our illnesses. Once the parasites and chemical toxins were removed, most of the patients recovered fully. It is very important to avoid and eradicate all parasites as well as chemical toxins. Parasites favour acidic and unhealthy blood.

What can you do?

Avoid raw or contaminated meat. Wash your hands before eating. De-worm your pets as well as yourselves regularly. Electronic zapping with a home device or QX apparatus kills parasites, but the eggs still survive within the contents of the bowel. The QX analysis can identify parasites. (See page 160.) It is best to make parasite control a part of your Happy Eating routine. Take worm remedies and herbal tinctures, tablets and teas. Use the remedies on pages 35 and 107. Look out for symptoms like itching, restlessness, emaciation, tooth-grinding, anaemia or constant hunger.

Indigestion or worms in the gut?

These whipworms were removed from the intestines of a man who complained of indigestion.

Microbial invaders that cause many diseases inside your body

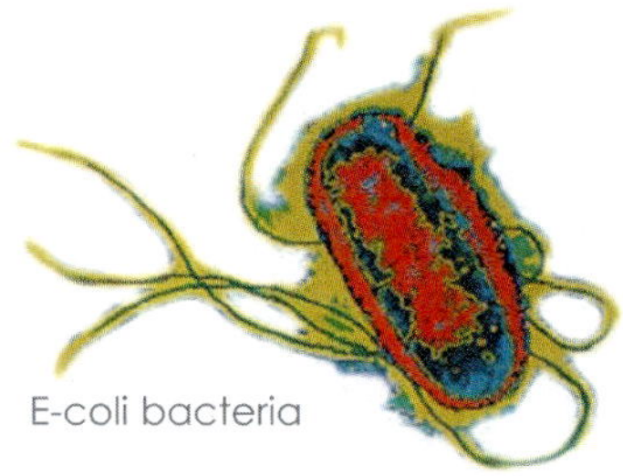

E-coli bacteria

E- coli bacteria

E-coli is a rod-shaped bacteria and moves around by means of hair-like protrusions called flagella. This bacteria proliferates in unsanitary conditions, especially in meat that is not properly cooked or left lying around. Once inside a friendly host, they divide and multiply rapidly until symptoms of diarrhoea are experienced. Drinking untreated water that has been contaminated with human and animal faeces also causes E-coli infections. Antibiotics are used, but according to laboratory trials, cinnamon can also kill e-coli bacteria in food. Try half a teaspoon of cinnamon with honey.

Helicobacter pylori

This little critter thrives in stomachs that can no longer produce strong enough stomach acid to kill it. When the stomach reacts by producing more, but weaker stomach acid, the pH is not low enough to eliminate it. The unfortunate host takes a lot of antacids to comfort the symptoms of heartburn and eventually gastric ulcers begin to develop. A simple test from the pharmacy will reveal its presence and antibiotics or a strong propolis tincture can be given to eradicate helicobacter.

Helicobacter pylori

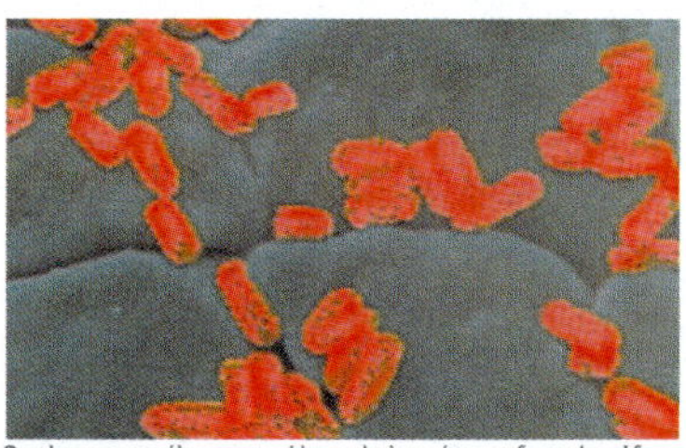

Salmonella on the blade of a knife

Salmonella

Salmonella usually lurks in uncooked meats, especially chicken, as well as raw eggs. One of the dangers of eating raw eggs is Salmonella poisoning. Symptoms are: stomach cramps, vomiting and diarrhoea. Antibiotics are usually the only way out. Wash knives, kitchen surfaces and chopping boards with a strong anti-bacterial soap after working with meat to prevent contamination of salads and raw foods.

Shigella

Shigella often has a delayed action as it attacks the lower intestines, setting off evil cramps, foul gasses and often profuse diarrhoea. Drinking infected milk, ice cream, yoghurt or raw meat causes this to happen. Layabout stews and samoosas may often be the culprits. Fortunately most curry spices also kill Shigella. For relief, mix a tablespoon of honey with a teaspoon each of: cinnamon, cloves, fennel and turmeric. Take 1 - 2 teaspoons every hour until symptoms abate, or see a doctor if it is debilitating.

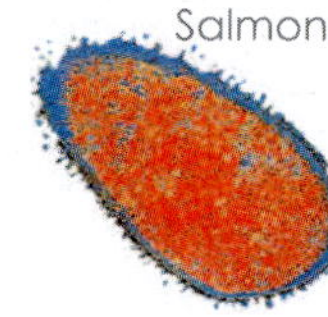

Salmonella

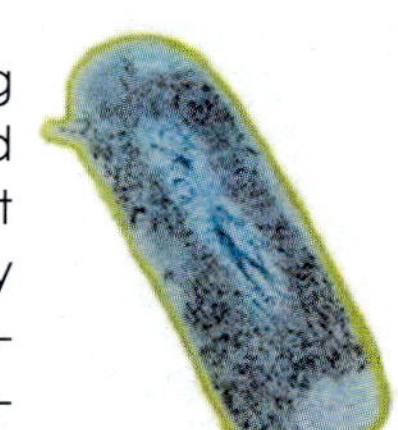

Shigella

Candida Albicans, also known as Thrush

Candida is a yeast-like plant, grown from tiny spores that attach to mucous linings in the mouth, intestinal tract and vaginal tissues. The spores grow rapidly into big white patches that can be easily seen. A profusion of this growth forms a vaginal discharge. People with weakened immune systems and pH imbalances are vulnerable to Candida and it can become a chronic condition. (See page 34.) Salt rinses with lemon juice are effective.

Candida albicans

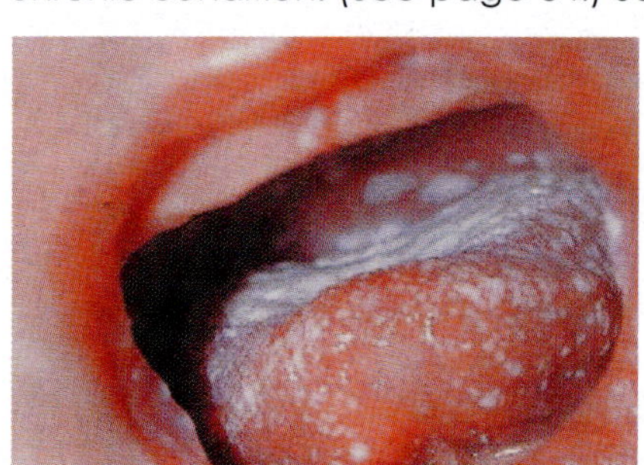

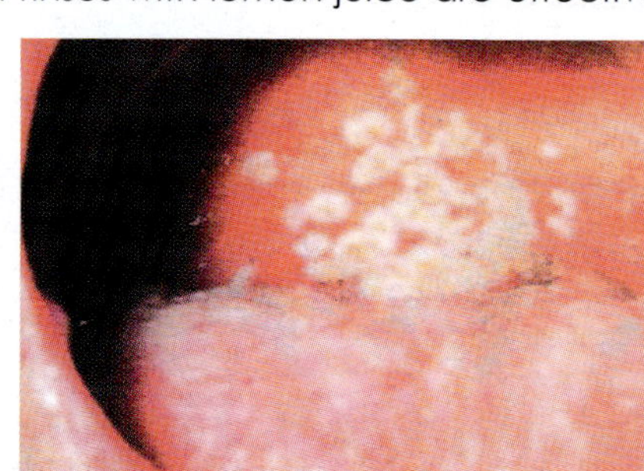

Supplement according to your blood type and specific needs

☹☺A Basic supplements

General: multivitamin and mineral complex and Omega 3. Vitamin C in 3 or 4 daily 250mg doses.
Calcium and magnesium, boron, iron, zinc.
Selenium and vitamin E in an anti-oxidant complex.

For stress and elevated cortisol: high potency B vitamin complex and tyrosine plus B12 with folic acid as sublingual tablets or injections.
Calming and destressing herbs: camomile, fenugreek, ginseng, ginger, hawthorn, milk thistle, St John's wort, valerian. Sterols and sterolins and melatonin if used under supervision.

Chromium to enhance glucose tolerance.
Herbal immune boosters: alfalfa sprouts and tablets, aloe, echinachea, olive leaf, burdock.
Digestion: Betaine HCL (hydrochloric acid) and digestive enzymes before eating meat. Take probiotics if you don't eat yoghurt.

☒A Harmful to this blood type

Cayenne, catnip, cornsilk, rhubarb, yellow dock.

☹☺B Basic supplements

General: multivitamin and mineral complex and Omega 3. Vitamin C in 3 or 4 daily 250mg doses.
Calcium and magnesium (only if dairy intake is low), boron, iron, zinc. Selenium and vitamin E in an antioxidant complex. Extra magnesium for ladies.
Lecithin and flaxseed oil or ground-up seeds (1 tablespoon of each, mixed in fruit juice).

For stress and high cortisol levels: adaptogenic herbs like ginseng, liquorice, astragalus, rhodiola, etc. Liquorice may raise blood pressure if potassium levels are low so take Slow-K. (See page 81.)

Ginger, mint, sage and all curry spices are good.
Digestive enzymes with large meals that contain meat. Also eat more pineapple and lentil sprouts.

Metabolic enhancers: coenzyme Q10, L-carnitine, biotin, chromium, zinc, lipoic acid, vitamin B6.

☒B Harmful to this blood type

Aloe, coltsfoot, cornsilk, gentian, fenugreek, golden seal, hops, rhubarb, senna, shepherd's purse.

☹☺AB Basic supplements

General: multivitamin and mineral complex and Omega 3. Vitamin C in 3 or 4 daily 250mg doses.
Calcium and magnesium, boron, iron, zinc.
Selenium and vitamin E in an antioxidant complex.
High potency B vitamin complex plus extra pantothenic acid (vitamin B5, 100mg twice a day).
Vegetarians: amino acids, vitamin B12, folic acid.

For stress: lipoic acid, L-tyrosine to increase dopamine, adaptogenic herbs like rhodiola, ginseng and astragalus.
Glutamine and chromium to control a sweet tooth.
Increase stomach acid concentration: bitter herb tonics, coffee, Denrobium or Betaine HCL (also present in kola nuts), digestive enzymes.

Beneficial herbs: alfalfa, burdock, echinachea, ginseng, olive leaf, ginger, hawthorn and liquorice.

☒AB Harmful to this blood type

Aloe, coltsfoot, cornsilk, fenugreek, allspice, anise, cayene, hops, senna, rhubarb, shepherd's purse.

☹☺O Basic supplements

Geneal: high potency B-vitamin complex. Calcium and magnesium, iodine (see page 110-112), manganese (usually found in grains, nuts and pulses)
Pancreatic enzymes if a lot of meat is eaten.

For stress: adaptogens like rhodiola, ginseng; sterols and sterolins, lipoic acid, L-tyrosine, Vitamin C.
Glutamine and GTF chrome for sugar cravings.
Anti-inflammatory: liquorice, turmeric, ginger, slippery elm, eugenia berries. (See page 84.)

Beneficial herbs: Bladderwrack and kelp, cayenne pepper, chickweed, liquorice, dandelion, fenugreek, hops, parsley, mint, sarsaparilla.

Vegans and vegetarians: amino acids, Vitamin D, vitamin B12 & folic acid. Spirulina and quinoa are complete protein. Vitamin K and lactoflora.

☒O Harmful to this blood type

Aloe extracts, alfalfa, St John's wort, gentian, golden seal, echinachea, senna, rhubarb and yellow dock. Vitamin A and E thins O blood too much. Use natural food sources: oils, liver, leafy greens.

The twelve tissue salts and how they keep us healthy

What are tissue salts?

The twelve tissue salts are finely mixed, potentised forms of mineral salts sold as food supplements. If an illness is caused by mineral deficiencies, then tissue salts are the cheapest and most effective way to replace them. Their profound action on the body can do the work of many prescription drugs that are used for treating symptoms of both acute and chronic conditions.

Are tissue salts like homeopathy?

Homeopathic remedies are not the same as tissue salts. Tissue salts represent the inorganic constituents in your body and they are present in your blood, tissues, bones and all your organs in different proportions and combinations. When a mineral salt is deficient, a malfunction occurs and this presents itself as a symptom of an illness. Typical conditions are inflammation, nausea, acidity, pain, swellings or discharges. When the correct tissue salt is taken and sucked under the tongue, the symptoms of the specific mineral or tissue salt deficiencies will no longer manifest themselves. Thus, tissue salts are nutritional supplements as opposed to a drug, a medicine or a homeopathic remedy.

Homeopathy treats a condition with a potentised remedy made from a substance that produces a similar set of symptoms. For example, if your eyes water, you take the remedy made from onions because onions make your eyes water. Your body is then stimulated to heal itself.

How can we obtain tissue salts?

Tissue salts are inexpensive and are available at health shops and pharmacies. The little pills are safe to suck under the tongue and are effective within hours, if not minutes. They are usually sold at the potency of D6 but if you dissolve a few pills in a bottle of water and shake it, you can increase the potency. It is easier to treat babies and pets with this mineralised water. Adding tissue salts to your daily bottles of drinking water is a good habit to adopt. See page 100 for a way to make some of the tissue salts yourself. Some brands sell convenient combinations of tissue salts to treat certain conditions like asthma, fatigue, constipation, etc.

Are tissue salts safe for everybody?

Tissue salts are totally non-toxic because very little of the mineral salt is actually present. At this fine dilution, the body picks up more of a vibration; a coded message to attract microscopic particles of the missing minerals to the affected area.

Use these tissue salts with caution:

Silicea stimulates the elimination of any foreign matter in the body like pus or splinters but larger and more frequent doses may also stimulate the removal of pacemakers, fillings, leg splints or other bodily implants like uterine contraceptives.
People who are allergic to sulphur may react badly to the "sulph" tissue salts: Calc Sulph, Nat Sulph, and Kali Sulph.

1 CALC.FLUOR. (Calcium fluoride / fluorspar)

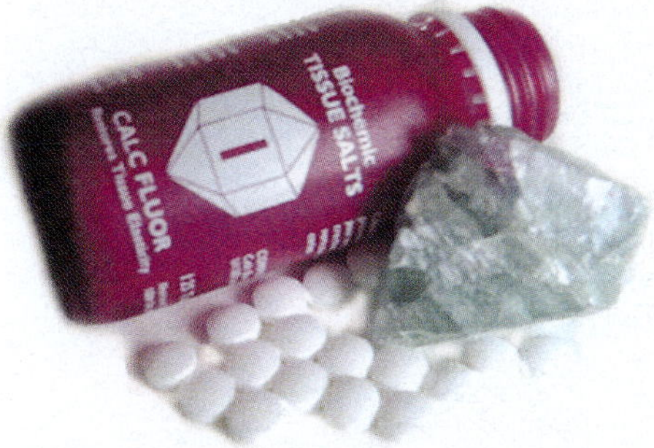

Calc Fluor is the major constituent of tooth enamel and collagen tissue. It is responsible for connective tissues and skin elasticity and gives flexibility and strength to muscles and blood vessels. Used for weak, relaxed tissues, cracked skin on palms of hands and at mouth corners, loose teeth, weak gums, piles, varicose veins, hardened glands, spurs (exosotses), blood tumours, sagging breasts, loose flabby skin and excessive wrinkles. Take as an antidote to toxic fluoride damage to gums and connective tissue caused by toothpaste, water or dental treatments.

Natural food and herb sources of Calc Fluor:

Garlic, parsley, sage, winter savory, chickweed, mustard, chives, buckwheat, lemons and lemon pith, grapes, oranges, pumpkin, squash, cabbage, onions and rye bread. These foods assist the uptake of fluoride.

2 CALC.PHOS. (Calcium phosphate / lime phosphate)

The crown of a tooth contains a lot of fluoride and the roots need calcium

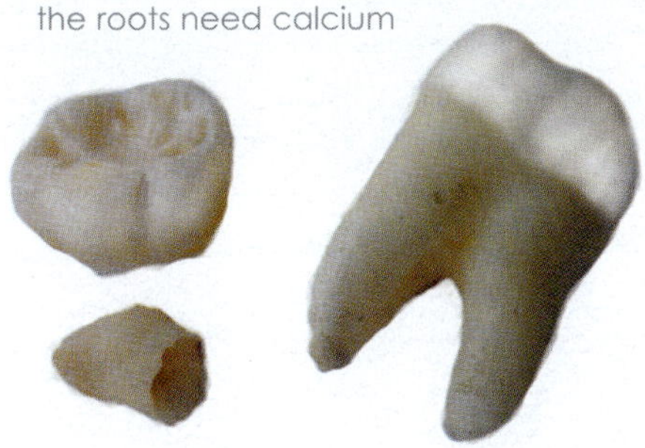

Calc Phos is found in teeth, bones, blood and especially gastric juice. It is a good all-round tonic and is used after treatment with other tissue salts like silicea for clearing up pimples, acne and boils. Calc Phos helps the bones to strengthen and assimilate calcium. Used for sore or underdeveloped teeth and all bone conditions like osteoporosis and osteoarthritis; for poor digestion, white skin patches on the face, anaemia and colds. Take Calc Phos during or after an illness as a tonic.

Natural food and herb sources of Calc Phos:

Comfrey, chamomile, alfalfa, borage leaves, oats, green leafy vegetables, carrots, lentils, most fruits, eggs, meat and dairy products.

3 CALC.SULPH. (Calcium sulphate / plaster of Paris)

Calc Sulph is present in all skin cells and in the blood. It purifies the blood, dissolves discharges of pus, drains tissues, heals and cures suppuration and stimulates the flow of oxygen to all parts of the body, especially the skin. Good for liver and bile production. Used for catarrh (mucous), lung problems, boils, carbuncles, abscesses, pimples and acne. It is often used after the tissue salt Silicea to heal wounds, boils and pimples.

Natural food and herb sources of Calc Sulph:

Urtica (stinging nettle), red clover, wormwood (artemesia), onions, garlic, leeks, radishes, watercress, asparagus, cauliflower, figs, prunes, celery, parsley, fennel, all green leafy vegetables.

4 FERRUM. PHOS. (Iron phosphate)

Ferrum Phos is a component of red blood cells. It is needed for all inflammatory and febrile conditions. It has anti-inflammatory properties and is required for expelling heat from the body as in cases of fever or hot flushes. It reduces swelling where there is redness, burning, itching and pain. A solution of Ferrum Phos and water can be applied topically to an inflamed area. Ferrum Phos is a major blood remedy. It strengthens blood vessels, helps form new red blood corpuscles and is an alternative to iron supplements for treating anaemia.

Natural food and herb sources of Ferrum Phos:

Parsley, horseradish, dandelion, celery, urtica, yarrow, garlic, chives, sesame seeds, spinach, lentils, radishes, walnuts, almonds, apricots, prunes, leeks, red meat, liver, yeast and kelp.

5 KALI. MUR. (Potassium chloride / salt substitute)

Kali Mur is present in all body tissues except bone. It is good as a decongestant and anti-inflammatory, especially when taken with Ferrum Phos. It works as a blood and lymphatic conditioner and as a digestive remedy when the stomach acid is weak. It strengthens nerve tissue. Kali Mur is used to relieve glandular swellings and lumps. Main symptom: a white coating on tongue and back of throat, glandular swellings and lumps in the tissue or on the bone and painful, swollen breasts or armpits.

Natural herb and food sources of Kali Mur:

Violet, yarrow, mullein, ginger, fennel, basil, borage, sage, green beans, carrots, beetroot, squash, cauliflower, kale, sweetcorn, asparagus, celery, peaches, apricots, pineapples, lemons and plums.

6 KALI. PHOS.(Potassium phosphate)

Kali Phos controls nerve function, especially brain tissue and intracellular fluids. It relieves brain and emotional fatigue, depression, sluggishness and confusion. A general pick-me-up to lift the spirits, calm the nerves and focus concentration. A deficiency of Kali Phos is indicated by: fatigue, depression, confusion, loss of memory, offensive breath, flatulence that has a really bad odour and partial paralysis.

Natural herb and food sources of Kali Phos:

Ginger, mustard, St John's wort, horseradish, red clover, thyme, chives, garlic, all green leafy vegetables, tomatoes, olives, walnuts, lemons, broccoli, apples, apple cider vinegar, dates and green beans.

7 KALI.SUPLH. (Potassium sulphate)

Kali Sulph oxygenates the cells, supports liver function and clears out mucous. It brings vitality to the skin, especially where there are offensive discharges or yellow pimples. Kali Sulph deficiencies show up as: dandruff, eczema, catarrh (mucous) of the lungs and digestive system. This tissue salt helps bring oxygen and vitality to the liver, to hair and skin cells and to the mucous membranes.

Natural herb and food sources of Kali Sulph:

Lemon balm (melissa), watercress, parsley, flaxseeds, mustard, lettuce, almonds, rye, wholewheat, endives, chicory greens, barley, all sprouts and leafy green vegetables are rich sources of potassium. Molasses, especially the crude blackstrap molasses, cottage cheese and yoghurt.

8 MAG.PHOS.(Magnesium phosphate)

Mag Phos controls the nerve fibres. A deficiency results in a contracted nerve fibre and causes cramps, spasms, convulsions, sharp shooting neuralgic pains, hiccoughs and stress-related pains and tensions. Mag Phos relaxes muscle cramps, menstrual pains, abdominal discomfort, colic, twitching, curled fingers and restless legs. Suck a few Mag Phos tissue salts at the onset of a cramp to relax the contracted muscles.

Natural herb and food sources of Mag Phos:

Lemon balm, mint, chamomile, oats, sage, nettle, valerian, dandelion, green leafy vegetables, apples, plums, bananas, oranges, grapefruit, walnuts, lemons, lentils and figs. Dill, fennel and aniseed have strong antispasmodic properties and work well for gas, spasms and cramps. They work well on their own or can be combined with the tissue salt Mag Phos.

9 NAT.MUR. (Sodium chloride / table salt)

Nat Mur regulates water balance in the body to prevent dehydration, bloating and water retention, dry skin and hair. It controls the mucous membranes and distributes water between the cells. Symptoms appear as runny nose, diarrhoea, oedema, watery or dry eyes, constipation, wrinkles and dry hair or skin. Emotions are: anger, irritability, withdrawal.
Natural herb and food sources of Nat Mur:
Table salt, comfrey, mustard, calendula, chickweed, celery, thyme, origanum and majoram, melissa and chamomile; beetroot, cabbage, spinach, parsley, almonds, figs and sesame seeds. Meat and seafoods contain a lot of Nat Mur. Salt contains sodium and must be balanced with potassium. Herbs have a perfect balance of sodium and potassium.

10 NAT.PHOS. (Sodium phosphate)

Nat Phos balances the acidity of the body, keeping the blood at an ideal pH. Deficiencies show as heartburn, acid belching, nausea, vomiting, indigestion, arthritic pains and stiffness. Used for nausea, arthritis, gout, billiousness or travel-sickness and to alkalise the body, helping to prevent worms and other parasitic invasions. The tongue usually has a creamy white or yellow coating.
Natural herb and food sources of Nat Phos:
Parsley, coriander, caraway, cumin, anise and ginger all contain Nat Phos and are excellent digestive aids as well as flavourants for food. Foods that are alkalising are: rice, celery, beetroot, apples, peaches, apricots, pawpaw, quinces, lemons, grapes, carrots and watermelon.

11 NAT.SULPH. (Sodium sulphate / Glauber's salt)

Nat Sulph controls the fluid levels within each living cell and the secretion of bile. It regulates all the secretions in the body and works with Nat Mur in expelling excess fluid and detoxifying the body. Deficiencies show as: a dirty greenish-yellow coating at the back of the tongue, diabetes (insufficient pancreatic juices), jaundice, dropsy, menopausal hot flushes, vomiting especially during pregnancy. Nat Sulph can be combined with Nat Phos for treating morning sickness.
Natural herb and food sources of Nat Sulph:
Parsley, celery, yarrow, dandelion, chillies, horseradish, broccoli, cabbage, Brussels sprouts, kale, onions, beetroot, pumpkins, green peppers, cucumber, bananas and apples. Add a pinch of Glauber's salt to a litre of water and shake it up well for a natural liver tonic.

12 SILICEA (Silica: quartz)

Silicea eliminates pus and toxins from tissues and strengthens, supports and sustains connective tissue. Important for strong hair, nails, teeth, nerves and bones. It promotes the discharge of pus, foreign objects like splinters, and is used for boils, cysts, abscesses, nasal catarrh, septic tonsils. Follow up with Calc Phos to resolve infection. It is used for profuse night sweats and debility. Consult a homeopath before taking large or frequent doses of Silicea if you have a pacemaker, an IUD, metal implants or a lot of amalgam in your mouth because they could become dislodged by the silicea.
Natural herb and food sources of Silicea:
Dandelion, nettle, horsetail (equestrium) comfrey, all grains, soya, spinach, pulses, nuts and seeds, lemons, guavas spinach and lettuce.

Who needs extra calcium and magnesium?

Most people experience calcium deficiencies throughout their lives. When the blood becomes too acidic, calcium is silently removed from the mineral deposits in the bones to alkalise the blood, should no other calcium be available. If this did not happen on a continuous basis, the heart would not be able to regulate the flow of blood and it would stop beating. Calcium is so essential for our survival that we have been provided with vast reserves of it in our bones but we no longer seem able to replace calcium at the same rate as we remove it.

Who needs extra calcium ?

By the age of 40 the average person's bones have already weakened and signs of calcium and magnesium deficiencies are blatantly evident: cramps, aches and pains, blood and tissue acidity, blood sugar imbalances, weakened immune systems, thyroid problems, fatigue, constipation, kidney stones and poor digestion. Magnesium regulates over 300 metabolic processes in the body and perfect calcium homeostasis of the tissues cannot be maintained without it.

High levels of hormones like estrogen block the access of calcium to the bloodstream. Steroid hormones like cortisone and testosterone rob the bones of calcium. When no other calcium is supplied via the diet or supplements and access to the calcium from bones is denied, the body undergoes a crisis in the form of heart attacks or metabolic disorders that can have fatal results. A constant lack of calcium makes tissues acidic, starved of oxygen and more prone to cancer.

Kidney stones and calcium

When the body needs calcium, it is removed from bones. This dissolved calcium gets trapped in the kidneys, forming stones because the system is acidic. No kidney stone has ever been known to contain calcium from a supplement that contains the correct ratio of calcium to magnesium.

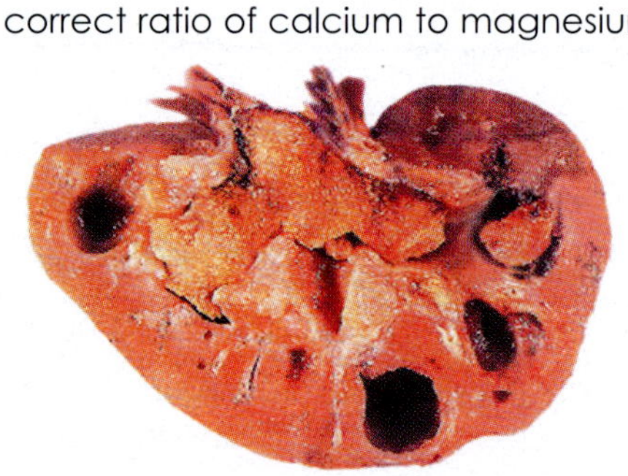

Kidney stones are acidic waste compounds like oxalic acid, phosphates or uric acid combined with calcium. This happens when body tissues are too acidic.

The first signs of a calcium deficiency:

Growing pains in children who are unusually tired, irritable and unable to concentrate. Young girls with menstrual cramps are not getting enough calcium as the surge of estrogen on the first day of the cycle inhibits the release of calcium and magnesium from their bones. As soon as the estrogen levels drop during the next few days, these minerals are once again removed from the bones if calcium is not present in the diet. This is the beginning of osteoporosis, at an early age!

We blame our stressful lifestyles for most of our diseases, not realising that our need for alkaline minerals, trace elements and tissue salts increases in direct proportion to the amount of stress that we experience. It is never too early or too late to begin taking calcium and magnesium supplements.

How can we prevent osteoporosis?

Osteoporosis, or the weakening of bones, is easily prevented by taking adequate calcium and magnesium whilst bones are developing to a peak density during adolescence. The most important time for women to take a good supplement is during and immediately after their child-bearing years. I did my bone-loading with a simple calcium and magnesium powder. Two children later, in my late forties a bone scanner charted a density of above one. It was higher than the machine could measure! Many women in their thirties are already teetering on the brink of the fracture line, having lost up to 30% of their bone density. Quite a few young women already have osteoporosis and they are full of estrogen! The theory of using HRT to prevent this disease is a mystery to me.

Bone density can be restored at a rapid rate of over 10% per annum with correct supplementation whereby the minerals and nutrients can once again attach to the weakened bone tissue.

Do calcium supplements help with osteoporosis?

Sceptics who insist that we can only assimilate calcium in an organic form should note that ladies with osteoporosis experience a positive increase in bone density very soon after taking a well-formulated inorganic mineral supplement. A mineral is a mineral and in your stomach, calcium is ionised by stomach acid and chelated (attached to) proteins and vitamin D supplied by the food you eat.

However, people with weakened stomach acid, especially blood type A can get osteoporosis regardless of taking calcium supplements due to this problem. They soon improve after taking a hydrochloric acid supplement such as Solgar Betaine HCL.

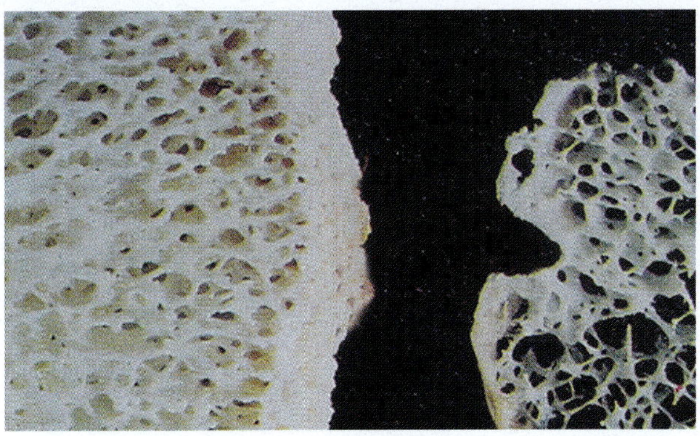

Osteoporosis is the loss of calcium

In the picture above, the bone the bone on the left has adequate calcium. Keep it that way by taking calcium and magnesium supplements to prevent your tissues and blood from becoming acidic and stripping calcium from your bones. The bone on the right is at an advanced stage of osteoporosis and well below the fracture limit. Don't let this happen to you or your children!

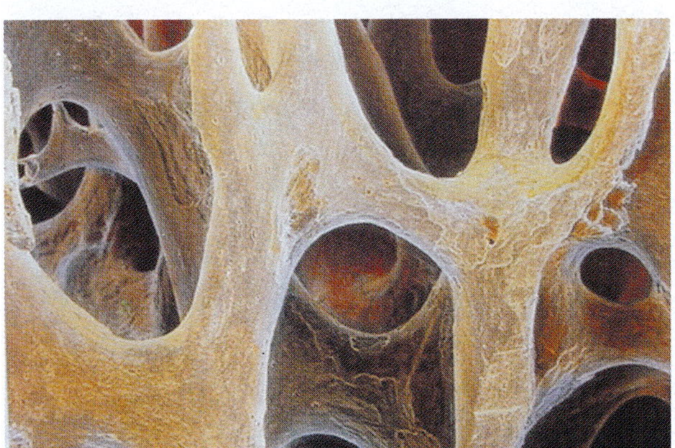

A magnified view of bone tissue. Collagen is the organic connective tissue that forms a framework for minerals like calcium to be deposited by the bone-forming cells called osteoblasts.

What type of calcium is best to take?

A well-balanced formulation with adequate calcium and magnesium for daily use need not be prohibitively expensive. Osteoporosis can easily be prevented and even reversed. Most people are warned not to take calcium carbonate because it is used as an antacid to relieve heartburn. It is best to look for a combination of calcium citrate, calcium carbonate and magnesium. Look for a pH of 7 (neutral) or lower if you have weakened stomach acid, or take some lemon juice beforehand.

Supplements that contain only an alkaline form of calcium can form kidney stones, constipation and can calcify soft tissue. Magnesium prevents faulty calcium assimilation and ensures that it connects to a transporter protein to latch onto bone tissue. Vitamin D3 and vitamin D6 play an important role in the transport of calcium.

Homeopathic tissue salts assist in the balancing, transport and assimilation of calcium. The most important tissue salts are: Calc Phos, Calc Sulph, Calc Fluor and Silicea. Stomach acid splits off the calcium atoms from the carbonate, lactate, gluconate or organic compounds and attaches them to digested proteins. This process is called chelation. It happens in your own body so why pay more for chelated "organic" minerals?

Boron is essential for preventing the loss of calcium in urine and it helps one to release more of the steroid hormones like estrogen and progesterone. The inorganic structure of bone resembles the crystalline mineral called apatite. It is composed of calcium phosphate, combined with magnesium, silica, sodium, potassium, chlorine and fluorine with bicarbonate, citrate and water. This porous section of the bone has to bond with the organic structure known as collagen tissue to give the bone strength and flexibility. Vitamin C, amino acids and organic sulphur known as MSM(methylsulphonylmethane) promote the production of collagen tissue both in the bones as well as connective tissues.

The bonding of minerals to the collagen-based bone matrix occurs within an electrical field for which the presence of zinc and copper is critical. Most of the calcium is lost from the bones during the maintenance and detoxification of your cells and tissues whilst you sleep. At the same time, new minerals are deposited back into the bone tissue. A more alkaline diet is recommended. Stomach acid needs to be made more acidic, especially in people over 40 and blood type A. (See page 69.)

Do we get enough minerals from vegetables?

Boron deficiencies in vegetables

We used to get adequate boron from apples, broccoli and just about everything that grows in the ground. Plants that are fed chemical fertilizers are unable to take up boron. For us, a lack of estrogen and other steroid hormones, especially cortisol stems from resultant boron deficiencies. Arthritis as well as menopausal maladies can be relieved with boron and vitamin B5 supplements.

Broccoli with a boron deficiency has a hollow stem, so check the bottom of the stem before you buy it. Beetroot that has white rings when you cut it, has been deprived of boron because of the use of fertilizers.

Sulphur for healthy cells and tissues

Many foods are rich in sulphur, especially yellow foods like eggs and mustard. Garlic and onions also contain natural sulphur compounds. Organic sulphur obtained from pine trees called MSM (methylsulphonylmethane) is available in many supplements today. It boosts the production of collagen tissue, eases joint pain and accelerates the action of other pain relievers. MSM with vitamin C lowers blood sugar effectively for diabetics when these supplements are taken with meals.

See page 75 for more about iron deficiencies.

Zinc, manganese, chrome, vanadium

Zinc and chrome are essential for making insulin. Consuming too many sugars and starches depletes levels of chrome and zinc. People deficient in zinc lose their taste and cannot detect levels of sweetness. They tend to tip many spoons of sugar into their tea and you will see white spots on their fingernails. Zinc gluconate is available in tablet form. Chrome controls blood sugar imbalances and is helpful to diabetics and slimmers.

Natural forms of chrome are combined with vanadium that is essential to balance chrome levels. These minerals are found in green vegetables like spinach and beans but especially in guava leaves. Guava leaves can be added to your digestive tonic (See page 106), dried for tea or ground up into a powder and packed into capsules or added to salt.

The folk remedy of tea made from guava leaves helps diabetics to regulate blood sugar.

Chrome supplements are available but watch out for exceeding the dose as there is no guarantee that any form of chrome is safe in the long run. It is far better to cut out carbohydrates that are not suited to your blood type. Eat a huge serving of green beans instead. The GTF chrome is safer and helps to control sugar cravings. It contains zinc, chrome and manganese and is reasonably priced.

Natural sources of iron

Iron is essential for making red blood cells and the transport of oxygen. Eat large quantities of parsley, dried apricots, prunes and raisins every day. They are rich in natural iron. Blackstrap molasses also improves anaemia and the tissue salt Ferrum Phos D6 increases the absorption of iron. Make juice out of wheatgrass that you can grow from wheat kernels. It is rich in chlorophyll, the most important factor for restoring your iron levels. Secondly, you need vitamin B supplements especially vitamin B12 and folic acid with vitamin C. Pernicious anaemia is a deficiency of vitamin B12 and folic acid and iron supplements are of little use.

The minerals: sodium and potassium control our water levels

Dehydrated grapes are called raisins. Soaking raisins in water makes them return to their original shape.

Salt is as important as potassium

Without water, these fresh grapes shrivel and dehydrate into raisins. Water is required to return them to their original shape. If the raisins absorb too much water, they get water-logged. This happens to the cells in your body when they do not have enough potassium to regulate the water levels inside them. Sodium and potassium regulate the amount of water in extracellular fluids like blood plasma. We are told to avoid salt if we have high blood pressure or water retention. Sodium accumulation is caused by a potassium deficiency and not always an excessive salt intake. Balanced levels of sodium and potassium are required to control dehydration as well as water retention.

Liquorice root, drops, sweets and salted liquorice

Aldosterone regulates sodium levels

The hormone aldosterone regulates the balance of sodium to potassium. Liquorice is a natural source of this hormone and salted liquorice is a wonderful tonic for ailing adrenal glands that are in need of both aldosterone and salt. Liquorice root powder is available from health shops and is 50 x sweeter than sugar. Cough mixtures and some breath fresheners contain liquorice. Caution: liquorice can raise blood pressure and increase mucous in the throat and chest. (See page 59.)

How do we get more potassium?

Potassium deficiencies manifest as fatigue, weakness, confusion and ultimately the dehydration of the colon, resulting in chronic constipation. We need potassium to activate the release of stored glucose from the liver to rectify a drop in our blood sugar, known as hypoglycaemia. To obtain more potassium, we need to eat a lot of fruit and vegetables, especially the dark green leafy varieties. Potassium supplements are usually given in the slow-release format known as slow-K. Kloref is an effervescent tablet containing 1 gram of potassium chloride that dissolves in water. Add potassium chloride and cream of tartar to half your table salt.

Potassium and high blood pressure

Add ½ tespoon of potassium tartarate (cream of tartar) to a litre of your daily drinking water. Bitter blackstrap molasses is also a good source of potassium. A tablespoon of molasses in a glass of hot water is a very good tonic, helping to lower high blood pressure and ease constipation. Adequate calcium and magnesium and a good source of Omega 3 from fish liver oil or salmon oil should also be taken. Ironically, high blood pressure and water retention are symptoms of dehydration, so drinking more water makes sense. (See pages 99-101.)

Salt only causes water retention when there is insufficient potassium in your system. For high blood pressure, more potassium can be obtained by drinking glasses of water with a pinch of cream of tartar. Add a tablespoon of crude black molasses, to absorb more organic minerals like iron and especially potassium. Add cream of tartar to your salt shaker.

Plant sources of potassium

Fresh herbs like dandelions are rich in potassium and they are safer to use than diuretics. Include a bunch of fresh leaves with your juice. All leafy green vegetables are rich in potassium. The herb buchu is a diuretic and kidney flusher. Cucumber and watermelon are also diuretic and help to detox the liver as well as flush the kidneys.

General supplements that most people need to take

Multivitamin and mineral complexes

Organic versus inorganic? Fruit and vegetables should be providing most of our vitamins and minerals, but only if they are grown in natural manure and compost. Fertilizers block the uptake of boron, molybdenum, manganese, etc. Commercial vegetables generally yield only 10% of the nutrients they once did. Take a comprehensive all-round supplement to guarantee your supply of micronutrients. A time-release coating on the tablet allows an extended rate of availability to the bloodstream as water-soluble vitamins are only active for about three hours. Some supplements are formulated with fruit and vegetable compounds to facilitate the biochemical uptake of vitamins and minerals. Other multi-supplements cater for the specific needs of sportsmen, children, women, the elderly, etc.

The organically-grown spinach on the left yields up to ten times more potassium, iron, calcium, magnesium, etc. than spinach grown with commercial fertilizers.

Vitamin B complex and the B vitamins

On blood-type diets where the intake of grains and pulses is restricted, the B vitamins need a daily boost. People who suffer from stress, depression and fatigue really benefit from taking high potency B-complex vitamins in a general formulation that has a reliable time-release effect. This will ensure a steady trickle of vitamins into the bloodstream. If you experience an immediate flood of yellow urine and then it goes clear, it means that the vitamins have surged in and purged out again. Try to maintain a steady, but pale yellow coloured urine.

Many people take supplements every day to ensure adequate supplies of micronutrients that are lacking in their diets. Some supplements are used as substitutes for drugs and medications.

Vitamin B3, known as niacin or nicotinamide is a great blood vessel flusher and dilator, helping to lower cholesterol as well as dopamine in mental disorders such as schizophrenia. Vitamin B5 (calcium D-pantethonate) facilitates the metabolism of carbohydrates, fats and sugars. It helps to produce more cortizone and is a good cure for gout, producing relief within 2 weeks, providing the diet is free of lectins, polyamines or rich fatty foods. Take 100mg with every meal for best results. Vitamin B6 prevents water retention and is anti-inflammatory. Vitamin B12 is usually injected or taken in slow-release form with folic acid so it can be absorbed by the lower bowel. Sublingual lozenges pass directly into the bloodstream. Pernicious anaemia is caused by a vitamin B12 deficiency.

Anti-oxidants galore

Vitamin C, known as ascorbic acid, cannot be made or stored in the human body and we need supplements if we neglect the intake of fresh fruits, vegetables and their juices. Ascorbic acid powder is handy to add to foods, especially salads, as it destroys moulds or aflatoxins. Vitamin E supplements are usually given with selenium. These substances are readily available in natural foods. There are many good combinations of antioxidants available. They usually include beta-carotene, lipoic acid, coenzyme Q10, procyanthin, etc.

Minerals like calcium, magnesium, etc.

See pages 78 and 79 for more about these minerals.

Supplements to help with specific conditions

Some supplements react with prescription medications. Consult a doctor or pharmacist for guidance when selecting supplements.

Boosting immunity in blood type A and B

For blood type A who has a slack immune system and the older B's who are prone to pathogenic conditions in later life, the immune system has to be kept sharp and active at all times. Take antioxidants, alfalfa, zinc and alkalising minerals, echinachea, olive leaf products, sterols and sterolins and procyanthin. Control parasites. (See pages 34, 35 and 106.)

Weight problems and gross obesity

Fat burners, food blockers, metabolic enhancers and detoxifying, stimulating and slimming supplements abound. When you stop taking them, the weight bounces back and the blubber ends up being more persistent. This is why blood type slimming makes sense. Do more exercise, cut out the fattening food lectins and eat sensibly. Get professional advice for suitable slimming supplements. First attend to vitamin and mineral deficiencies as well as bad eating habits.

Stress, cortisol and the adaptogenic herbs

A's and B's pump out a lot of cortisol under stress and this can deplete supplies of adrenal hormones. Good adaptogenic formulations contain special herbs like ginseng, rhodiola rosea, astragalus, schizandra chinensis, etc. Adaptogens increase stamina and energy levels and help to overcome stress and depression. They improve our resistance to disease and strengthen the adrenal glands. The herbs in a good formulation interact with each other to produce a synergesic effect. Some products also contain vitamin B5, tyrosine and DLPA (DL-phenylalanine) to help ease stress and depression.

When suffering from adrenal burnout, avoid herbs that contain stimulants such as caffeine that is found in guarana and kola nuts or ephedrine that occurs naturally in ma-huang. Also avoid caffeine in any form. (See page 105.) Excessive doses of St John's wort can increase joint or muscle pain.

Ginseng root is a popular adaptogen. Ginseng and iquorice may raise blood pressure but victims of adrenal burnout or chronic fatigue usually have low blood pressure.

Circulatory disorders, blood pressure and high cholesterol

Niacin or nicotinamide (vitamin B3) is a popular blood vessel dilator and it reduces bad cholesterol along the way. Drinking fruit juice mixed with flaxseed oil and lecithin is recommended by Dr. Peter D'Adamo. Hawthorn berries and leaves work miracles with congestive heart conditions, weak blood vessels, etc. Gingko biloba, ginger and olive leaf supplements boost microcirculation. Lower the blood pressure with Omega 3, potassium, calcium and magnesium. Attend to potassium deficiencies. (See page 81). Drink more water to prevent water retention. Ginger prevents platelet aggregation of the blood cells and is a good alternative to aspirin or warfarin. (See page 60.) Eating pineapple helps to prevent fibrin strands from forming. Go back to the kitchen!

Blood sugar imbalances: diabetes and hypoglycemia

Cutting out faulty carbohydrates and fats will solve half the problem. Balancing blood sugar levels is also important. Many natural substances help make insulin more effective: green beans, cinnamon, bay leaves, fenugreek, etc. (See page 66.) Chrome supplements combined with zinc and manganese, known as the GTF, work very well. The new herbal supplement: Gymnemia Sylvestra is proving to be successful in restoring pancreatic function. MSM (methylsulphonylmethane) mixed with vitamin C also helps to lower blood sugar levels when taken with a meal. Diabetics need extra antioxidants as well as vitamin and mineral supplements.

Nature's miracle workers to use as a food or a supplement

Kelp, bladderwrack and seaweed provide a natural type of sugar called fucose that we all need to deflect lectins in food. Seaweed is especially good for blood type O. It is also rich in minerals and trace elements.

Spirulina or blue-green algae provide amino acids and vitamin B12, especially for vegans who don't eat meat. Also try amino acid supplements. The grain quinoa is the only vegetarian food that contains all the amino acids.

All cooked tomatoes are rich in lycopene, the great antioxidant. It is also available in beetroot, grapefruit and guavas. Drink the fresh juice with lecithin and flaxseed oil or take salmon oil and lycopene supplements.

Ginseng root is the ultimate adaptogen for stress, low blood pressure, fatigue and a healthy happy sex life.

Milk thistle is the ultimate liver remedy. The active ingredient called silymarin, can help to regenerate an ailing liver. Take with vitamin C to avoid hangovers if you are having a party.

Cranberry juice helps to combat urinary infections. Eugenia fruit from the clove tree family is good for bladder infections, candida, stomach ulcers and inflammation.

CLA (conjugated linoleic acid) burns off the bad fat that makes us obese. It is found in cream, butter or supplements. Eat more ground-up flaxseeds, walnuts and avocados.

Lecithin from soya or eggs lowers cholesterol. Also use Omega 3 essential fatty acids or fish liver oil. Eating eggs does not raise cholesterol. (See page 48.)

One tablespoon of bitter blackstrap molasses per day provides extra iron, potassium, enzymes and trace elements. It can be mixed with herbs and spices and used as a medicine.

4 Happy Eating

How to get up and go

Fruit fasting in the morning if you need to detox. How to adapt food to a more active type of metabolism. This is the key to staying slim and energetic. Pack up nutritious school lunches and meals to take to work or for meals away from home.

The fruit and veg healing diet

Detoxify your body with natural foods. Set up a healthy and satisfying eating plan that you can stick to.

What to drink

Water is the most important drink. New ways to enjoy water, juice, and hot beverages to increase your fluid intake.

Soups and salads

Inspiration for Fresh and healthy light meals and attractive salads for all blood types.

Main meals

Healthy and satisfying and delicious meals for the whole family to enjoy. Coping with blood type individuality or vegetarianism within a meat-eating family. A variety of vegetable dishes that suit all blood types. Meat, eggs, fish or tofu can be served separately.

Please note that this information should not be used to diagnose, treat or cure a condition. Consult your doctor or an experienced practitioner, especially if you are pregnant, breastfeeding, epileptic, diabetic or have blood pressure or heart complaints. (See page 2.)

Fruit fasting to heal and detoxify

The correct way to eat fruit

Eating fruit that suits your blood type will make a big difference to your health in general. Many of us do not tolerate oranges, bananas or even papaya as well as the other fruits. Fruit salads that hang around for hours often contain random combinations of fruit that can cause severe indigestion. If the fruit is not freshly prepared, it ferments and attracts mould, fungi and bacteria.

Fruit can be either harmful or healing to us and that depends on when and how you eat it. Eating beneficial fruits for your blood type regularly and especially during the morning will enhance your health, energy levels, weight control and metabolism. Try to avoid fruits that are not recommended for your blood type or eat a less of them. Fruit is cheap, very tasty and enjoyable to eat. When you embark on a fruit healing regimen for a few days, select the fruit that suits your blood type or stick to the all-type healing fruits. (See page 87.)

Do not eat all this fruit at once! In a healing fast, start with as much as you like of one type of fruit. Have another variety of fruit two hours later after your previous fruit has been digested or you feel hungry again.

Fruit fasting as a healing therapy

The easiest way to keep the body free of stagnant wastes and toxins is to start the day with fresh fruit. Our body is in elimination mode from before sunrise till midday, so no extra food can be metabolised until then, regardless of eating so-called "energy" breakfasts. Fruit fasting in the morning promotes the regular peristalsis of the intestines. Natural fibres, enzymes, antioxidants and bioflavonoids in fruit keep the mucous linings healthy and active.

Eat only fruit in the morning

Eat as much as you like of a suitable fruit. Two hours later you can change to another type of fruit. Eat like this for the whole day or just the morning to ensure regular bowel habits and to keep your system clean and efficient. Some people are not comfortable on a fruit-only breakfast as they have a very rapid metabolism. People like this and especially ectomorphs are not well-suited to fruit fasting for too long, using unsuitable fruits. Take it slowly in the beginning. (See page 7.) A slim blood type A ectomorph, for instance, will not do so well on pawpaw or papaya exclusively. Start by eating more fruit during the day between meals instead of cakes, chips, doughnuts, pizzas and biscuits. Blood type A must avoid fruits like pawpaw, papaya, oranges, bananas and mango. Rather eat the all-type fruits like apples, grapes, pineapple, peaches, pears, plums, watermelon and grapefruit. Oranges only suit blood type B in large quantities. (See pages 12 and 39 for the fruit lists.)

The advantage of a fruit detox

The liver begins to process food correctly during the morning session and you will have a lot more energy because you are not being slowed down with a heavy breakfast, piled on top of the meal you ate the night before. Do not be alarmed by the amount of waste you begin to excrete!

The top fruits used for healing and fasting suit all blood types

Apple is king of the healing fruits

The natural pectin in an apple balances blood sugar and lowers cholesterol. It also removes heavy metals and toxins from the body. Apples contain vitamin C, E and folic acid. Folic acid must be taken by pregnant women to prevent neural tube disorders in the growing foetus. Apples may help prevent if not cure many types of cancer, due to high levels of the antioxidant, quercetin. Apple fasting makes sense, but first consult your doctor. The sour green apples help to control low blood sugar levels and are better for slimmers. For nausea or morning sickness, eat a sweet red apple to stimulate the liver.

Grape diets have cured many diseases

Grapes provide a unique form of natural sugar that resembles your own blood plasma. Grape fasting is recommended by naturopaths as a cure for extreme toxicity or even cancer. Sour grapes are better for people with blood sugar imbalances. Blue, purple and black grapes have higher levels of polyphenols, especially in the skin and these have anti-fungal and anti-viral properties. Red wine helps to free up testosterone in older women and thus enhances their sexuality. Grape seeds contain a powerful antioxidant.

Pineapples for natural digestive enzymes

Pineapples contain the enzyme bromelain that helps us to digest protein. For this reason, eating pineapple for breakfast can make you very hungry. If you suffer from low blood sugar, don't eat pineapple if you have skipped a meal. Pineapple can be eaten with other foods, especially meat, if you have problems digesting fat and proteins. Harmful levels of fibrin in the blood are reduced by eating this fruit regularly. Wash the pineapple skins and combine them with other fruits in the liquidiser when you make your juice every day. (See page 90.)

Watermelon for cleansing and providing energy

Start the day with watermelon for a surge of natural sugars and fluids that totally nourish the body whilst they flush out the liver and kidneys. Regarded as a single cure for some types of kidney stones, watermelon fasting is safe and effective. Chop up and the white part of the rinds and liquidise them with a few slices of ginger and lemon for a natural source of water. Watermelon is best eaten on its own and can be toxic if combined with other foods or left lying around. Watermelon contains citrulline, a chemical that regulates nitric oxide levels. There is also a mood-enhancing amino acid that boosts the release of endorphin.

Grapefruit and lemon for slimming and cleansing

Grapefruit contains natural fat-burning phytochemicals and blood sugar balancing mechanisms. They have a low Glycaemic Index rating, using little if any insulin from the body because they have high levels of citric acid. Use grapefruit for fruit fasting in the morning and you will have stable blood sugar levels! The ruby grapefruit is rich in the antioxidant lycopene, a popular cancer deterrent. Include the white pith in the blender as it is a valuable source of bioflavonoids. (See baking recipes on page 146, more about lemons on page 32.)

Preparing food to take along when you are at work or away

Some people are well suited to a fruit-only breakfast. Every two hours you are advised to have another type of fruit. So clean, peel and pack up some pieces of fruit to take with you. The best way to eat breakfast cereal is dry, believe it or not! Starch can only be digested in the mouth by the enzyme called ptyalin that is contained in saliva. This is why dry toast or biscuits are easier to digest. Cooked porridge, slushy cereal, doughy buns, sandwiches and even pasta also have to be well-chewed or they cause heartburn, headaches and mucous problems. Big breakfast eaters need more time to have substantial meals.

Many of us will need a breakfast box, or snack boxes as well, to help ward off the ten o'clock cake and doughnut syndrome at the office or the afternoon blood sugar slump. During the evenings or week-ends, have wild and wonderful baking sessions and make cookies, muffins and homemade treats with the recipes and suggestions given in this book. (See pages 144-151.)

Sugar awareness: do not eat foods that contain only sugar or refined white flour if you are hungry. First, have some cheese, a few nuts, sunflower or pumpkin seeds, sprouts, or something nutritious to get rid of those carbohydrate cravings. Eat healthy little meals every two hours. The odd teaspoon of sugar in a muffin or cookie does little harm. It is the abuse of sugar that is a direct cause of diabetes, asthma, rheumatoid arthritis, heart conditions, cancer, obesity and mental illness.

Diabetes has become the third most common cause of death in our society. In South Africa the monthly per capita consumption of sugar exceeds 4 kilograms. Look for healthy alternatives to junk foods from tuck shops that you and your family can make yourselves. Nobody has to go hungry, but just about everybody is addicted to junk food because they can't tell the difference between real hunger and an addiction to foods they cannot tolerate.

Eat out in style and enjoy foods that are nourishing and sustaining: rye bread sandwiches, soya, rice or rye cookies. Enjoy fresh fruit, cheese, seeds, nuts and homemade muffins, biscuits and treats.

Starches and carbohydrates

Eat health bread, rye bread, pumpernickel bread, rice cakes, rye biscuits. Avoid white bread, rolls and all wheat or gluten products if you have allergies or suffer from heartburn, postnasal drip, hay fever, headaches, constipation, ear infections and sinusitis. Use the recipes on pages 144-151 to make and bake satisfying, nourishing take aways.

Fresh fruit and vegetables

Apples, bananas, peaches, oranges, pears, plums and grapes are easy to grab. Pineapple, carrots, cucumber, celery and tomatoes can be cut into wedges and packed in plastic bags with washed lettuce. Have with dips, made in bulk and packed in small plastic containers. (See page 114.) In cold weather, pack soup in a flask.

Meat, eggs and cheese

Pack in some cheese, cold meats, biltong and hard boiled eggs. Small tubs of yoghurt or tofu can also be added.

Nuts and other munchies

Raisins, dried prunes, apricots, apples, figs, dates, and minced dried fruit, etc. for treats and nibbles.

Peanuts and sunflower seeds.(Only good for blood type A.) Walnuts and almonds are very good for everybody. Grind up pumpkin pips, sesame seeds and flaxseeds(linseed) and add them to dips or sprinkle onto sandwiches. Oven roast puffed rice (rice crispies) and cornflakes for tasty alternatives to chips. (See page 149.)

Make your own juice in the blender every day

Fresh fruit and vegetable juices supply live nutrients

A simple electric blender is a total asset and costs the same as one month's supply of vitamin, mineral and enzyme supplements. Unleash all these nutrients from your own fruit, vegetables, herbs and wheat or barley grass. You also have the advantage of drinking it immediately so that none of the key antioxidants, enzymes and bioflavonoids can spoil. Every day you can whip up exciting and tasty blends of fresh juice. Try the recipes on the following pages for special remedies and tasty drinks. Nothing is wasted as some of the pips and peels contain special phytochemicals that can control hormones and eliminate parasites.

Get the best and more from juice

1 Add 200ml water to the jug

It is important that the blades are covered with at least 200ml of liquid before switching on the motor or the fruit cannot be liquidised.

2 Add chopped fruit, etc.

Half fill the jug with diced fruit, vegetables, herbs, spices and sprouts. Use the scraps from other meals like the peels and pips. Pineapple skins make a lot of juice, but wash them first. Blend for about a minute on high speed.

3 Sieve through a cloth bag

You can make a straining bag out of strong cloth like petticoat material and stitch the seams very well because they tend to break after a lot of use. A stocking is fine to use but it will only last for a few times before breaking.

Take the bag in both hands and wring out all the juice. Very little waste remains.

Make this juice in a blender: sieve it and take your medicine!

Apple and spinach for a heavy metal detox

The best way to remove heavy metal deposits from the body is by trapping, binding and excreting them. Pectin is a natural soluble fibre, found in apples, that does just that. The oxalic acid in spinach aids the process. These substances also help to clear old hardened waste material from the bowels. Take this juice before and after you have dental done for a good detox and to help alleviate the effect of anaesthetics. Take calcium and magnesium at bedtime to complete the process. (See page 78.)

250ml water   2 chopped apples   8 spinach leaves   1 slice of lemon

Natural HRT to boost estrogen and progesterone

Red sweet potato helps to stimulate progesterone secretion and fennel raises estrogen levels both safely and naturally. This juice is a good booster, especially during menstruation or when you feel hot flushes creeping up. Ginger prevents blood clots and helps relieve nausea, PMS and hot flushes. You don't have to sieve the mixture. Sip or chew it slowly so the phytochemicals enter the bloodstream via the mouth mucosa.

250ml water   1 chopped sweet potato   5ml fennel powder
1 slice fresh ginger(or 2ml powder)   20ml lemon juice   5ml honey

The classic naturopath's blend

Raw carrot, beetroot and potato juice have a profound detoxifying effect on the whole body. Blood type O and A should not eat potatoes. O's can substitute with sweet potato and A's should try butternut or apple. This formula has been successfully used by natural therapists throughout the world for many decades to treat chronically ill patients. Some people take it regularly for its tonic effect, especially for the liver.

250ml water   1 raw beetroot   2 large raw carrots
1 chopped raw potato (not A or O, use sweet potato or apple

Eliminate large parasites like flukes and tapeworm

Fresh squash, butternut and pumpkin seeds contain an amino acid that helps eliminate tapeworms. Watercress and nasturtium leaves get rid of liver and pancreatic flukes. A pinch of cloves discourages parasites and gut infections. The pips need to be fresh and the liquidising releases the phytochemicals they contain. This includes betasitosterol that helps to control testosterone levels. Blood type B should avoid pumpkin seeds.

250ml water   1 cup pips from butternut, pumpkin or squash
1 bunch watercress/nasturtium   2ml clove powder   half a lemon

Digestive enzymes from pineapples and lentil sprouts

Wash the pineapple well before removing the skin and dicing it. The peels make a lovely juice and contain the digestive enzyme bromelain that helps to digest protein in the stomach. All sprouts contain digestive enzymes as well as a host of phytochemicals, minerals, vitamins and trace elements. (See more about sprouts on page 110.)

250ml water   1 cup diced pineapple skin   2 tablespoons sprouts
half a lemon chopped   Plus: any other fruit peels and pips

Natural juice therapy for just about every ailment

The greatest energiser and cleanser we have

The natural sugars and amino acids in watermelon give one a marvellous energy boost. Watermelon juice has been known to flush out some types of kidney stones. It is good for the liver, helping to provide fresh vitamins and enzymes. For juicing, use all the watermelon, including the white area but remove the thin green rind. Drink the juice immediately. You can use the white edges of watermelon slices as a substitute for cucumber in the following recipe as cucumber does not suit blood type O.

200ml water 500ml chopped watermelon, plus white pith
500mg vitamin C or half a lemon or lime if desired

A natural diuretic formula, with loads of potassium

Dandelions are a rich source of potassium and they help to relieve us of excess water, oedema and bloating. They are a common weed and easy to find on lawns or pavements. (See herbs page 57.) Dark green leafy vegetables and herbs are full of iron, potassium, chrome and other minerals that get flushed from the body by the excessive use of drug-based diuretics that have harmful side-effects.

250ml water 250ml chopped cucumber half a lemon
a big bunch of dandelion leaves with parsley and celery

Red grapes zap viruses and boost energy

Start the day with grape juice or have a grape juice fast for very rapid results. The juice is wonderfully energising and speeds up your elimination processes. Grapes help to expel yeast, mould, viral and bacterial infections. When you make red grape juice, pour more water over the strained-out pips and skins. Allow them to soak for a few hours, then blend again and strain. Phytochemicals in this second brew will include extra polyphenols that are beneficial to the heart and immune system.

200ml water a few big bunches of grapes, particularly red grapes

Carrot juice with a twist of lemon, apple or pineapple

Carrots are a rich source of vegetable-based vitamin A known as beta carotene. Their natural sugars provide a good energy boost and carrots contain many vitamins, minerals, enzymes and trace elements. For a quick change, add pineapple or pinepple skins, chunks of lemon, apples or raw butternut. Carrot juice is a great pick-me-up and can sustain convalescents for many days. Diced carrots can be lightly cooked and blended with other juices for a nutritious smoothie or for baby food.

250ml water 2 diced carrots any other scraps of fruit like apple,
grapes, lemon, strawberries or pineapple

Make your own wheat or barley grass juice

Grow your own wheat or barley grass from seed. (See page 113.) Include it in your daily juices to receive all the amazing health benefits that expensive supplements provide. It is best to drink the juice from freshly cut grass to unleash the enzymes. It is lovely with lemon juice and celery or add a few grapes to make a sweeter taste for children.

250ml water a few bunches of wheat or barley grass half a lemon
a small bunch of celery, parsley, watercress or other herbs

Adapting a health regimen for pregnancy and breastfeeding

The body changes during pregnancy

Many drugs or innocent foods and herbs can affect pregnant women adversely because their bloodstream is linked to the placenta that also feeds their unborn child. When Mom consumes alcohol, smokes cigarettes, takes painkillers, stimulants or sleeping pills, she shares them with Junior.

Morning sickness: all-day sickness

During the first few weeks of pregnancy, one suffers the onslaught of many physiological changes that result in morning sickness or an all-day nausea syndrome. The liver is overburdened with ketones, known as fats that break down from body tissues to produce fuel for the metabolic changes. Mom feels green, has low blood sugar, loses her appetite and suffers even more, because the fasting releases more fats into the bloodstream. Too much vomiting can result in dehydration.

Nausea during pregnancy can be modified when blood-type eating is combined with fruit and vegetable healing regimens. Ladies can fight nausea best by eating fruit, especially when they feel queasy. It is best to stick to all-type fruits. Freshly made juices with ginger are wonderful for nausea and boost energy at a cellular level, helping the liver to process all the new metabolic functions.

By now you know about lectins and incompatible foods so only nibble at suitable snacks. Salty foods often help and many ladies feel better when they suck a stick of biltong or sip a cup of hot clear vegetable stock with a dash of ginger, lemon juice or chilli. There is no formula, other than to know your blood type and stick to fresh, nourishing foods that are free of lectins.

Avoid rich foods if you feel liverish. Here is a fake egg. It's half a peach in fat free yoghurt. Serve it with fruit, sprouts, blended dates and ground-up flaxseeds

All those cravings, are they for real?

A pregnant woman who demands sweet things all the time is advised to watch out for low blood sugar symptoms: weakness, confusion, dizziness, shaking and bad moods. Sugar is not the solution as it sets off insulin that in turn, lowers blood sugar. When you can handle solid food, opt for lovely plates of freshly prepared vegetables and whatever nutritious morsels suit your blood type. There are plenty of suitable foods to choose from. (See page 117.) Try the juices, soups and salads and throw away the sweets, cakes and biscuits.

Watch out for herbs or supplements

Drug and supplement manufacturers usually warn pregnant women not to take certain substances and for a good reason, as they may cross the placental barrier and affect the baby. It is best to consult a qualified health practitioner who is experienced in nutrition and supplementation for pregnant women. Take a good multivitamin with plenty of folic acid to prevent neural tube defects. Avoid alcohol and don't undertake gall bladder flushing or any severe fasting or detoxification.

Get the book: Eat Right for your Baby

"Eat Right for your Baby" is a book by Doctor Peter D'Adamo. Get it even before you become pregnant, to give yourself a headstart. Follow the blood type guidelines in this book and for goodness sake, clean out your whole system and detoxify your liver before you get pregnant. Hopefully you will not have to suffer the nauseous phase. We wish you well with your pregnancies and may you have loads of bouncy babies that can all "eat right" for their blood types throughout their healthy lives.

The Happy fruit and veg healing, slimming and detox diet

It is your responsibility to let your doctor know if you wish to adjust your current medications. Please check up on potential drug reactions and intolerances you may have to any of the foods, herbs and supplements that are recommended. The diet is based on blood type compatability, being free of harmful and fattening lectins. Should you need allergy testing, your blood group identified or advice on supplementation, herbal and homeopathic remedies or medications, consult an appropriate health professional.

Time to get rid of sugar cravings

Insulin resistance causes the waistline to expand, resulting in the "apple shape". It is the result of consuming too many simple sugars and carbohydrates. Known as Syndrome X, the symptoms of insulin resistance are high cholesterol, high blood pressure, carbohydrate and sugar cravings, low energy, weight gain and feeling hungry soon after a big meal. (See page 98.) Syndrome X is a major health hazard, especially if combined with stress and adrenal burnout. Therapeutic diets can often reduce the need for drugs to control diabetes, high blood pressure and cholesterol. Natural bowel habits are soon established without needing laxatives. (See pages 65-68.)

Discipline and detoxification

Firstly, make sure you know your blood type, especially your secretor status. Use the imformation on pages 7-9 or have the professional tests done. Write down what you have chosen to do and eat in a special diary and stick to the program. Take a few photos of yourself, like I did. Three months later, the 8 kilograms and all the centimetres I had lost, really showed! Measure and weigh yourself every week and you will be pleasantly surprised. List your complaints and cross them off, one by one as you see the body begin to heal itself. Keep updating your progress report. Make a healthy new shopping list that you compile by using the blood type lists. Throw out junk foods and stop buying them

Clear the sludge out of your bowels

For healthy, clean and very regular bowels, see pages 65 and 97. When you have fasted on fruit and vegetables and taken the appropriate steps, you will truly have helped yourself back to health. Keep it that way with healthy, disciplined eating habits. Share your success with others! You have to go on a personal journey to get rid of your excess baggage. Over time, you got yourself into a mess. No more excuses, use this safe and natural process to become the new you.

Flush your kidneys clean

By the time we reach the age of 60, most of us only have 25% of our kidneys functioning. Get busy with the juices on page 89 to clean out and rejuvenate your kidneys.

Clear the toxins out of your liver

The liver gets so congested with waste material it can no longer break down and eliminate toxins, let alone produce vital nutrients and enzymes. Time for the liver and gall bladder flush on page 31.

Clear the lungs

For ten minutes a day, inhale over a simmering pot with 1litre water, 1 tablespoon bicarbonate of soda and 1 tablespoon of hydrogen peroxide for 10 minutes with a towel over your head.

First thing in the morning we have a workout and then...

The early morning detox with fruit

First exercise for 20-30 minutes. If you can continue for longer, then all the better. For a quick start, have a tot of warm water with a teaspoon of honey or fructose and a teaspoon of apple cider vinegar. Alternatively, have watermelon or grapefruit or some juice. Choose an activity that suits you: aerobics, running, cycling, power yoga, martial arts or a combination of calisthenics and stretching. Don't forget to breathe as it's one of the best ways to expel toxic wastes, speed up the metabolism and oxygenate the tissues. Then have some juice, water or herb tea. For the rest of the morning, eat all-type healing fruits. (See pages 86 and 87.) Insulin stimulation is what makes you hungry and you begin to crave bread and cereals. Eat only fruit in the morning on a healing fast and your appetite will begin to adjust accordingly.

Do not eat anything but one kind of fruit. Eat as much of it as you need to. Try to have your first bowel movement early in ther morning. This may not happen the first day, but you can establish the habit. After every two hours, change to another variety of fruit. You can drink as much water, juice or herb tea as you like. Stick with the fruit and liquids and do not eat anything else until your bowels move. (See page 65 if you need to cleanse your colon.) Exercise on an empty stomach, before you start eating. If you have no time in the morning, get up half an hour earlier and do at least 20 minutes of hard jogging or aerobics to warm up the system and to wake up your sleepy body.

Forget it!

No more pork, fried foods or big, heavy breakfasts

Hang in there!

Watermelon is a great energy booster!

Why the fruit routine works so well

On this healing and slimming diet, we try to fast on fruit for as long as possible in the morning. This is because the body processes all your food during the night and in the morning the waste is ready to be expelled. We first have to answer the call of nature before reloading the system with more food. By eating only fruit, this elimination is stimulated and increased.

Unlike other diets that recommend fruit salads, yogurt and muesli, we just have a single type of fruit selected from those best suited to you. This is the key to healing your body, to gaining power and energy and to getting rid of illness and disease, fat, cellulite, acne and the like. At times, you may feel a little weak and shaky during the detoxification process. Learn to take a few really deep breaths of air, all the way down into your diaphragm. Your blood pressure and your wobbles will be rectified. Then eat more fruit, drink some purified water or make yourself some fresh fruit and vegetable juice. (See pages 89-91.)

The midday meal and lots of delicious food to chew on

Add creativity to every meal: sauce it, spice it and enjoy it!

Olive oil is best for salad or vegetable dressings. Add fresh lemon juice, herbs and herb salt with a spoon of honey should it suit you. (See pages 117-121.)
In cold weather, go for lean green soups or hearty vegetable stir fries. Avoid black pepper as it lies around the gut for seven years and could be the main culprit in cases of colic, flatulence, spastic colon and many other mysterious ailments. If you have trouble with gas and colicky pains, remember not to drink water with meals or eat bread with fruit or salads. (See pages 29 and 69.)

Select seeds and nuts for your blood type and try making your own seed and nut butters and dips. (See pages 114 and 115.) Add cooked legumes like beans and peas to meals at a later stage, after you have shed a few kilos. Nibble a few slices of rye bread or rice cakes if you get very hungry during the afternoon. (See page 145.)

No more white flour products, especially: biscuits, bread, pasta, cakes, muffins or cookies. Cut out all that sugar as well.
Substitutes: 100% rye bread, (not for B) thinly sliced and toasted, soya bean products, cooked sweet potatoes or a little brown rice. Eat just a little, as this diet is ideally starch-free. If you really scream with hunger, chew a few sprouts, walnuts or almonds. Never chew nuts with fresh, acidic fruit.

At midday, we add vegetables to the meal

After a morning of fruit and juices, the body has had a chance to detoxify and process all the nutrients from the previous day. Midday is when the digestive juices are at their peak and you are now ready to handle food. Treat yourself to salads or lightly cooked vegetables if you are strictly on the healing diet. Otherwise, you can modify meals to suit your metabolism and appetite. Later on, you may change to cereals in the morning.

For the healing diet it is recommended that you stay away from all types of bread, rice, pasta, potatoes and other carbohydrates during the first few days. Also try to avoid meat, cheeses, eggs and dairy products. However, essential fatty acids are required and that means olive oil for salads and stirfries, plus plenty of ground-up flaxseeds with every meal. Take Omega 3 fish oil supplements. This will speed up the elimination process.

For a maintenance diet, a selection of wholesome cereals and grains that suit your blood type can be eaten separately or used for snacks throughout the day. Starches and sugars interfere with the digestion of fruit, so eat your toast or dry biscuits separately. Chew them slowly. It is only your saliva that can digest starch. Nibbling a few sprouts or nuts and seeds will keep away the hunger pangs and stop sugar and junk food cravings.

Eat alkalising blood-type foods to lose weight

Fresh fruit, salads and green leafy vegetables are all alkalising. The only alkalising legume is the humble soya bean. You can have it in various forms (not for blood type B[2] and O[2]). Watch out for lentils, sweetcorn and certain dried legumes as they cause health and weight problems in some blood types.

Keep up the good work!

Your body has a few years of old junk, toxins, pus and mucous to get rid of, so come clean and stick with fruit in the morning, salads, soups and stirfries at midday and vegetables at night.

Out with junk food, in with fresh natural food

The hazards of eating out

Be cautious when you eat in a restaurant. Fruit salad, prawn cocktails in mayonnaise, fruit juices that are not fresh, salads that are harbouring pesticides and parasites, complex combinations of salads, gourmet dishes, old fatty fried foods and killer desserts can cause days of discomfort and add to your toxic load. It is best to avoid any fruit, vegetable, meat, starch or condiment that you are intolerant to. Some of them may be recommended for your blood type, but you may have particular intolerances. It is best to be allergy tested. (See page 8). Black pepper, tomatoes, oranges, raw cabbage or peanuts may cause trouble for you. Use the blood type lists as a guideline and try to be at least 80% compliant, even when you eat out. Individuals with weakening stomach acid will benefit from taking digestive bitters before the evening meal. Eating foods that do not agree with you or those eaten at inappropriate times usually result in discomfort and indigestion. It is always better go to the kitchen and learn to prepare your own nutritious gourmet meals!

Give junk food the boot!

Load up with all the fresh ingredients at fruit and veg markets for your daily meals and you will not have to rely on takeaways or eating out.

Lightly cooked vegetables at night

For the healing diet, lightly cooked vegetables are better for you at night. You have a delicious variety to choose from. They can be prepared in so many different ways: soups, stews and curries, stirfries and baked dishes. (See pages 40 and 116 for vegetable dishes.)

The late evening routine

If you had an early supper, have a few late night snacks before you retire to prevent the low blood sugar syndrome that often wakes up menopausal women. The release of cortisol in response to the drop in blood sugar causes a state of alertness. This is why you don't snack on sweet things at bedtime, especially blood type A and B who are sensitive to surges of cortisol. Have milk, soya products or something bland like a banana or avocado smoothie or a little creamed tofu before retiring.

Watch out for foods laden with white, denatured starch, white sugar and harmful trans-fatty acids.

Beware of an addiction to junk food

Constant hunger pangs and cravings for foodless foods laden with starch, grease and sugar may still haunt you. Be a step ahead and always keep healthy alternatives with you when you are away from home. (See page 88.)

Fermentation in the gut

Eating piles of raw cellulose (as in salads) combined with sugary foods and tummy-fillers like pasta, white bread or rolls can cause instant fermentation in the gut, especially if such a mismatched medley of foods is washed down with juice or water and is not properly chewed. If your constitution is acidic to begin with you will have plenty of alcohol and gas forming inside your digestive tract! Symptoms usually begin with intense abdominal pains, a distended belly and flatulence. (See pages 29, 64, 69 and 97.)

Common problems you may encounter on a healing diet

Constant hunger and sugar cravings

We all have individual metabolic types, regardless of blood type. If you are a large person and have a rapid metabolism you will need more food than those with a slower metabolism who do not burn up food as quickly as you do. If you are battling with a weight problem, watch out for junk food cravings that will upset your insulin balance and make you even more hungry. Take chrome supplements if you suspect you have Syndrome X and you have too much padding around the waistline. (See pages 19, 23, 66, 80, 93, 98.)

The transition to salads and fruit can make one feel a little empty and deprived. Your body is used to feeling "full". A rebellion sets in once you begin to detox and your life-long addiction to breads, pasta, sugars and fatty foods will come to the fore. Take yourself in hand and fight these symptoms of addiction, just as a drug addict or alcoholic has to overcome their withdrawal symptoms.

Constipation

It takes time to adjust to a new way of eating. Once the fruit and vegetable healing system sets in, you will find you excrete far more than you eat. A joyous farewell to all the muck and toxins that have been trapped inside your whole body for all those years! To speed things up, have a gall bladder flush. Then take a tablespoon of ground-up flaxseeds every day. (See pages 26, 31 and 101.) Drink enough herb tea and water. A few teaspoons of blackstrap molasses with a cup of warm water is also helpful. Have a colon flush with fresh water to clean out obstructions in the bowel. (See page 65.) As soon as you begin to eat fresh, healthy food, no more laxatives, purgatives, fibre supplements or so-called "energy" foods will be required.

Avoid temptation, stay away from forbidden foods.

Hormonal upsets from food?

Many vegetarian diets include a lot of herbs and leguminous plants that contain phytoestrogens. These may have an anabolic effect on the body, causing one to gain weight. The thyroid gland can become inactive from too many phytoestrogens. Uterine fibroids may also develop. The most common offenders are: fennel, sage, alfalfa, lentils, soya and whole wheat bread. The blood type system indicates your intolerance to many of these foods. For instance, O^2 and B^2 get into trouble when they eat soya. (See pages 11-23.)

Fatigue, black rings under the eyes

Blackness under the eyes indicates a lack of oxygen in the capillaries due to poor circulation, a build-up of toxins, extreme dehydration and allergies from eating unsuitable foods. Some people are prone to pernicious anaemia or a vitamin B12 deficiency. Most women in later life seem to get tired for no reason, because of a vitamin B12 and folic acid deficiency. An autoimmune disorder can disrupt this vitamin supply. Injections can be given or take supplements. (See page 82.)

Frequent colds, sniffles, postnasal drip

Human beings are resistant to colds, but the combination of parasites, exposure to an adenovirus that comes from them and eating mouldy food is what produces the cold. Vitamin C destroys moulds in foods. Wheat or milk allergies cause mucous. Add vitamin C powder to your veggies, salads or juices. Take a daily bug-busting tincture. (See pages 30, 34 and 107.)Blood type A and B need to stimulate their immune systems.

Gas, colic, pain in the gut, bloating

Take the tissue salt Mag Phos D6 for cramps and spasms. Kali Phos works well for chronic flatulence with a bad odour. If you are reacting to some milk or meat that may have been infected, the best cure is 2 teaspoons of honey with half a teaspoon each of: cinnamon, cloves, ginger, turmeric and fennel powder. Take a teaspoon and drink some warm water. Repeat after an hour. This is very good for gut infections, Shigella, diarrhoea and vomiting. When you feel ill, take a break from eating, but drink plenty of water and fresh fruit juice.

Syndrome X and obesity are creeping up on junk food eaters

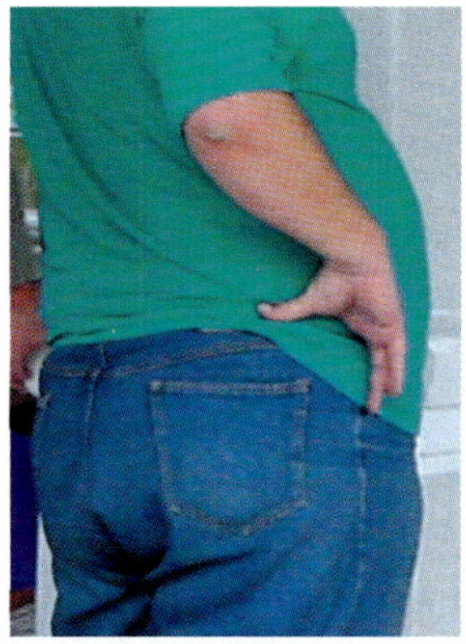

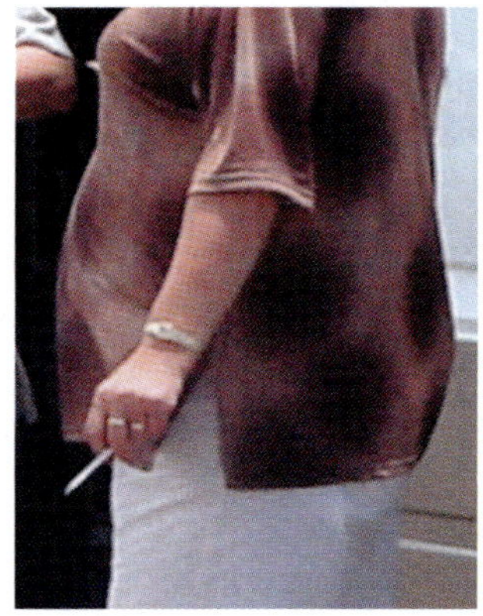

Syndrome X is a self-inflicted disease

When you notice your waistline expanding, your cholesterol and blood pressure rising and you experience a feeling of weakness and hunger soon after a big meal, it's time to look at Syndrome X. All these symptoms, as well as Type 2 diabetes, indicate insulin resistance or Syndrome X.

When the cells in your body lack glucose for energy, it does not mean that you are short of sugar, energy foods or carbohydrates. It means that the body can no longer process or assimilate them, due to an insulin malfunction. The early stages of diabetes begin to affect people with this type of insulin resistance, caused by eating too many fats and denatured carbohydrates like sugar and white flour, too frequently. The average person's sugar intake has increased steadily; up to 50kg per person per year, in some cases.

Lots of "empty" food makes us tired

An overload of white flour, sugar, fatty fries and cooked proteins causes havoc in the digestive as well as the immune sytem. A hungry and neglected body is always looking for beneficial nutrients in food but it has to process all useless and harmful substances as well. Most of this is either stored as excess body fat or it lodges in the system, bound by lectins. (see page 7) It then plugs up the bowels and spills over into the lymphatic system.

If the intestinal walls and blood vessels are damaged by parasites, then toxins and food particles escape into the bloodstream to set off the "leaky gut syndrome." The immune system triggers an inflammatory reaction especially around joints where these particles accumulate. The bowels harbour between 9-18 kgs of toxic residue. It can stay there for years, blocking up and exhausting the energy systems. It makes you acidic, it attracts parasites and weakens the immune system.

The role of insulin in the body

One of the functions of insulin is to transport glucose into the cell for energy. If the cell receptors are blocked by lectins or trans-fats, the glucose stays in the bloodstream. The second function of insulin is to bind the spare glucose molecules into packs of three. These are known as triglycerides and they float in the blood as LDL or "bad" cholesterol. Excessive triglycerides are transported by insulin to areas like your waistline for storage.

If the primary function of insulin fails, you lose your insulin sensitivity. Insulin needs zinc and chrome in order to be effective and too many carbohdrates deplete these minerals. This results in glucose spilling into the bloodstream and if it is not bonded into triglycerides, you develop Type 2 diabetes. If the triglycerides remain in the bloodstream and are not packed onto your waistline, you develop high cholesterol. High blood pressure is often caused by congested kidneys trying to flush out the excess sugar. In Syndrome X, the symptoms vary according to the extent of insulin failure and the amount of sugar, fats and carbohydrates you eat. Arthritis develops when glucosamine is stripped away from the joints by these foods and the system becomes too acidic. (See page 78.)

Diets that exclude carbohydrates

Some diets recommend the exclusion of carbohydrates and encourage more fat and protein to be eaten instead. This would be more effective if blood-type choices were made and kilojoules were restricted. The Atkins diet is proving to be very successful with people who have a problem with insulin and carbohydrates, but remember that blood type B should not eat chicken and type A does not tolerate beef. Type O non-secretors would be best off on this type of no-carb diet but be careful of relapses and sneaky carbohydrate cravings if you are not restricting the kilojoules!

Water is the most important nutrient of all, apart from air

Why do we call water a nutrient?

As much as 70% of our body weight consists of water. We know that water is the most important substance in the body yet we seem to worry more about eating than drinking. The most important liquid we drink is indeed water and we need to do so frequently throughout the day because we are losing it every time we exhale, sweat or urinate. Our body's transmission systems rely almost entirely on water for their normal functioning. Water conducts electricity and our nervous system relies on water to convey the nerve impulses. Water is a major constituent of our blood whereby food, oxygen and waste material are transported from one area to another.

When you are severely dehydrated, every cell in your body begins to suffer. The nervous system, your blood pressure and circulation, digestion, respiration, hormonal output, etc. will not be able to function normally. The thirst mechanism only activates itself long after you have become severely dehydrated, so discipline yourself to sip water more frequently even if you are not thirsty. Drinking water that contains caffeine as in coffee, tea, cola drinks and some of the medicines we take causes dehydration. We need to compensate by drinking a glass of water beforehand. Water retention is a symptom of advanced dehydration because your body tries to conserve water.

Eating fruit throughout the day helps to replenish your water supply. Leafy vegetables like spinach help to introduce water and minerals back into the intestines to prevent as well as cure constipation. Most fruit is composed of 90% water and it is free from chemicals and preservatives. Fruit, herb teas and fresh juices can provide a lot of your daily water in a pleasant way. There are many water therapies available but nothing beats a lovely summer swim. Watermelon provides water as well as natural sugars and energy boosters. It cleanses the kidneys and helps to control water retention. As a bonus, watermelon contains amino acids that make you feel good!

Water within and water without

Modern man needs more water than his ancestors

When we exercise and are exposed to hot dry conditions, stuffy rooms and air conditioning, we need to compensate for the additional loss of water. We no longer eat or live naturally and so we should drink more water to compensate.

We dehydrate ourselves

Drinking unnatural and unhealthy beverages that contain caffeine or a lot of alcohol, especially spirits, will dehydrate one regardless of the amount of water they contain. Many medications like codeine have a dehydrating effect. Headaches are usually triggered by dehydration and the cure is often the glass of water that washes down the medicine! Most people get headaches when they are constipated as this is one of your body's requests for more water.

Our primitive raw-eating ancestors did not suffer from diseases that related to dehydration and indigestion, like we do. Although we are encouraged to once again eat like them to rid ourselves of degenerative diseases, not many people today would survive as well as they did by drinking so little water. Drink freshly-made fruit and vegetable juice and herb tea with lemon juice as part of your daily water quota. Make juice out of cucumbers and especially the white inner rind of a watermelon for one of the best forms of natural fluid you can get. (See pages 89-91.)

Drink more water!

People spend a fortune on expensive creams for wrinkles, dry skin and those dark rings around the eyes. A wise old friend of mine had the answer"Drink more water!" It's surprising how much better the skin looks when you do! We need to make water a more valuable and interesting aspect of daily nutrition. Water is common, plentiful and costs next to nothing, but we should never underestimate its unique properties. Water, like air, is truly a vital nutrient.

Is it natural to drink a lot of water?

Ideally, on a raw and natural diet consisting of only fresh fruit, nuts, seeds, roots and plants, early man did not have to drink much water and could not sip it constantly whilst he hunted. Fruit and most vegetables contain over 90% water. They provide adequate water plus a constant supply of essential organic minerals, vitamins and enzymes. When meat, eggs, dairy products and grains crept into our diet, more water was required to process the extra fats, proteins and carbohydrates that contain far less water than fruit and vegetables.

Water as a quantum medication

Water is the carrier of information, at the quantum level, based on very finely tuned vibrations that it retains. This is why water plays such an important role in Bach flower remedies, homoeopathy, colloidal silver and other forms of natural medicine. It can be infused with the vibrations of plants, minerals and other energies. Although no substance can be seen or measured in the treated water, it can have a profound effect on us and enhance our physical as well as mental wellbeing.

We can even treat water with colour and sound vibrations. For instance, a tuning fork for the note A vibrates to the frequency of the immune system and so will the water if you dip the vibrating tuning fork into it for a few seconds. When coloured glass bottles of water are charged up in the sun, the water retains the individual colour vibrations: yellow for the solar plexus, green for the heart area, red for the genital region, blue for the mind, etc.

Make a homoeopathic remedy

A glass of water is a medicine in its own right. Water is used to make a homeopathic remedy more potent. For example, a pinch of salt is added to a bottle of water. By shaking it up, the salt molecules begin to imprint energy wavelengths into the water. When half the water is tipped out and replaced with new water and shaken up, a higher potency is achieved.

Repeated shaking and diluting will ensure that no measurable traces of salt remain in the water, yet this water will now contain one of the most important Homeopathic remedies we have: Nat Mur. It is used to cure chronic as well as acute water imbalances in the body. We know that salt imbalances include runny noses and water retention, so conversely, a homeopathic remedy of salt, in an activated or finer potency will ease the symptoms.

Make water-based remedies

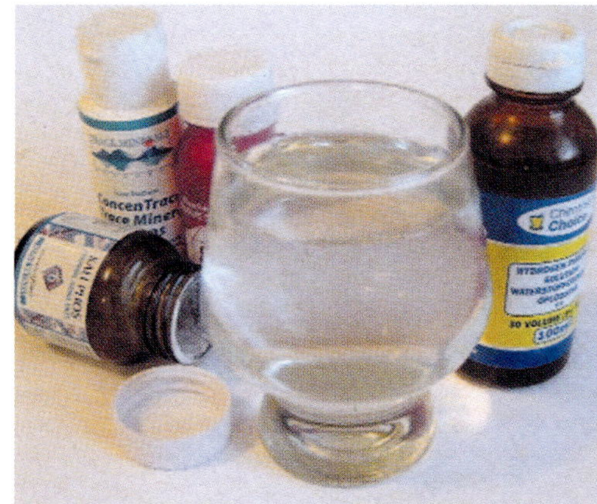

Add herbal tinctures or remedies to glasses of water. If left to stand for a while, the alcohol will evaporate away. Try colloidal silver, peroxide or trace elements.

Add ½ teaspoon of honey and ½ teaspoon of apple cider vinegar or lemon juice to a glass of water. This helps balance the electrolytes to facilitate the passage of water in and out of cells. It helps nutrients to enter cells and encourages waste material to be excreted by the skin, kidneys and intestines.

Watermelon and cucumber juice contain one of the purest forms of water to drink.

Are you getting enough water?

The correct intake of water helps to prevent, if not cure, the following common conditions: asthma, allergies, dry skin conditions as well as pains associated with heartburn, colitis, joint pain, backache, headaches and fibromyalgia or heart stress. Ironically water retention, high blood pressure, constipation and cellulite are indications of advanced states of dehydration. The body tries to conserve water the more we try to get rid of it, so diuretics are not the answer. Water is! Don't only drink when you get really thirsty as dehydration of the cell happens long before the thirst mechanism kicks in as a belated warning. By then, dehydration has already taken its toll on all of your basic metabolic functions. Elevated histamine levels due to dehydration manifest as allergies, hay fever and itchy skin, shortness of breath, confusion, weakness and debility. Taking anti-histamines and ignoring such symptoms of dehydration will undermine your health in the long run. For more information about water and how important it is to us, visit the website: www.watercures.com

Infuse your water with sun energy

Each colour of the rainbow relates to the energy contained in your seven chakras. Colour-treated water becomes infused with this healing energy when we leave water out in the sun in coloured glass bottles. Blue and green wine bottles are easy to find and you can paint the others with glass paint. If you do not have a water filter, place boiled water in a glass bottle or bowl out in the sun for a few hours with herbs or flowers in it, to make a flower remedy. If the surface tension of water is not ideal, due to incompatible hydrogen bonds, it is unable to enter the cell. A few drops of anything acidic like lemon juice or apple cider vinegar will reduce the surface tension of the water and improve its uptake into your cells.

Can we drink too much water?

Forcing down large quantities of water will only flush out your kidneys, taking most of your valuable electrolytes and minerals with it. This will make you feel tired and weak. It is not good to drink more water than the kidneys can cope with at one time as it overburdens them. Water-logging may result, especially if too much salt has been consumed or absorbed by the skin during hours of exposure to sea water. This also causes potassium deficiencies. (See page 81.) The tissue salt Nat Sulph is helpful in drawing excess water from the tissues and returning it to the bloodstream. Watermelon, cucumber and dandelions are natural diuretics. After sport, drink water that contains traces of mineral salts (electrolytes) to prevent the loss of minerals like calcium, magnesium, etc. via sweat and urine.

What is the best water to drink?

Drinking only tap water all day will expose you to too much chlorine, fluoride, aluminium, heavy metals and micro-organisms. These as well as many other toxic substances should be filtered out of your drinking water with a home filtration unit. Boiling water will not remove the inorganic components, but it will destroy the bacteria. Commercial bottled water is not always free of bacteria or contaminants. Always try to drink the best water that is available.

Herb teas for all reasons and for all blood types

Make Turkish apple tea by grating up apples and drying them in the warming drawer for a few days.

Rooibos tea with apple juice makes a pleasant drink.

Beetroot makes a beautiful pink or red tea. Grated beetroot can be dried on a plate in the warming drawer. Add a pinch of this to enhance the colour of herb teas.

Make your own herb tea blends

Herb teas have such beautiful colours, so are best drunk in clear glasses or cups. They should be appreciated for their delicate fragrances, colours and tastes in the same way as people savour a good wine. If you are a tea snob, you would never consider using a tea bag!

Tea bags contain a finely milled mixture of leaves and many of the subtle aromatic oils disappear, leaving the chemical taste of the fabric. They may be convenient, but change over to brewing fresh, exciting blends of tea in a pot and you will soon become a tea connoisseur.

Rooibos tea, the pride of South Africa

In South Africa, rooibos is regarded as a cheap tea to drink and we seldom appreciate its remarkable healing properties. The "Green Tea" drinkers of the East are now extolling the virtues of our African "Red Tea!" All the goodness of nature is packed into this unique herb: antioxidants, minerals and vitamins as well as soothing anti-inflammatory compounds. Rooibos tea does not contain caffeine or other stimulants so it is safe for everybody to drink. Many products containing rooibos extracts are now on the market. Blends of rooibos tea are popular, but you can prepare your own fresh tea. It only takes a few extra seconds to sieve the brew. Throw the tea leaves onto the garden; plants love it.

Rooibos tea for allergies and sensitive babies

Babies suffering from incurable allergies or bowel and chest infections can recover by drinking rooibos tea, we are told. It can certainly do less harm than cow's milk or wheat, sugar and salt-laden baby foods. Try replacing cool drinks, milk and tea with a fresh brew of rooibos tea, mixed with a little fruit juice. Omit all sweets and commercial baby foods. Use rooibos tea for cooking vegetables for baby food. Rooibos and molasses are high in potassium, one of the minerals that are essential for restoring the body to health. They also contain a lot of calcium, magnesium, iron and trace elements. For skin allergies, rashes, burns, genital itches and vaginal irritation, there is nothing more soothing than applying a strong brew of: rooibos tea with a few spoons of salt and some lemon juice to treat the problem area.

Savour the delights of traditional teas from other countries

Hibiscus tea, known as karkadesh

Karkadesh, from Egypt, known as hibiscus tea

Karkadesh is a warm, rich and mellow red beverage that tastes of vitamin C. It is intensely sour and is traditionally brewed with a lot of sugar. I was able to buy the dried petals at Egyptian spice markets but have not seen them in South Africa. Red hibiscus petals let out a beautiful red colour and a sour tang. A similar effect can be obtained by blending beetroot tea with lemon juice or ascorbic acid (vitamin C) powder.

How to make a red colourant for tea

Grate up a few beetroot. Dry out the shreds on dinner plates left in the warming drawer. As it dries, stir so that the beetroot does not stick to the plate. Keep the dried beetroot in a sealed container and add to herb teas to make them pink. Concentrated beetroot juice can be used to colour water, juice, milk and yoghurt pink, much to a child's delight.

Moroccan mint tea made with Chinese green(air-dried) tea teaves.

Mint tea as it is served and enjoyed in Morocco

Mint grows abundantly in Morocco and guests are offered glasses of hot, sweet mint tea. It is very refreshing in the desert but the sweetness is as always, the downfall. Originally this tea was made from Chinese tea. Long ago a consignment of Chinese tea was abandoned in a Moroccan port. They added sugar to it, to "improve" the taste and threw in a few sprigs of mint. Next time you make some black or green tea, add some mint for a refreshing, brain-boosting drink.

Turkish apple tea, the national hospitality drink

Turkish apple tea is served in little glasses. A delicious, tasty and tangy drink that is usually taken with a few lumps of white sugar. Many of the Turkish apple teas sold to tourists contain only apple flavouring, citric acid and sugar, so read your labels! The traditional method is to take minced apples that have been dried in the sun. These granules are brewed and boiled for a few minutes, to produce a weak-tasting apple tea. The flavour can indeed be improved by adding vitamin C, citric acid or lemon juice with some honey or a suitable sweetener.

Chinese green(air dried) tea and oolong tea

The classic cup of Chinese Tea

God bless the Chinese: they are the only people who offer you black tea without sugar. On arrival, guests are presented with petite little cups of precious tea. Some of the teas cost over R2000 per kg as each leaf is hand processed. When you drop the little rolled-up leaf in a cup with boiling water, it unfurls into two leaves and a bud. Up to six cups of tea can be repeatedly made out of a measure of expensive Chinese tea leaves. Jasmine tea, according to our Chinese friends, is made out of older or "rough" tea leaves and mixed with jasmine for gullible Westerners to consume.

Chinese tea is brewed in fussy little pots but the leaves are first infused in a lidded bowl. Tea ceremonies are the answer to stress, even if Chinese tea contains a lot of caffeine; up to 30mg per cup!

The tea and coffee we drink every day: does it really suit you?

First test your tolerance

Not all of us are well suited to drinking vast amounts of normal tea and coffee every day. Blood type eating includes your regular beverages. A cup of coffee is good for people with weak stomach acid, but contains over 100mg of caffeine. Ceylon tea contains 60mg of caffeine and Chinese tea as much as 45mg. A splash of milk in tea or coffee is usually overlooked for type O and A, as it falls within the limits of being 80% blood-type compliant. Sugar is not a health food, cut it out or cut down on your sugar intake. Try fructose or stevia.

Delicious variations for coffee: Turkish or Kama Sutra

Turkish coffee is a finely milled powder. It is usually boiled in a little copper pot with sugar till it froths over the top. The pot is then removed from the heat and boiled up once again, before serving in small cups. A muddy, but chewy residue remains in the bottom of the cup. Turkish and Greek coffee is traditionally served with a glass of water.

In the Middle East coffee is brewed with cardamom seeds.You can add other aphrodisiacs like vanilla, star aniseed, nutmeg or coriander to the coffee before brewing. Try grinding up a mixture of these spices with sugar to serve separately. Enjoy the rest of the evening!

Mongolian salted butter tea or liquorice tea

On the icy plains of Asia, Mongolians fight the chill with cups of salted butter tea. Yuk!, you might say but give this recipe a try when you are freezing cold and dog-tired after a long cold day: Use your coffee grinder to grind up 1 tablespoon Ceylon tea leaves, 1 tablespoon of full cream milk powder and large pinch of salt. Brew with half a litre of boiling water for 5 minutes and strain. This tea should not be sweetened. Another great pick-me-up: add a pinch of salt and a tiny sprinkle of natural liquorice powder to a cup of tea. Salted liquorice helps the adrenals when they are stressed. (See pages 59 and 81.) For fatigue, drink black rooibos tea with a pinch of cream of tartar and some molasses.

Indian Cha is hot, sweet, strong and milky

In India very sweet Cha is what keeps everybody's blood sugar rising and falling. Tea or coffee without sugar or milk is seldom an option. I was glad the milk was boiled as the cows roam the streets and feed on litter. Not exactly nourishing, especially the pages of an English dictionary that the one cow was chewing! You are what you eat. Pukka Cha is an aromatic brew of spices in a milky tea. If you drink milk, give it a try by adding a blend of ground-up spices like: cinnamon, nutmeg, fennel, vanilla, cardamom, etc. to some hot, sweet, milky tea.

Alcohol and caffeine: good or bad?

Red wine suits all blood types, but...

Red grapes contain more healing substances than other varieties. The best way to benefit from the antioxidants and polyphenols is by drinking fresh grape juice. (See page 91.) Red wine has many health benefits, especially for the heart and is highly recommended for women. A glass a day before the evening meal sounds reasonable, if not beneficial. For people who abstain from alcohol, there are capsules available, known as French Paradox, that contain a powdered residue of red wine.

Red wine and olive oil are recommended in the Bible for treating wounds and helping to clear up many common ailments. During wars, the Spaniards drank a little red wine with their water and thus stayed free of cholera and diarrhoea. Red wine has profound anti-microbial effects, as laboratory tests are now able to prove.

Alcohol is a toxic substance

It is said that everything should be done in moderation, but a toxin is a toxin. Alcohol-related deaths rank as one of the highest of all statistics. Alcohol is an addictive substance and has adverse effects on one's judgement, moods and reasoning capabilities. When driving, one is not allowed to drink too much alcohol as it slows down the reflexes. An accumulation of alcohol in the liver eventually develops into cirrhosis, where excessive scar tissue causes congestion. Fluids leak into the abdomen because hormones that normally stimulate their removal are not able to function.

Unfortunately liquor is cheap and readily available. Only the medicinal use of alcohol can be justified, as in the preparation and preservation of herbal tinctures. (See pages 106 and 107.)

Caffeine in tea, coffee and cocoa

Coffee is the richest and most delicious source of caffeine. A cup of your favourite filter coffee yields 100-130 mg of this drug. Black Ceylon tea contains 60mg of caffeine per cup. Do not be fooled by Oolong or Chinese Green Tea as it contains 45mg of caffeine per cup. Cocoa contains 10mg of caffeine. Caffeine has a dehydrating effect on the body and actually makes you thirsty. Drink a glass of water to compensate; before or after your tea and coffee. Decaffeinated coffee is full of harmful chemicals. It is safer to substitute coffee with a blend of roasted chicory, herbs and cereals.

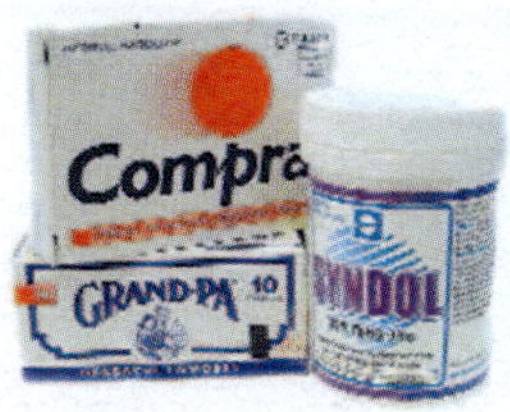

Some headache and slimming preparations are loaded with caffeine. Read your labels. Coffee encourages insulin to convert sugar into fat. Coffee may be free of fats and kilojules, but it can produce a fattening effect, especially when sweetened with sugar. Caffeine can make you irritable, jittery, unable to sleep at night and takes its toll on the adrenal system. Being a stimulant and an addictive substance, caffeine is not recommended for people suffering from the chronic fatigue syndrome or insomnia.

The good side of coffee? It's wonderful for opening up the lungs and dilating blood vessels. Many athletes have a good shot of coffee before they run. It gives most people a lot of comfort and pleasure and is hence one of the world's largest trading commodities.

How to make herbal tinctures for medicinal use

A word of caution about herbs:

Although kitchen herbs and spices are innocent enough to enjoy with your food, they do have profound medicinal effects. If you are pregnant, breastfeeding or take medications for epilepsy, diabetes, blood pressure or serious conditions, then discuss your herbs with a qualified professional. The information provided is to give you a brief outline of the scope of common herbs and spices. Do not try to diagnose, prescribe or treat a condition that a practitioner should be attending to.

Alcohol is the best tincture base

Alcohol is traditionally used to make a tincture as it acts as a preservative, keeping the mixture free of moulds, bacteria, etc. for a number of years. Without it, the herbal extract will spoil within days.

You do not have to drink this alcohol

Many people do not approve of drinking alcohol and for a good reason, as it is a toxic substance. Fortunately alcohol is volatile, meaning it evaporates easily. When you take a tincture, all you have to do is put the dose in some warm water. Stir and wait. The alcohol will evaporate by the time the water is cool. It's that easy!

Unleash the healing power of plants

Some of us need a little phytochemical boost from time to time, so we make fruit and vegetable juices. Another trick is to prepare herbal tinctures and keep them handy. For instance, if we take a daily shot of herbal tincture to control parasites, boost the immune system and detox the liver, then we do not have to buy other expensive products!

Herbs are soaked in alcohol and then sieved, diluted and bottled: ready to use.

A daily shot of herbal tincture can boost energy, stimulate immunity and awaken your libido!

How to make a fresh leaf tincture

1 Pour a cup of Vodka or Cane spirits into the jug of your electric blender.
2 Process a cup of chopped, fresh leaves of your choice with the alcohol till it is finely milled.
3 Now you can add more herbs if the blender mixture is still thin enough for the blades to turn.
4 Pour the mixture into a glass jar. Label it and allow it to soak for at least two weeks.
5 Strain everything through a fine cloth, squeezing out the last precious drop. This mixture can be diluted 1:1 if you prefer. Bottle your tincture and use one or two teaspoons at a time.

A dry herb tincture

1 Soak a cup of dried or powdered herbs in a cup of warm water for a few hours.
2 Place a cup of Vodka or Cane spirits into the blender jug and keep adding the soaked herbs, half a cup at a time.
3 Bottle and keep for two weeks, then strain.

Fresh and dried herbs with powder

One can combine fresh herbs, dried herbs and spices or herb powders. Always start with the alcohol and fresh leaves, then add the dried herbs and powders. Keep processing until the blades begin turn with difficulty, then add a little warm water if you still have more herbs to add.

Herbal tinctures to make and take

A broad spectrum bug-buster

Olive leaves and artemesia are potent anti-parasitic herbs and help to stave off colds and flu. Cloves have an intense anti-microbial action and keep the gut as well as its contents free of parasites. They don't fancy the taste! Nasturtiums and watercress discourage liver flukes. Take 1-2 teaspoons every day, especially when visiting other countries or when you have eaten something bad.

1 cup Vodka/Cane
1 cup warm water
1 cup chopped fresh olive leaves
½ cup chopped nasturtium leaves
1 cup fresh Wilde Als/Wormwood/Artemesia
or: ½ cup dried herb with ¼ cup water
1 cup fresh watercress/nasturtium leaves
50ml clove powder

Allow the tincture to soak for at least two weeks, in a glass jar, then strain it and keep in dark bottles. Take a teaspoon every day before the evening meal to keep the bugs at bay

Ways to take these tinctures

1 Before a meal. Have a cup of herb tea or a glass of warm water with a few teaspoons of the tincture. To further aid digestion, take digestive enzymes and a Solgar Betaine HCL supplement.

2 With a glass of wine. Red wine suits all blood types and a small glass before a meal is in itself beneficial. A swig of the tincture can be washed down with water or wine, if it tastes to harsh!

3 Add half a teaspoon of honey to a teaspoon of tincture. Some fresh lemon juice can also be used. For extra benefits, mix in more powdered spices like turmeric, cloves, etc.

The "Achey Breakey" blend

People with sore joints and stiff bodies, headaches and sluggish systems will enjoy this one.

1 cup Vodka/Cane
1 cup warm water
1 cup mixed: chopped mint, basil, rosemary
¼ cup fresh chopped ginger
or: 30ml ginger powder with ¼ cup water
1 teaspoon each of: bitter aloe powder, cream of tartar, turmeric, chilli powder

A general digestive/diabetic tonic

This blend is aimed at improving insulin function and it helps to stimulate the release of digestive secretions. It should be taken before lunch or dinner. Do not take this mixture without having food, as it lowers the blood sugar levels.

1 cup Vodka/Cane
1 cup warm water
1 cup mixed: chopped fresh parsley, rosemary, majoram, thyme, oregano
or: use ½ cup mixed dried herbs
2 teaspoons each of: cinnamon, fenugreek, turmeric, ginger and bay leaf powder
if available, try to add:
½ cup fresh lentil sprouts or guava leaves, olive leaves or dandelion leaves

The great grand waterfall

This mixture is rich in potassium. Potassium is essential when expelling water, to maintain the equilibrium of cellular fluids and minerals. (See page 81.)

1 cup Vodka/Cane`
1 cup warm water
1 cup chopped dandelion leaves
1 cup chopped celery and parsley
50ml dried buchu
5ml cream of tartar
50ml bitter blackstrap molasses
5ml each of: turmeric and ginger powder

Master these basic kitchen skills to cook vegetables in a jiffy

There are many ways to enjoy carrots. When you prepare a lot of carrots, keep the tips for a separate dish and then slice and dice, snipper and grate the rest. Use for salads, dips, stirfries and as a quick nibble while you are busy in the kitchen. Add your creative touch to onions. Boiled onions make creamy vegetable dressings. (See page 114.)

Anybody can cook: especially men and kids

People who prepare their own food enjoy a firsthand experience with all the exciting colours, textures, aromas and flavours of food. All it takes is the effort to buy loads of fresh and healthy ingredients. With a bit of guidance, you can become totally independent and able to feed yourself and entertain lavishly. Make Happy Eating come to life!

All the best meals begin with chopping

Have a look at these carrots. After scrubbing or peeling, rinse them off and start chopping or grating. Carrots, parsnips, turnips, butternuts, beetroot and sweet potatoes can be sliced into just about any shape. They can be enjoyed raw, steamed, stir fried or roasted. The thin raw slices make a wonderful substitute for chips when you serve dips.

Chop up a load of onions, etc. to keep

Before you peel onions, soak them in water to avoid the tears. Some people light a candle to absorb the evil fumes. To take the burn out of raw onions, pour boiling water over the slices and soak for a few minutes before draining. Always keep a large container of chopped onions, herbs, celery, parsley, green pepper, etc. in the fridge so you can toss out salads, omelettes and stir fries in a jiffy.

Clean and peel on newspaper

Spread a few sheets of newspaper onto the working surface, then put down the chopping board. As the vegetable waste accumulates, wrap it up, ready to bury in the garden compost. (See pages 116-135 for more delicious quick meals.)

No more takeouts, deliveries or junk food. No more slavery while your man watches TV. Men are very good at preparing food, besides eating it! They really enjoy chopping and getting stuck into the ingredients, knowing that they can choose their favourite foods. To stay out of trouble, only take out the foods that suit your blood types and learn how to use them in a number of basic dishes before getting too ambitious. Involve the children as well and teach them how to stirfry. See pages 128-131 for some exciting ways to entertain with stirfries and Oriental food, to suit your own blood types.

Have fun with food together in the kitchen

Save time by cleaning and chopping vegetables in bulk and keeping them in the fridge

Butternut suits all blood types, so get chopping!

Blood type A should not eat potatoes or sweet potatoes. Try these delicious alternatives from the humble, nutritious butternut.

Butternut slices

Slice the butternut neck into thin slices for roasting in the oven. Brush them with a little olive or canola oil. Sprinkle on herb salt or a pinch of curry masala. Cook on medium heat at 180° C. To save energy, bake other dishes like casseroles, curries, rice hotpots or cookies at the same time.

Butternut chips

Cut 6cm thick slices of butternut neck and remove the skin. Slice downwards into chips. These can be stir fried in a little olive oil or baked in the oven as an alternative to greasy potato chips.

Stuffed butternut

Hollow out the bulbous end of the butternut and cook whole in a steamer till soft. Fill with rice or millet, chopped onions, parsley, canned tuna, cooked soya mince, walnuts, etc.

Grated butternut is delicious raw

Grated butternut can be eaten raw, as a salad, or combined in equal quantities with rice to reduce the starch content. You can lightly stir fry or steam grated butternut or add it to a soup, just before serving. Lightly cooked butternut is a good baby food.

Use up the bits and pieces in other dishes

Chop up all the bits and pieces of butternut that remain and toss into soups or stews. Try adding the butternut chunks to the pot next time you cook rice or millet. It is delicious with any meal.

Even the pips are used as a folk medicine

The butternut pips are very special. Add them to the pieces of chopped fruit and vegetable scraps when making juice. When using an electric blender, always pour a cup of water into the jug so that the blades are covered. Then add your fruit and vegetables. Sieve the juice through a stocking or a cloth bag before drinking. (See pages 35 and 90.)

Always keep a mixture of chopped onion, celery and parsley handy in the fridge. Add green peppers and chillies if they suit you. Use for quick salads, fries, sauces or dips.

Grated vegetables can be very colourful and are delicious to eat raw. The secret is to serve them with sumptuous salad or vegetable dressings. (See pages 115, 125 and 140.) Try this combination of grated carrot, beetroot, parsnip and butternut.

Soup in a jiffy! Fry up the chopped onion, parsley and celery mixture, add herb salt and a stock cube, some water and simmer for a few minutes with the grated vegetables. Add some curry powder and ginger.

How to grow your own sprouts in just four or five days

Sprouts are the ultimate in nutrition

Welcome to the world of sprouts. The transformation that takes place once a seed begins to germinate happens at a rapid rate and the vitamin C level alone increases over 600 times. A single lentil expands up to five times its original size as the fats and starches transform into sugars, vitamins, minerals and valuable enzymes. Sprouts boost the nutritional value of all your meals or snacks and are very low in kilojoules. They are excellent value for money, costing a few cents a day for all that goodness.

Anybody can grow their own sprouts and it becomes a pleasant part of your weekly kitchen routine. The nutritional benefit is overwhelming: amino acids, vitamins B, C and E, enzymes, minerals like phosphorus and iron, trace elements and antioxidants in a n organic "food state" form we can assimilate and use. Sprouts are so fresh, they're still growing! They are a wonderful way to supplement the diet, especially if you can't afford to buy expensive vitamins and minerals all the time.

Growing a regular supply of lentil sprouts, for instance, will cost you a few cents a day per tablespoonful. Although lentils may not agree with blood types O and B, the lentil sprouts suit everybody as the harmful lectins are removed by the sprouting process. The same goes for soya, wheat, maize and barley sprouts. Mung bean sprouts are not for blood type B. Blood type O should avoid alfalfa sprouts because they can overstimulate their immune systems.

Half a cup of soya bean sprouts contains more vitamin C than six glasses of orange juice. A tablespoon of alfalfa or lentil sprouts provides all the vitamins and minerals we need for the day. Lentil sprouts are very rich in B vitamins, especially vitamin B6 that is essential for controlling water retention. Ladies on a regular intake of these sprouts should experience some relief from premenstrual bloating, swelling and oedema. Lentil sprouts are a cure for depression because they help one produce the mood-elevating neurotransmitter serotonin. This is due to the high niacin (vitamin B3) content. These sprouts also contain amino acids, enzymes and high levels of calcium, magnesium and potassium.

Sprouts help to energise us and can improve our concentration because they contain phosphorus, the ultimate brain and nerve tonic. Being rich in chlorophyll, they help to ward off infections, keep the breath fresh and stimulate the immune system. No commercial supplement can equal the dynamic quality of live enzymes that are contained in home-grown sprouts.

1 Begin by sprouting lentils, mung beans, alfalfa or fenugreek as they are ready to eat after just 4 days. Soak the seeds in water overnight. Add a few drops of aqueous (Lugol's) iodine to the water and soak for another day if you have a sluggish thyroid. The sprouts then contain organic iodine and will be free of any stray fungal or bacterial infections.

2 After soaking for 1 or 2 days, rinse the swollen seeds in a sieve and place over a soup bowl. Cover the sieve with a plate. Rinse with water every morning. After two days, the shoots begin to appear and the sprouts can be eaten. Keep them covered in the fridge.

3 The best time to eat your sprouts is after 4 days as this is when vitamin C levels are at their best. When sprouts turn green like these ones, they are overexposed to light and may cause indigestion, gas and flatulence.

Sprouts have it all and cost so little

Where do we buy seeds and sprouts?

Most vegetable markets and supermarkets keep a variety of fresh sprouts but if they have been exposed to light, make sure they are not too green. The large, long white fleshy mung bean sprouts are fabulous in oriental stir fries. It is always better to grow your own sprouts if you have the time. Always keep them in a dark refrigerator as soon as they are four days old to maintain the highest vitamin C levels. You can buy seeds like alfalfa, cumin, fenugreek, mustard and mung beans from a health shop or a spice shop and have a lot of fun experimenting with them. Throw in a few cumin, mustard or fennel seeds to the sprouting mixture to make more interesting flavour combinations.

Lentils do not suit all blood types but if you soak and sprout them, the harmful lectins are removed. Lentil sprouts grow to four or five times the volume of the original seeds.

Teach children about the miracle of sprouts

Ordinary soup lentils from the supermarket are freely available, cheap and very easy to sprout. They are ready to eat in four days and are one of the most delicious, nutritious and rewarding of all sprouts to use every day in the home. Children enjoy watching them grow. They learn about the miracle of life from seeing the lentils spring to life once they get moisture, warmth and air. Sprouts can grow in sea water and will provide more minerals and trace elements than those grown in fresh water. Alfalfa seeds produce wonderful foliage if you plant them in a pot. The shoots can be eaten in salads or included in juices. Wheat and barley kernels grow into nutritious grass and make a very energising juice, when included in the blender with other fruits and raw vegetables. (See page 113.) If children don't like sprouts, add them to their juice. They are the ultimate immunity-boosters.

Bright green mung bean sprouts have a delicious nutty taste and are easy to grow. They are delicious to nibble and are good all-rounders for many dishes. Bood type B should not eat them.

Try not to cook sprouts, rather eat them raw

Overheating vegetables, including sprouts, will destroy the live components of the plant, including some vitamins and enzymes. This is why sprouts are added to cooked dishes at the last minute or served separately. Some sprouting fundis recommend you allow sprouts to stand in the sun for an hour or two to increase the chlorophyll content, just before you eat them. Do not expose them to too much light for too long because bright green sprouts can cause severe indigestion and may cause abdominal discomfort and gas. Remember that we also get plenty of chlorophyll from parsley, spinach and other dark green leaves.

Fenugreek sprouts are very beneficial for diabetics and help to control blood sugar. They have a distinctive bitter, or curry-like taste and blend in well with strong spicy foods and sauces.

Sprout pulses before you cook them

We can sprout dried pulses before cooking them for soups and stews. The sprouting process destroys harmful lectins in dried pulses like peas and beans. It makes sense to soak dried peas and beans in water for a day. Rinse them well and sprout for a day or two until the baby roots emerge. After cooking, the pulses taste better and are easier to digest and they do not produce any gas. An additional benefit is that most of the starches will have been converted into a more digestible form of sugar. (See pages 29 and 118.)

A tablespoon of alfalfa sprouts contains all the micronutrients you need for the day: vitamins, minerals and enzymes. In Arabic,al-fal-fa means the father of all foods, but not for blood type O!

Wonderful ways with sprouts to enjoy with almost every meal

Add a thick layer of sprouts to a slice of bread or toast or a rice cake spread with cottage cheese, mashed avocado or bean paste. Season with herb salt and a sprinkling of olive oil, lemon juice and even chopped onion and parsley.

For breakfast or light meals: add a few tablespoons of sprouts to an omelette before flipping it over. Sprinkle a mixture of sprouts with chopped celery, onion and parsley on top, with a little olive oil and lemon juice. Serve the omelette on a bed of lettuce.

In summer make cold soups out of cooked beetroot, celery, parsley and onion or try a blend of avocado, yoghurt or tofu and cold stock. Add a tablespoon of lentil sprouts per person and blend until smooth and creamy. Season with lemon juice, yoghurt, olive oil, freshly chopped herbs and herb salt.

Sprouts can be added to cooked samoosa fillings or curries to increase the nutritional value. They should not be overcooked, so add them at the last minute and mix them in. Use soya protein to stretch the meat. Here you see a sambal paste that was made from fresh sprouts, onion, chillies, spices and celery.

Sprouts can be added to the blender when making fruit and vegetable juices. Sprouts are especially good for sick people and small children. Try adding sprouts to fresh chunks of ginger, pineapple, grapes and lemon. Add a spoon of honey after sieving the juice or use stevia if it needs sweetening.

Always add a handful of sprouts to salads. You can make a lovely salad dressing out of sprouts with chopped onions, apple and herbs. Round it off with herb salt, kaloontjie pepper, lemon juice and olive oil. Blend in some mashed avocado or yoghurt.

How to grow your own wheat and barley grass

Make fresh juices for the best kicks

No supplement can deliver the active nutrients and live enzymes that your own fresh wheat and barley grasses can. They are rich in chlorophyll which helps to restore flagging iron and protein levels in the body and purges the system of toxins.

Fresh grass juice made in the blender

If you do not have a special grass juicer, just use your electric blender. Add a bunch or two of the freshly harvested grass to just about every juice you make. Add some fresh alfalfa leaves but remember they are not recommended for blood type O. For a delicious green chlorophyll bomb, combine the grass with celery, parsley and any other herbs you have on hand. If you have dandelions growing in the garden or on the pavement, always include a few of the fresh leaves as well. Add a slice or two of lemon and process it all together with a cup of water in the blender. Sieve through your juice bag or stocking. This is the best way way to come alive!

1 Buy seed at the health shop

For a few rand you can buy a large packet of wheat or barley kernels. Make sure you have live, organic seeds and not the pearled wheat or barley. You can also buy alfalfa seeds to grow in the same way, but the shoots take a long time.

2 Soak the seeds overnight

For every medium-sized flower pot, take a handful of seeds and soak them in water overnight. To enrich them with iodine, add a few drops of aqueous iodine, called Lugol's solution, to the water.

3 Prepare pots and plant the seeds

Fill each pot with garden soil to 5cm from the rim. If you have vermiculite or compost, mix it in as well. Now add the seeds in a generous layer.
Cover with a light 1cm layer of soil.

4 Just add water and wait!

Keep the pots well-watered and after a few days, green shoots appear. After a few weeks they are ready to cut. The grass will grow again for another cutting. Plant pots of seeds regularly for a constant supply of this nutritious grass throughout the year.

In addition to wheat and barley shoots, you can plant a pot or two of alfalfa seeds. Add alfalfa shoots to the grass when juicing. (Alfalfa is not for blood type O.)

Basic kitchen equipment for Healthy Happy Eating

Two blenders and a coffee grinder

Buy a basic electric blender for making juices and smoothies every day. Use your coffee grinding attachment to grind flaxseeds, nuts, etc. Invest in a hand-held blender when you can afford one, to do pesky little jobs like making small amounts of sauces, baby food, nut butters or creamed soups and vegetables - directly in the pot or container.

You also need a few sharp knives and a chopping board, a potato peeler, a grater and a few sieves. Make yourself a straining bag for juices out of old petticoat material, to fit inside and over the top of a 1-litre jug. (See page 89.)

To make thick pesto sauce or bean dips in an electric blender, start with enough oil and lemon juice to cover the blades. Slowly add onions, garlic, spices, herbs, etc. Add a few bits of spinach at a time. For thickening the paste once you have removed it from the blender, stir in grated parmesan cheese, ground-up sesame seeds, sunflower seeds or walnuts. To make bean dips, use the same method, adding mashed beans afterwards. You can also press it through a sieve with a spoon.

Bean dips: an alternative to hummus

1 can butter beans or baked beans
1 small onion, 50ml lemon juice
2 teaspoons cumin powder, salt to taste
1-2 cloves garlic
50 - 100 ml olive oil

Process in a medium-sized bowl with your hand - held blender till smooth and creamy. You can add paprika, tomato paste (if it suits you) and celery, green peppers, chillies and exciting spices.

Salad and vegetable dressing

2 medium onions, chopped and boiled
1 clove garlic, 1 small chilli
5-10ml grated lemon rind
juice of 1 large lemon (50ml)
100ml olive or canola oil
5ml honey
herb salt to taste

Combine all the ingredients and process with a hand-held blender or use a liquidiser. This is a delicious alternative to mayonnaise for vegans.

Make your own sauces, drinks, dips, nut cheeses and butters

Thick pea soup, which can be served cold as a dip.

A quick and nourishing soup

1 Fry a cup of chopped onion mixed with celery, parsley and garlic in a splash of olive oil.
2 Toss in a can of cooked dried peas. Add a stock cube and half the empty can of boiling water. Allow to simmer for a few minutes.
3 Plunge in the hand-held blender, or whirr up the mixture in your blender goblet. Season to taste.
4 Serve with lemon wedges and rye toast.

Variations: canned butter beans, chick peas, sweetcorn, lentils, etc. Add curry spices or chilli.

Nut and seed butters or cheeses

If you have thrown out the cheese and butter, don't despair. Make this gorgeous nut butter.

100ml sunflower seeds or walnuts
50ml olive or canola oil
2ml salt for savoury or 5-10ml honey for sweet

Process in a narrow container with the hand-held blender. Variations: cashew nuts, sesame seeds, almonds, peanuts, etc. To make cheese, keep adding seeds and nuts to 100ml oil. Add chopped onion, seasoning and herbs to taste. Form into rolls.

Walnut butter

Sunflower seed cheese

Quick soups and shakes for your type

Whisk up smoothies with bananas, yoghurt, molasses, honey, tahini, lemon juice, etc. For people deprived of dairy products, use soft fruits that suit their blood type. Try paw paw, pears, stewed apples or apricots. Combine with rice or soya milk, tofu, boiled rice or a little cooked sweet potato.

Make cold soups out of avocado, tomatoes, cucumber, etc. Use the blender jug or hand-held blender. Any leftover vegetables and even sprouts that your family may dislike, can be blended into nutritious soups and exciting health drinks.

Most children love flavoured yoghurt, rice or soya drinks. Add natural fruit or honey and leave out the sugar.

Nutritious Omega 3 energy boosters

To any glass of juice, add: 30ml flaxseed oil, 5ml olive, walnut or sesame oil and 15ml lecithin. Process in the blender. The lecithin emulsifies the oils and makes a deliciously creamy drink that is really satisfying. Honey improves the taste.

Frozen fruit "slush"

Lightly frozen juice, iced tea or beetroot juice can be buzzed with the hand-held blender to make ice "slush". Sweeten plain beetroot juice with a little fructose and add vitamin C to sharpen the taste.

Easy vegetables for all blood types to begin with

Butternut
Broccoli
Carrots
Turnips
Parsnips
Onions
Spinach
Courgettes
Squashes
Lettuce
Lemons
Garlic
Ginger
Parsley
Celery

Welcome to the kitchen!

Some of us have had bad experiences with vegetables and we rarely see, taste or touch them before they reach our plate. We all know we need at least 5-8 servings of fresh fruit and vegetables every day and it is best to eat those that are beneficial to you. Blood type eating is about avoiding harmful lectins, including those in fruit and vegetables. (See page 7.)

Start with simple meals for all types

The recipes and cooking techniques in this booK will help you to become familiar with a few vegetables at a time so you can gain confidence in your ability to prepare food for yourself, your family and friends. Learn to whip up these quick and delicious dishes by yourself, if this is your first session in the kitchen. Refer to the lists on pages 11 -14 to add the neutral and beneficial foods according to your blood types. Make delicious sauces and dips for the vegetables and try out new food combinations. Try to stay away from foods that are not recommended for your blood type. If you are cooking vegetables for people of a different blood type, then make sure items like tomatoes, brinjals, potatoes, etc. are served separately wherever possible.

Keep tasting the food you are preparing to really enjoy your cooking. Get your family involved in selecting new, healthy foods that suit them.

Relax and enjoy the fun

Even if you know nothing about blood science or why certain foods are bad for you, the selection of vegetables on these pages contain no harmful lectins and can be considered as medicinal foods. They help to provide vitamins, minerals and valuable enzymes to the diet. They boost your immunity, improve mental alertness and eyesight and help you to lose weight. In this section we learn how to make salads, soups and quick stir fries. Now relax as you enjoy cutting, tasting, cooking and blending the beautiful colours and textures into dishes of food that you can enjoy and be proud to serve, even to the fussiest little eaters!

Two easy soups for beginners to make and enjoy

Golden beta carotene soup

Ingredients for 2 servings:
1 clove finely chopped garlic
1 teaspoon chopped ginger
1 tablespoon olive oil
1 medium sweet potato, peeled and diced (not for A - use apple)
1 chopped onion
2 carrots, scrubbed and diced
1 cup chopped butternut or pumpkin (not for B)
1 teaspoon curry masala
1 teaspoon fenugreek (methee)
1 cup boiling water
1 vegetable stock cube or equivalent
chopped parsley or celery for garnish

How to make this golden beta carotene soup

Beta carotene is the precursor to vitamin A. A single serving of carrots, pumpkin, butternut or yellow sweet potato provides enough vitamin A to protect the lungs from the damaging effects of smoking or air pollution. This delicious soup can be enjoyed as a starter or as your main meal.

1 In a heavy-bottomed pot, fry the garlic and ginger in olive oil at a medium temperature.

2 When sizzling, add the sweet potato, carrots, onion and butternut or pumpkin. (Substitute the sweet potato with apple or pear for blood type A). Mix in the curry powder, fenugreek and a little salt. Stir for a few minutes and savour that aroma.

3 Pour on the water and watch the steam rise. Add the stock cube. Close the lid, turn to low and simmer for 15 minutes.

4 Mash the cooked vegetables to a finer texture by hand or use a hand-held blender. Blood type B can add orange juice, if liked. Serve with a topping of chopped parsley, onion or celery. Add a swirl of cream or yoghurt, but not for blood type O.

Broccoli and pears: these ingredients can be served as a stir fried vegetable dish or as a soup because the cooking method is the same. We just add more stock or hot water to make the soup.

Broccoli and pear soup

A slimmer's delight, with an unusual fresh tang from the pears (or apples)

1 Chop and fry one onion with a little garlic and ginger in olive oil. Cut the broccoli into separate litle florets and slice them very thinly.

2 Add half a cup of water and some herb salt or vegetable stock to the onion mix and toss in the broccoli.

3 Turn off the heat and cover the pot. Peel and thinly slice a pear. Add a few teaspoons of rice flour to the broccoli to thicken it. Mix in the pear slices.

4 Serve as a vegetable dish, or as a warm salad or starter.

5 For soup, add more boiling water, a bit of soya sauce or more herb salt and serve with a slice of lemon.

Three-bean soup

Curried root vegetable soup

Green pea and spinach soup

Beetroot soup

How to make different kinds of hearty vegetable soups

The basic quick vegetable soup technique

We always begin by frying chopped onion, parsley, garlic and celery in a little oil. Then we add chopped fresh vegetables like carrots, green beans, beetroot, butternut and sweet potatoes or potatoes for B^1 and AB. Cover the vegetables in hot water, add herb salt and a stock cube, plus other herbs and forms of seasoning. Later add softer vegetables like, broccoli, courgettes and spinach. Add noodles made from rice, rye or mung beans. Add lettuce and sprouts at the end. You can also add a can of baked beans, white broad beans, lentils, chick peas or cannellini beans and tomato paste. (Tomatoes are not for A^1 and B^1.)
A cream of vegetable soup is made by adding a little rice flour and milk or soya milk. Process the mixture, using a blender.

Dried legume soups or dhal

Yellow pea soup with rye bread and bean sprouts

To avoid fattening lectins, choose pulses that suit your blood type. All blood types: white broad and cannellini beans, dried peas, soya beans (not B^2 or O^2). Lentils are not for B and O^1. Chick peas only for O^1. Red kidney beans are only suited to B.

Dried peas, beans and lentils

1 For soup made from cooked dried peas, beans or lentils, also begin by frying onions, celery, garlic and parsley. To this mixture, add stock, curry spices or tomato paste, etc. to make wonderful hot spicy soups, hummus, dips or dhal.

2 Use canned peas and beans for your soups if you are in a hurry, but it is best to cook your own so you can first sprout them to get rid of lectins. (See page 29.) Sprouted or well-soaked pulses take less than half an hour to cook, instead of a few hours.

NB! Never add salt to dried beans whilst they are cooking because they will stay hard. Season after they are cooked. When done, soften beans to a pulp with a potato masher or hand-held blender to make dhal or soup. Add fresh garlic, curry powder, lemon juice and olive oil.

Lean mean veggies keep you slim

Use these slimming dishes to replace: rice, pasta, bread or potatoes

Slimmers, diabetics and people on the healing diet must reduce their carbohydrate intake at meals. Eat mostly green, non-fattening vegetables.

Non-fattening vegetable selection

Lettuce in all its beautiful varieties, courgettes, onion, garlic, parsley, celery, baby patty pan squashes, lentil sprouts, watercress, baby spinach, carrots, broccoli, green beans, parsnips and turnips suit all blood types. Pears and apples: all except O^2. Green peppers: not A^1 , AB. Radish: not B , AB.

Add water to a stir fry to make a soup

Versatile lean soup or a stir fried meal

Eat as much as you like, so make large amounts!

1 Start with the usual splash of olive oil to fry chopped onion, celery, parsley, garlic, chilli or other herbs.

2 Toss in a range of thinly sliced vegetables like: carrots, turnips, broccoli, pears, parsnips courgettes or green beans.

3 Now add a cup of water and a vegetable stock cube. Cover with a lid, turn to low.

4 Chop up thin slivers of lettuce, spinach or cucumber (not for O). Stir it into the pot, just before serving. Add more water or stock to make soup.

Variation: add noodles to the dish

Add quick-cooking noodles like rice vermicelli to the pot when you add the water. Mung bean or cellophane noodles are high in protein and free of gluten but they don't suit B and AB. Wheat noodles only suit A^1 and AB. Rye pasta does not suit B.

Other ways to fill up in a healthy way

For a more satisfying meal, add some cooked or canned peas or beans. Be creative with your seasoning and add soya sauce or try a little barbecue sauce or chutney. Chop up a lot of parsley and sprinkle it over the food for decoration. Try serving soups and stirfries onto shredded lettuce leaves to avoid carbohydrates. Rice can be mixed with grated carrot and chopped onion and parsley to stretch it out. To cook rice in a flask, see page 119. Cook noodles with shredded green beans.

Lettuce and courgette salad

Wash a head of lettuce and arrange a layer of the best leaves onto a platter. Shred lettuce leaves, spinach, watercress, etc. into thin strips and pile them onto the leaves. Sprinkle the greens with olive oil and lemon juice. Use a potato peeler to cut long thin strips of courgettes and carrots or parsnips. Now add onion rings and a variety of raw fresh fruit and vegetables and chopped herbs.

Simple and healthy salad dressing

Use a separate bowl to mix up a dressing of olive oil and lemon juice with some herb salt. Use a tablespoon of olive oil and a squeeze of lemon juice for four people. Add a splash of soya sauce and a teaspoon of honey or brown sugar (not O^2).

Soak thinly sliced onion rings in boiling water for a few minutes to remove the strong-tasting gas. Drain, squeeze out and soak in lemon juice and honey. This makes a lovely garnish for many dishes.

Take it with you to make on the spot!

Teach your man to make a mean salad to suit your blood type

What is a salad?

By definition: salads are either totally raw or made out of cold, cooked foods. A warm salad is a fusion between lightly steamed vegetables and crunchy fresh raw salad ingredients. More fructose is released in carrots after light cooking so they are sweeter have more B-carotene and vitamin A.

Salads for all blood types

Start by chopping onions, parsley and celery. Wash all varieties of lettuce and spinach. Tear up or shred. Chop up or prepare fresh herbs : water-cress, mint, thyme, majoram, nasturtiums, basil, etc. Grate or finely slice: courgettes, beetroot, butter-nut, parsnips, apples (not for O²), pineapple, etc. Lightly steam green beans, carrots and broccoli.

For more substantial salads, add: sprouts, hard-boiled eggs, baked beans, cheese, tuna, sardines, mackerel or pilchards. Grind up flaxseeds for a salad sprinkle and combine with ground-up seeds and nuts that suit you. Make salad dressings or dips. (See pages 114 and 119.) Enjoy salads as a main dish, a starter, a snack or a side dish.

A All type foods plus:

Cooked or raw sweetcorn (only A¹), peanuts, sun-flower seeds, avocado, cauliflower, radishes, cucumber, alfalfa sprouts, leeks, tofu

B All type foods plus:

Tomatoes (not for B²), oranges, cheese, yoghurt, bananas, dates, cabbage, cauliflower, cucumber, leeks, pickles, aubergines, green olives

AB All type foods plus:

Avocado, dates, pawpaw, cabbage, cauliflower, cucumber, olives, aubergines, tomatoes, leeks, potatoes, alfalfa sprouts, cheese, yoghurt

O All type foods plus:

Tomatoes, red and green peppers, bananas, radishes, mung bean and lentil sprouts
O² : Avocao pears, button mushrooms

Have salads every day to keep slim and trim, alive and alert

Cucumbers, courgettes, tomatoes, onions and cream cheese. Serve with an onion dressing. (See page 114.)

Apple, cucumber and green beans. Line bowl with lettuce leaves. Cook green beans. Add cucumber, apple and soaked onions. Pour on a dressing and then garnish with tomato roses, etc.

Begin with chopped onions, herbs, cucumber, pineapple, sprouts, cooked green beans, etc. Add a dressing, some boiled eggs and serve with hummus and rye bread or toast.

Traditional Warldorf salad. Lettuce with chopped apple, onions, herbs, walnuts and anything else that suits you. Try tomatoes, radishes or cucumber with a dressing of olive oil, lemon juice, herb salt and yoghurt.

Pineapple with tofu or cream cheese and sprouts. Make bean pastes or nut butters as an alternative.

A South African braai (barbecue)that caters for vegans and all blood types

Put an end to fat beer bellies and heart attacks

When entertaining, people usually do not cater for blood types or for vegans, slimmers or those with wheat and gluten allergies. In fact, most South Africans and especially blood type A individuals who eat a lot of meat, potatoes and bread are totally unaware of their blood type! Madness takes its toll as cholesterol levels rise, hearts pack up and "boeps" (beer bellies) expand.

Take yourself in hand and control the hazards of weekend eating and drinking binges. The food you eat every day should be sufficiently exciting and tasty without needing fatty meat and denatured wheat or maize products to bulk it up. Blood type O is well suited to meat, but their mealiepap (maize porridge) contains disruptive lectins that cause obesity. Alcohol, sugar and carbohydrate cravings can be our downfall as we get older and more sluggish. The "Happy Eating" option ensures good digestion and effective nourishment to keep you alert, energetic and beautifully slim and trim. No deprivation is required, but a more intelligent and disciplined approach to your "braai" is essential.

Entertain at home or pack up food to take with you

1 Prepare a few packs of vegetables in foil. These are easy to take along anywhere and are a vegan's aid to sanity. Chop up a pile of your favourite veggies into tiny pieces, especially harder things like beans and carrots. Add a splash of olive oil and some herb salt. Fold over edges and place the packs on burning coals for a few minutes. My daughter calls them pressure packs as they cook in steam pressure generated inside the foil, so don't prick the packs!

2 Pre-cook sweetcorn (only for A^1) or halved sweet potatoes and thick slices of butternut for everybody else. Keep them undercooked, brush with olive oil and place on the grid over hot coals.

3 Make kebabs out of diced ostrich meat, turkey or fish like cob, salmon, tuna or monkfish as they suit all blood types. Mutton suits all blood types except A^1. Vegans, except O^2 and B^2, can have soya substitutes, but watch out for wheat and MSG. Marinade in a nice BBQ or herb sauce with chunks of onions, green peppers, pineapple, etc. Thread pieces onto skewers and cook on the coals. Use a bunch of herbs to baste kebabs with the sauce.

Select healthy ingredients

Salads, starters and snacks

Make healthy salads. (See page 120.) Whip up delicious dips for fruit and vegetable platters. (See pages 114-115.) Serve them as starters and snacks or with the main meal. Try to avoid the usual chips, rancid peanuts and wheat-laden muck that does you no good. (See pages 149 and 156 for alternatives.)

Vegetable stews and sauces

Make vegetable stews and gravies, especially if you cook wors (sausage) and a variety of other meats. People enjoy cooking in a potjie (cast iron pot), over the coals. Use olive oil to brown the onions and garlic. Add a selection of chopped herbs, spices and vegetables and simmer gently in a little stock, or as some people may prefer, beer or wine. Adding tomato paste or fresh tomatoes with a little curry powder is my favourite. Too much tomato is bad for blood types A^1 and B^1 so compensate by using paprika and grated carrots. (See page 46.) The stew or gravy can be thickened by sprinkling in a little rice flour shortly before serving.

Offer vegetables, salads or a bed of lettuce to accompany the cooked meat or vegetarian foods as an alternative to always having potato, wheat or maize products that may not suit everybody.

Prepare a delicious marinade or basting sauce

Create a grand concoction of your favourite herbs and spices in the blender and whip it into a frenzy for aromatic flavours to marinade your meat, veggies, soya patties or tofu.

A basic barbecue or grilling sauce

½ cup olive or canola oil
50ml soya sauce
50ml honey or 25ml brown sugar
30ml tomato paste (or 20ml paprika plus grated apple)
5ml herb salt and 5ml pepper blend (page 141)
50ml lemon juice or apple cider vinegar
fresh chopped garlic, ginger and chillies to taste

Process everything together in an electric or hand-held blender.

Delicious, healthy alternatives to mealiepap (maize porridge)

Grind up soya protein granules

Grind up soya textured vegetable protein (TVP or soya mince) in your coffee grinder. Use it with rice and millet flour for a nutritious alternative to the traditional South African "braaipap", a porridge made from maize.

Cook what suits you best

Use the recipe below to substitute maize meal with rice, soya or millet. Keep the leftovers in the fridge and have it hot or cold, with any meal. Individual portions that are baked or steamed in cookie cups are handy to take out with you when food choices may not suit your blood type or allergic condition.

Soya and rice pap (porridge)

This dish is ideal for people who are intolerant to wheat and maize. If you add fenugreek and herbs, it helps diabetics to control their insulin. Soya protein is especially good for all vegetarians, except blood type B^2 and O^2. Millet flour is also rich in protein and can be used instead of soya protein.

50ml olive oil
1 cup rice flour
1 cup ground-up soya mince(TVP)
(made from 2 cups soya granules)
alternative to soya: 1 cup millet flour
3ml sea salt
5ml bicarbonate of soda
2 cups boiling water
30ml lemon juice or apple cider vinegar
optional herbs and spices:
5ml fenugreek powder (methee)
5ml ground-up basil, majoram and thyme

1 Mix the oil into the dry ingredients.
2 Stir in two cups of boiling water, then add the lemon juice to make the mixture fluffy and light.
3 Bake for 20 minutes in a flat, greased dish that is covered, in a medium oven. The mixture can be spooned into muffin trays or individual ramekins. Alternatively, cook in a well-greased foil dish or a cast iron pot directly on the grid over the coals. If you are in a hurry, microwave the covered dish or six individual ramekins or cookie cups for 5 minutes.

A quick easy "pap" substitute

1 Mix 1 cup rice flour with 1 cup millet flour and 2 tablespoons of olive oil. Add a pinch of herb salt and a teaspoon of bicarbonate of soda. Stir till crumbly and add 1 cup of boiling water. Stir in a tablespoon of lemon juice or apple cider vinegar (or Balsamic vinegar) till the mixture becomes light and fluffy.

2 Grease a cast iron frying pan or "potjie" and add the mixture. Close the lid and cook over gentle coals. A lovely crust forms if you use a flat pan or foil baking tray, but use plenty of oil or baking spray. First arrange chopped onions and herbs in the bottom of the pan if you want to tip it out onto a plate.

Alternately, cook it in a covered glass dish in the microwave for 3-4 minutes if you are in a hurry and still use a microwave oven. You can bake this dish beforehand in the oven during a family baking session. It keeps well and can be heated up or served cold.

Healthy Happy entertaining begins with fresh ingredients

Colours to delight the eye

Take pride in your presentation. The Chinese philosophy is to present contrasts of colour, size, texture and tastes. Use fresh, colourful fruits and vegetables and transform them into visual masterpieces. Forget about tumbling everything out of plastic bags. Be spontaneous and original and serve everything with love. It works!

Make herb vinegar or oil by adding fresh herbs, garlic, chillies and lemon rind to oil or vinegar.

Make your own healthy party dips and sauces

Use the guidelines on page 114 to get the hang of making a variety of creamed dips. Use canned beans as a base and take off from there: add a can of tuna, anchovies or smoked mussels. Creamed avocado and yogurt always goes down well. Season with soya sauce and lemon juice.

These creamy concoctions can be served for starters, as dips, or used as dressings for salads and vegetables. Throw away the packets of chips and rather serve your dips with paper-thin slices of rye toast or rice crackers. Have plenty of carrot and celery sticks available for your lean and mean guests who are trying to lose weight or are staying away from starches and greasy food. Offer fresh fruit, sprouts and a variety of raw or steamed vegetables.

Blood-type guidelines

Most people fret about entertaining or catering for all blood types. The rules are very simple and easy to follow:

1 Stick to all-type foods to begin with. (Consult the lists on pages 11-15.)

2 Cater for your own blood type or that of your partner, if nobody else cares. This means you cook as you normally do for your own family.

3 Allow people to pick and choose. Opt for self service. If you serve cheese, tomatoes, green peppers, avocados and cucumbers, then leave them visible so people can select what they want. (Most blood type eaters are still viewed with suspicion!) White butter beans suit everybody. So do walnuts, lemons, olive oil, garlic, parsley, celery, lettuce, courgettes, onions, pineapple, green beans, rice, broccoli, spinach, grapes and carrots. Red wine suits all blood types, but may offend people who abastain from drinking alcohol, so serve grape juice and water as well.

How to cook soya protein mince

1 Soak 1 cup of soya mince in 2 cups of boiling water with a vegetable stock cube. Note: soya TVP or textured protein does not suit blood types B^2 or O^2. Soya chunks are available, but they taste better if they are crushed finer. Bash the bag of soya chunks with a hammer or rolling pin.
2 Fry chopped onion, garlic, celery, etc in a pan with a little olive oil. Add a few green or sweet red peppers or mushrooms if they suit you.
3 Mix in the soaked soya protein. Stir in some grated carrots, parsnips or turnips.
4 Add herbs and spices, especially those with medicinal qualities. (See pages 57-62.)
5 Adjust the seasoning with soya sauce or miso paste. Add a bit more water to make a good creamy texture then turn very low to simmer with the lid on for about ten minutes.
6 Thicken with a few tablespoons of rice flour, stirred directly into the pan.

Basic cooking for an all-type meal

Use the vegetables listed on page 12. They suit all blood types and are easy to prepare. Use the cooking suggestions on page 40. Cook rice or millet. (See page 127.) Offer slimmers some shredded lettuce or grated carrots as an alternative to rice.

Soya protein can be made to look and taste like meat.

How to cook savoury mince

1 Fry 1 chopped onion and some parsley and celery in a pan with a little oil. Chop and fry 1 green or sweet red pepper and 4 mushrooms if they suit you. Then add about 250g of ostrich, lamb, turkey or beef mince and keep stirring until no longer pink. Add a lot of medicinal herbs and spices like: coriander, bay leaves, rosemary, majoram, thyme, fenugreek (methee), cumin, ground mustard or black kaloontjie seeds. (See pages 57-62.)
2 For thickening: soak a cup of soya mince in a cup of boiling water or soak rye bread crumbs, oats or ground-up barley flakes as an alternative. (Soya not for O^2 or B^2, rye not for B^1 or B^2.)
3 Add the soaked soya mince or rye bread or ground-up barley and stir in well. Turn heat to low.
4 Add a stock cube, some herb salt and 2 teaspoons of paprika powder or a small tin of tomato paste. (not for A^1 and B^1).
5 Stir in 1 or 2 cups of grated carrots, parsnips or turnips. Adjust the seasoning with soya sauce or miso paste. Add a bit more water to make a good creamy texture then turn very low to simmer with the lid on for about ten minutes.
6 Thicken with a few tablespoons of rice flour, stirred directly into the pan.
7 If more guests suddenly arrive, add a can of white butter beans or baked beans to the dish.

Ostrich meat has no fat. Other meat can also be used.

Different ways to cook rice

Normal way to cook rice in a pot

Rinse a cup of regular white, long grain or Basmati rice (not parboiled) in a sieve. Add it to two cups of boiling water in a pot. Add a pinch of salt or a stock cube and bring to the boil with the lid on. Turn to low and simmer for about 20 minutes. Variations: add chopped pumpkin or butternut, mushrooms or aubergines to the pot of rice.

Bake rice in the oven in a hotpot

Reduce the energy load by using your hot oven to cook the rice when you are baking or roasting. Place 1 part rice to 2 parts cold water and a pinch of salt in a covered ovenproof dish. Cook as the oven heats up and check to see if it is done after about half an hour in a medium oven. Variations: make a complete rice hotpot meal by adding bits of sausage, leeks and other vegetables.

Cook health rice in a Thermos flask

Pour a cup of brown rice into the flask. Add two and a half cups of boiling water and a pinch of salt or a stock cube. Close the flask and it will be ready in about four hours. This cooked rice keeps well in the fridge. Use a little every day. Warm it up, toss it into a stir fry or add it to a salad.

Cut down on carbohydrate servings to lose weight

Serve half the rice, potato or pasta

Get into the habit of only having a token amount or rice, pasta or potato on your plate and fill up on quantity with some low-kilojoule starch substitutes.

Grated carrot or shredded lettuce

Use grated carrots or shredded lettuce, even under a stew or curry. It tastes pleasant with hot food. First sprinkle with lemon juice and olive oil.

Chopped-up onion, herbs or greens

This adds flavour to the meal as well as nutrients so keep a nice mixture handy in the fridge.

Dish up more marrow or gem squash

Marrow and squashes are not fattening, but taste bland. Add lemon juice, ginger or chopped onions and herbs. Serve as a base for stews and curries or stir fries and make sure the fatties take note! White starchy foods are no good, so make this change!

Entertain with an easy Mongolian stir fry and hotpot at home

Prepare it all, then relax and let them cook!

This meal is guaranteed to suit all blood types because your guests can pick and choose the foods that suit them best. Furthermore, they can do their own cooking or they can eat the food raw. The guests select a bowl of raw vegetables and meat. They pour on some stock and a little oil. Each person has a chance to cook their dish of food in the wok. Let them fill their bowl with rice and add the stir fry after a minute or two of cooking. A communal pot of soup stays on the boil and everybody adds to it or takes from it as they fancy. Noodles are cooked in the soup as well.

How to set up the table

1 Rig up a small electric two plate stove on the table with a large soup pot with a lid as well as a wok, soup ladle and a wooden spatula.

2 For each guest lay out a soup bowl, a pair of chosticks and serviettes. Chinese people do not always use soup spoons. They like to drink from the bowl and pick out the pieces of food with chopsticks.

3 Cook a large pot of plain rice in advance. (See page 127.)

4 Set up the bowls of stock and olive oil with garlic next to the stove. It is best to cook all Oriental foods with olive oil, even if they don't! Make a few jugs of stock with hot water, veggie stock cubes, a dash of honey and slices of ginger and garlic. Put the finely chopped chillies in a separate bowl with lemon juice.

5 Line up bottles of soya sauce, sesame oil and Chinese barbecue sauce.

6 Supply buckwheat (soba), rice or mung bean noodles to add to the soup.

7 Prepare and chop loads of vegetables and try to keep them separate. Offer thin slices of fish and meat as well.

Preparing and selecting the stir fry ingredients

Soup is made as and when you please. The guests can decide what they want to add to the pot of stock. Noodles are also cooked in the same broth.

Start chopping well in advance

Cleaning, chopping and preparing vegetables takes a lot of time, so plan ahead. Wash, peel, chop or shred the root vegetables. Be creative with the cutting and make cubes, thin strips, slices and wedges. Cubes of sweet potato can mimic tofu in a soup and thin strips of turnip can be added just before serving to replace noodles.

A selection of vegetables for the soup pot

Make the blood type selection easy

All-type vegetables should be offered to people on the blood type diets with a separate selection for them to pick out other items that agree with them. On my dinner table, the first two rows of dishes are: butternut, parsley and celery, onions and turnip strips with green beans, carrots and sprouts. I offer extra garlic, lemon and ginger separately but the bowls of oils and stock already have plenty in them. The back row of dishes is for serious blood-typers to select or avoid: tomatoes, chillies, mushrooms, leeks, cabbage and sweetcorn. Noodles for the soup are: rice vermicelli for all types, or mung bean noodles for A's and O's.

Make soup and add what you fancy

In a large bowl, arrange bigger pieces of carrots, sweet potato and whole beans. These are added to the pot of soup after frying up some garlic, onions and celery and pouring in a kettle of hot stock. Type A can add the chunks of sweetcorn. After a few minutes, add the noodles and just before serving, some strips of spinach or lettuce. Diehard slimmers can eat shredded lettuce instead of rice or noodles, should they want to.

Authentic Chinese food is very healthy and is easy to cook

Mastering the art of chopsticks

Chinese people eat with chopsticks from an early age. It is not difficult, even for left-handers, but it takes some practice. Hold one stick between your thumb and index finger like a pencil. Press the other one between the middle finger and the ring finger and cradle them both together in the crock of the thumb. Traditionally, the bowl is held close to the mouth and the food is nimbly tweezered into the mouth; long noodles, large green leaves and all, in a steady stream of biting, slurping and swallowing. Soup is drunk from the bowl. The beautiful porcelain spoons are only used for dishing up or for picky Westerners who insist on spoons. Knives and forks? Never! (Knives at the table are regarded as weapons in Eastern and Arabic cultures.)

Cooking a quick Chinese meal

Chinese rice is ususally the short-grained variety, but you can cook any rice you like. It is nice to add vegetables like butternut, beans or leeks to the pot. (See page 127 for ways to cook rice.) Always serve a large platter of stir fried green leafy vegetables separately. Try spinach and lettuce, Chinese cabbage, bok choy, etc. Make a sweet 'n sour sauce for the fried meat, chicken, fish or tofu dish. A whole fish is often cooked and served on a platter with a dark soya and ginger sauce, garnished with spring onions. A clear vegetable soup is served throughout the meal and is enjoyed between just about every little bowl of rice and meat or vegetables. Hot green Chinese tea is drunk with the meal and beer is served on special occasions.

Fried tofu with sweet and sour sauce, a rice and vegetable hotpot and salty black beans

Sweet 'n sour sauce for meat or tofu

When meat, fish or tofu is fried, it is served on a platter and a hot sauce is poured over. The sauces are clear and shiny and usually sweet and sour. This is all done at lightning speed at the very end, so a bit of planning is required.

1 Chop up the ingredients you are going to fry: onions, leeks, ginger, garlic, celery and a choice of: green peppers, mushrooms, pineapple, etc.
2 Fry in a pan with a splash of olive oil. Add seasoning. MSG is controversial (see page 13), so use a good brand or stick with vegetable stock powder and a little soya sauce. Once the vegetables are sizzling, add a few teaspoons of honey or brown sugar and a cup of water or stock.
3 Thicken with a few teaspoons of rice flour and adjust the sourness with lemon juice or vinegar.

Basic ingredients for Chinese cooking: soya sauce, ginger, chillies and garlic. Cook with olive oil; it's much healthier.

Add some Oriental excitement to your health regimen

Soup is enjoyed throughout the meal

Traditional Chinese meals never begin with soup. A hot, clear soup is served during the meal to stimulate the appetite and aid digestion. In cold weather, cream of sweetcorn or more elaborate meat or fish soups are offered. Serve a clear soup during your meal made from fried spring onions, ginger and garlic. Add the hot stock and simmer with slices of cucumber or mushrooms. Add shredded lettuce and spinach just before serving.

For special occasions, add shrimps or thin strips of chicken or turkey meat and try to get hold of exotic ingredients such as: bamboo shoots, water chestnuts or pickled tofu. Use soya products like miso, black beans and Tempeh to be authentic. Seaweed is a great favourite in Japanese and Korean soups, but it's not for everyone! Serve the seaweed separately. You can cut or tear thin strips of the seaweed paper that is used for making Japanese makimono rice rolls.

A Chinese ice mountain dessert

This dessert is really unique and can be so refreshing on a hot day. Simply pile a load of crushed or shaved ice in a bowl and offer side dishes of fresh, chopped fruit to pack onto it. You then sprinklle on nuts, dried fruit preserves and a few spoons of fruit syrup or honey. To prevent the ice from melting, place it in a bowl of ice cubes.

Do not be intimidated by Japanese makimono rolls. They cost the earth to buy, so try making your own varieties. At least they will be fresh!

Rice rolled in seaweed wrappers

Have a go at making your own makimono rolls. Just follow the cooking instructions on a packet of sushi rice. Spread a 2cm layer of cooked rice onto a sheet of seaweed or plastic wrap in a square shape and add a few fillers like: avocado pear, raw fish and pickles down the one side. Roll and press into a sausage with a special sushi mat and cut into slices. Serve with pickled ginger, sweet soya sauce, spring onions and some evil green Wasabi mustard. Stuff steamed turnips with soya bean paste made out of boiled and mashed soya beans with dark, sweet soya sauce.

A bowl of shaved ice packed with fruit and nuts

Turkish food is hearty and healthy but... it's not for all blood types!

Here are some changes you can make

Fried fish, grilled lamb: yummy!

"Yummy, it's good for your tummy" is the welcoming cry to this delicious spread of ready-to-eat Turkish food. Vendors grill fish or koftas on the streets and slap it into a wad of bread with the ubiquitous chopped tomato and lettuce leaves that accompany just about every street meal. Salt and raw onions are offered separately. The big doner kebab of mutton or lamb is a winner, and if bread is not for you, simply ask for more meat or salad. Turks splash lemon juice onto meat and vegetables before cooking them and season with a lot of cumin spice. Turkish coffee and Turkish apple tea are offered to guests. (See pages 103 and 104.) Tomatoes form a large part of Turkish cuisine, so if you need a substitute, see page 46.

Simple Turkish meat and vegetable dishes to make at home

Koftas are Turkish meatballs

Koftas are prepared just like meatballs or hamburgers, using lamb or beef sausage meat. Add cumin spice to your meat and form it into oblong patties that can be fried, roasted or grilled on skewers over glowing coals. You can substitute with soya burgers, spiced up with cumin if you do not eat meat. Soya is not for blood type O[2] and B[2].

Koftas are usually eaten on pieces of white fluffy bread with tomato, lettuce and onion. Wheat products are served with every meal, so you will have to substitute with rye bread or whatever suits you best. Try baking koftas in the oven with a selection of roasted vegetables like: aubergines, onions, green peppers, tomatoes, sweet potatoes, etc. Turkish lamb dishes with rich casseroles of tomatoes, aubergines and green peppers are not ideal for blood type A, but the Turks are mostly blood type B. The white cannellini bean is a popular food which suits all blood types, vegetarians or vegans.

The elements of Turkish food

Most meals are served with fresh salads. Typically Turkish are: grated carrots and yoghurt with mint, or salads of chopped lettuce, tomato, cucumber, celery, parsley, shredded cabbage and rocket leaves. Serve salads with oil and lemon juice, yoghurt or creamed aubergine. For those who love hummus made from chickpeas but are not O secretors, make hummus with white butter beans or baked beans. (See page 114.)

Stuffed tomatoes, aubergines and green peppers are popular. Stuff them with rice and scraps of minced lamb, chopped onion and mint. People who do not tolerate these foods can try stuffing the outer sections of large onions, cut in half. Boiled chick peas or cannellini beans are usually served in a rich tomato-based casserole. Pita bread, rolls, couscous, rice and potatoes accompany the main meal. Couscous is made of wheat, so cook dehusked millet as an alternative, if you are wheat-intorerant.

Canned fish can come in handy for an emergency meal

Keep a cupboard of cans on standby

Tuna suits all blood types and can be whipped into omelettes, quiches, dips, soups or served as salads. Keep a stock of other canned fish like salmon, mackerel or pilchards in your grocery store as well as cans of baked beans, butter beans and cannellini beans.

You should be confident about being able to offer a quick meal to anybody at short notice without the need for junky takeaways, or eating out. The secret is to be prepared for emergencies.

Quick starters or smart lunches out of a can

Use canned fish fillets like salmon, herring or mackerel, set off in an array of frilly salads and gorgeous garnishes for quick lunches or starters. Tuna can be mixed with chopped celery, onions, pineapple, etc. and served on lettuce leaves with a creamy salad dressing. Add gelatine, if you want to make a cold fish mould.

Fish burgers, fish dips, spreads and soups

Make fish burgers by mixing a can of tuna, pilchards or salmon with chopped onions, celery and parsley and then bind the mixture with oat, rye or soya flour. Form into patties and fry in a little olive oil. Add canned fish to the dips and spreads made with your hand-held blender. (See page 114.) Add canned fish to clear vegetable soups or cream- or tomato-based soups.

A fluffy salmon or tuna cake without eggs

Make this dish without eggs, and substitute tuna with feta cheese if you are a vegetarian or cooked soya mince if you are a vegan.

50ml rice flour
30ml rye or soya flour
5ml bicarbonate of soda
3ml herb salt or seasoning blend
20ml olive oil
½ can of tuna in brine or oil, drained
100ml chopped onion, celery and parsley
30 ml fresh or bottled lemon juice

1 Blend the dries into the olive oil.
2 Add the tuna and chopped onion, etc.
3 Stir in the lemon juice and allow the mixture to rise.
4 Transfer the mixture to a greased dish and bake in a very hot oven (200° C) for 10 minutes , or until the top is browned.

Creamed tuna: stir fry chopped onions, celery, parsley and sliced mushrooms in a little olive oil. Add a can of tuna and some milk or water. Thicken with rice flour.

Quick meals with spinach, cheese, beans and eggs

A rice and egg mountain begins with leftover rice, vegetables and eggs.

Add chopped spinach to salads, soups, etc.

Use spinach in your stir fries, chopped up into salads or blended into juices. The more tender varieties of spinach are good to eat raw and they are rich in chlorophyll, magnesium and iron.

Be more creative with omelettes

Indian-style omelettes are made by pouring beaten eggs over fried bits and pieces of onion, celery, chicken, etc. in a hot pan, with a little oil. Then add cheese, sprouts or whatever you have. Fold over when the underside is crispy and golden.

Stir fried spinach as a meal

Wash a whole bunch of spinach. Fry chopped onion and garlic in a large pan with a little olive oil and herb salt and one or two sliced apples, add a little water and simmer whilst you rinse and chop the spinach. Add spinach to the pan. It shrinks very quickly so keep chopping and stirring as you keep packing it in. When all the spinach is reduced in volume, turn off the heat and serve immediately. Add feta cheese, tofu or chopped walnuts.

Poach an egg in the spinach

Stir fry the spinach the same way but without the apples. As soon as the spinach has wilted, make a well in the middle of the pan and break in an egg or two. Close the lid, switch off the stove and the eggs will be ready within a few minutes. Crumble on some tofu or feta cheese to make a meal of it.

Rice and egg mountain

Mix equal quantities of cooked rice and grated butternut or carrot in a bowl. Add chopped parsley, onion and whatever else you fancy. Press the mixture around the sides of a greased bowl. Fill the cavity with chopped mushrooms, grated cheese and leftover vegetables or baked beans. Pour a few beaten eggs over everything. Cover with a saucer and microwave on full for 2-3 minutes, or 10-15 minutes in a steamer. When firm, run a fork around the rim of the bowl and turn it out onto a plate.

Eggs and spinach suit us all!

Eggs can be fried, poached, scrambled or made into omelettes. Boiled and poached eggs are highly recommended, being free of trans-fatty acids that are produced when food is fried. Spinach can be enjoyed as a dish on its own, or added to soups and casseroles. Eat some raw spinach for a good cleanout of heavy metals, or add it to juices. (See page 90.) Canned beans are a meal on their own or they can be added to soups and stews or used as a filler for making dips and sauces. White butter beans, canned baked beans and cannellini beans suit us all.

Garnish, garnish, garnish!

We eat with our eyes

The visual aspect of eating is as important as the taste of food and its nutritional value. Food that delights the eye will delight the stomach. All the basic shapes, colours and textures from fruit and vegetables are at your disposal. Add that extra special bit of love and effort and get garnishing!

Begin with simple projects

Use a potato peeler to cut thin strips from carrots, parsnips, etc. Cut a section from a leek and make fine cuts downwards, for flower-like stamens. Add petals cut with the potato peeler around this, to make a carrot lily. Secure the ends with a rubber band.

Thailand is famous for fruit and vegetable carving

This masterpiece was made by a Thai lady who comes from Bangkok. The Thais are happy, gentle people and this is reflected in everything that they do. Try making some of these items. All you need is a sharp knife, patience and a sense of adventure when unexpected shapes and objects begin to develop.

Be spontaneous, have fun

Lettuce, cucumber, tomatoes with basil and dandelion flowers. Go salad, go!

How to make tomato roses

Run the back of a knife all over the tomato to loosen the skin. Peel it off in a spiral, starting at the top. Gently wind it into a rose by first rolling up the skin removed from the tip of the tomato. It requires a delicate and confident touch. Slice the peeled tomato into a salad. Water lilies can be made by cutting tomatoes, lemons or sections of cucumber, in half using zig-zag cuts.

Easy lemon twists, radish roses, onion rings, etc.

When you clean and prepare your regular fruit and vegetables every day, select the odd piece and see what you can do with it. Red onion rings can make the most boring dishes look stunning. Keep your little creations in an airtight plastic container and pop them out onto swanky dishes that you make at the last minute. If in doubt, use fresh herbs like basil and parsley or a twist of lemon!

Children of all ages can play with their vegetable soup

Never force young children to eat certain vegetables. If there are tantrums about all-type vegetables, then the problem may be with the way you cook and serve them. Offer dips or sauces that they really like to have with the vegetables. Never overcook vegetables. Show them how vegetables are grown and get them involved with planning and preparing a meal to their liking.

Children love to watch beans growing on the windowsill in a saucer with wet cotton wool. Sprouts are wonderful for children to grow and the results are quick and rewarding. (See page 110.) They may take to them straight away and enjoy nibbling their own sprouts from an early age. Offer a variety of vegetables to them at an early age and let them decide what they would like in their special soup.

Make some delicious salad dressings, sauces or dips to go with the freshly cooked vegetables. (See page 114.)

Add a little olive oil to the pot. Stir fy onions, leeks, celery, parsley, ginger, garlic, etc.

Have fun cooking vegetables in clear soup

Prepare attractive platters of chopped vegetables. Place an electric hotplate on the table and make a pot of hot, clear soup, starting with chopped fried onions, garlic, celery and parsley. Add boiling water and a stock cube and simmer gently on low heat. Help the children to thread vegetables onto skewers. Press a piece of cork onto the sharp end of the skewer to secure the vegetables. Stay next to the stove whilst the children dip their skewers into the hot soup. Within a few minutes they will be eating load after load of delicious vegetables, cooked to their liking.

Pour on some hot stock and help the little ones thread up the skewers. Stay with them all the time.

Different blood types at the table and nobody wants a fuss

At home you learn to cater accordingly

If two parents have different blood types, their children will be the one or the other. You then have to cater for two eating patterns, should everybody wish to become blood type compliant.

Blood type A is not well adapted to heavy food

Ask any blood type A how they feel after roast beef, fluffy Yorkshire pudding made out of white flour, a few roast potatoes and lashings of gravy. Most will admit to feeling very full, almost distended, for many hours. This type of meal is difficult for A's to digest as their stomach acid is weaker and they battle with the lectins in potatoes at the best of times. Beef is out for them, much to the disgust of robust A-type meat eaters. The traditional hamburger embedded in a dead white roll and served with soggy fried chips is another digestive nightmare for a constitution better suited to fish, chicken, vegetables and other types of starches.

Most restaurants do not cater for "blood-typers"

Most restaurants serve everything on one plate, with loads of lectins, polyamines and gorgeous indigestables. I have a particular problem being an O-type vegetarian, an eating mode I have adopted to add a touch of reality to my research. Most restaurants do not cater for vegetarians who do not eat wheat. It is difficult to find food that suits me so I prefer a self-service option. My advice is: do the best you can. If you feel lousy, you will know exactly why. Thankfully you can make up for it the next day.

O-type hamburger option

A grilled beef patty squatting on a rye roll and surrounded by fresh greens like steamed spinach, snow peas, parsley and celery with lashings of tomatoes, grated carrots and onions. As for chips? Well, you can make some out of sweet potatoes or butternut if you feel deprived. Serve this meal with a lovely platter of baked vegetables.

The A-type hamburger

The soya hamburger patties we buy at supermarkets are quite palatable, but they usually contain some wheat. Most A's can tolerate wheat. This one is on a home-made tortilla made out of maize, to delight the A type. Grated carrots, onions, avocado and luscious greens set off this nutritious version of a boring old burger. Blood type A does not really tolerate potatoes or sweet potatoes, so you can serve roasted butternut chips with it. Top with a green pesto sauce. Serve with an attractive platter of vegetables.

Vegans and vegetarians eat no meat

Vegetarians, vegans and blood-type eating

Although blood types like the O group are well suited to eating meat, it does not mean that everybody has to eat loads of beef and red meat. Blood type O vegans can really thrive on their blood type diets, even if meat, eggs and dairy products are never eaten! Most people turn their noses up at the restricted selection of carbohydrates offered for their blood type, but it's not the end of the world. Cutting out lectins in carbohydrates and foods that are bad for your blood type applies to meat eaters and vegetarians alike. Not eating meat is a matter of choice, either for health reasons or for religious convictions. We can choose what or "whom" we eat.

Fried tofu substitutes for chicken or fish.

No need to panic about missing out on protein

Too many people believe we have to eat a certain amount of protein in order to be healthy. The fact is, too many people with major health problems are eating too much protein! Homocysteine is a deadly and destructive toxin that is released by the faulty breakdown of proteins, especially from meat. Uric acid crystals build up in the bloodstream from the faulty metabolism of proteins. Polyamines from rotten, infected meat and fish protein cannot be digested. These polyamines attract bacteria and pathogens in the gut. (See page 7.) If the blood vessels or membranes in the digestive system become permeable, undigested protein particles escape into the bloodstream and set off a host of autoimmune diseases that can destroy adrenal and thyroid glands along the way. Do we really need to worry about protein?

Make your own veggie burgers out of mashed, cooked dry beans or soaked soya mince. Add chopped onions and spices and bind with oats before frying in a little olive oil.

Where do we get our protein from?

Obviously our bodies consist of a certain percentage of protein, but we are quite capable of building and maintaining this tissue without eating foods that are known to be rich in protein. Just like other mammals, we too, can thrive on amino acids, the simple building blocks of protein, found in fresh natural fruits and vegetables. We cannot deny that some people are devout fruitarians, yet they are not lacking in protein. They do not have to worry about the dark side of eating too much protein; a health issue that is often ignored. It will always be a matter of choice. We tend to take food too seriously because our nutritional requirements are far less than we usually consume every day. Some people can live on fruit for months at a time and show no loss of protein in their muscles.

Offer a variety of vegeatables and serve with exciting sauces. If you do not tolerate wheat, cook millet grains as a substitute for couscous. Pad out the meal with lentils or a tofu casserole.

First do no harm, is what Hippocrates said

Many of the drugs and medicines we take have harmful side effects that can undermine your health and wellbeing. This is not what the Father of Medicine, Hippocrates had in mind when he said "first do no harm." In the long term, chronic medications cannot cure faulty eating habits, a lack of exercise or a stressful lifestyle. If you feel ill, the best way to do no harm is to allow your body some time to heal itself. People do not get sick from eating a healthy, happy selection of fruit and vegetables and the proof thereof is in the eating thereof! Vegetarians who eat according to their blood type seldom suffer from high blood pressure, arthritis, high cholesterol, diabetes, obesity or heart complaints.

Spice up your life, add natural flavours

Bottles of your homemade oil and vinegar blends are also very decorative. Recycled bottles full of pretty goodies make great gifts for everybody.

No self-respecting Indian lady of the house would ever open a packet of ready-made curry powder! Make a curry paste with lentil sprouts as a base.

Carrots and paprika are used as a substitute for tomato paste.

All you need are fresh, tasty ingredients and time!

If you always use commercially-produced pots of spice mixtures and bottles of sauces and oils, you really miss out on all the fun. Convenience is a lame excuse. Launch out into the fragrant and aromatic world of natural seasonings and flavourants. Take a little time to indulge in aromatherapy from the kitchen as you unleash these natural fragrances.

Buy these items and always have them handy

Loads of lemons, also try to get the little green limes, fresh ginger roots, garlic cloves, chillies and a bunch of parsley and celery. Stock up on larger items like onions, green peppers and try to find fresh herbs. It is best to buy them growing in a pot, or plant your own: basil, mint, sage, rosemary, majoram and thyme. Keep a supply of spices to grind up into different blends with dried herbs and sea salt: kaloontjie, coriander, mustard seed, fennel, fenugreek, cinnamon, cloves, paprika, bay leaves and turmeric. (See pages 57-62.)

Make herb vinegars and oils

Pour pale grape or apple cider vinegar into pretty bottles. Add sprigs of herbs like rosemary and sage or mint. Allow them to mellow in the sun and then use them for salads, cooking or hair rinses. To bottles of oil, add garlic, chillies, lemon rind and bay leaves.

An unusual curry paste

Use lentil sprouts and chopped onion, garlic, ginger, chillies and celery as a base for a curry paste. Add oil and lemon juice and curry spices like chilli powder, turmeric, fennel, coriander, etc. Work into a smooth paste with your hand-held blender. Keep it in the freezer.

Make a substitute for tomato paste

Mix a few teaspoons of paprika with half a cup of cooked, mashed carrots. Add a little sugar, herb salt and vinegar to taste. Use as a substitute for tomatoes in your recipes if you do not tolerate tomatoes.

Make herb salt and frozen stock cubes

Frozen stock cubes to keep handy

The big challenge is always to make everything yourself in the kitchen without having to buy condiments, stock cubes, etc. Make these stock cubes in large quantities and freeze them. Half fill your electric blender goblet with chopped herbs and spices and tasty veggies like celery, parsley, onions, garlic, leeks, basil, green peppers, ginger, chillies, etc. Add water, lemon juice, a little salt and some olive oil to cover the blades and process till smooth. Keep some in a jar in the fridge and freeze the rest. This fresh, aromatic vegetable stock can be used in dips, salad dressings or use the frozen cubes in soups, stir fries and stews.

Delicious ingredients for using in herb salt blends

1 Dried celery, parsley, bay leaves, majoram, thyme, sage, rosemary.
2 Combinations of these herbs with: celery seeds, mustard seeds, cumin, sesame seeds, flaxseeds, kaloontjie seeds, dried chillies and sea salt.
3 For a special tang, use dried, grated lemon or lime peel or dry some lemon leaves. For an instant salad sprinkle, add some ascorbic acid powder, known as vitamin C. This is a good substitute for vinegar or lemon juice and it kills fungi and moulds, as well as being an antioxidant.

Make up a few potent pepper blends

No more black pepper? (See page 29.) Nobody will miss it with a fake pepper grind of: kaloontjie seeds, coriander seeds and black or yellow mustard seeds. You can also add cumin seeds, bay leaves, mace and chillies. Grind them together and use for cooking meat, fish or tofu slices. Keep it on the table, next to the herb salt shaker.

Substitutes for monosodium glutamate

Some products are free of MSG (monosodium glutamate), however, If you are intolerant to it, rather make your own stock and seasonings. MSG is a substance which occurs naturally in foods like grapes, soya, tomatoes and potatoes. (See page 97.) The Chinese people use a special kind of MSG, derived from soya beans. Ironically, it helps one to digest cellulose and relieves gas, cramps and flatulence. It is the consumption of black pepper that causes most of the discomfort!

How to make herb salt

1 Buy or gather fresh green herbs, especially soup celery leaves. Dry out on newspaper in the warming drawer of your oven.

2 Rub the dried leaves by hand through a sieve and use as is, or grind them up in the coffee grinder with coarse sea salt.

3 Add a teaspoon of calcium or magnesium powder, for free-running salt that does not clog up the salt cellar. Add cream of tartar to increase the potassium.

The basic technique for baking poppadums, tortillas or nachos

These delicious crispy wafers keep well in a sealed container and can be used for general nibbles, served with dips or as a replacement for tortillas or poppadums. Most commercial products contain wheat and maize, so here are the alternatives.

Poppadums have to be very thin, so we use two sheets of plastic. This prevents them from sticking and breaking. It takes practice. When you have an even sheet of dough, peel off one sheet of plastic. Place onto the baking sheet and remove the other piece.

A new special non-stick baking paper is available. Otherwise, spray the pan or baking sheet with a non-stick spray or sprinkle the sheet or pan with flour.

An all-type recipe you can adapt

Mix the dry ingredients together and then rub in the oil. Add a little warm water by feel, till the dough is plastic, and not too crumbly or sticky.

250ml oat flour / barley flour / millet flour
250ml rye flour / soya flour / pea flour
3ml bicarbonate of soda
2ml citric acid or 5ml lemon juice
1-2 teaspoons of a selection of spices:
chilli, fennel, coriander, mixed herbs, fenugreek, black cumin (kaloontjie), vegetable stock.
100ml sesame seeds / ground-up flaxseeds
100ml olive or canola oil
about 200ml warm water

Roll the warm, plastic dough into 12 balls. Oil your fingers if they get sticky. Some people prefer to work with flour on a floured surface. Try for yourself. Roll each ball between 2 sheets of plastic with a rolling pin or an empty bottle. Making them round takes some practice. Press the ball down by hand to make a flat disc then roll it out gently to achieve an even thickness of just over 1 mm for a poppadum or 3mm for a tortilla. Gently peel away the plastic and place onto a greased baking sheet.

Baking: microwave individually for ½ minute, on a sheet of baking paper. This gives you time to roll out the next one. When done, immediately peel off the baking paper and cool on a wire rack.

Oven baking: bake the tray in a medium (180°C) oven for about 20 minutess or leave for longer in a switched-off oven after cooking casseroles, etc. You can use a hot pan, browning one side at a time on medium heat. Use a spray release agent or line the pan with special non -stick baking paper.

5 Fun food

Please note that this information should not be used to diagnose, treat or cure a condition. Consult your doctor or an experienced practitioner, especially if you are pregnant, breast-feeding, epileptic, diabetic or have blood pressure or heart complaints. (See page 2.)

Bake for blood types and allergies

An all -type recipe for muffins and cookies. Fairy cakes from grapefruit and lemon pith and a general cake mix to adapt for all types. How to select the right baking ingredients. Natural alternatives to baking powder.

Making savoury snacks

Fried rice noodles, savoury rice puffs, roasting peanuts. Baking whilst roasting.

Chocolate suits all blood types

Chocolate treats to make: puddings, cookies, dips and icing, sweetmeats. Healthy ways to deal with chocolate addiction.

Fruity desserts and iced drinks

Natural colour from beetroot. Frozen water ices and fruit ices. Frozen yoghurt.

Ice cream alternatives

Soya ice cream or frozen yoghurt.

Make your own healthy sweets

Cut out the sugar. Use more dried fruit, nuts and seeds.

Parties for all types of children

No more junk food parties. Loads of lovely fun food to make. Party themes.

Healty Happy Baking:
for your blood type
for vegans
for allergies

The recipe that agrees with all of us

On an anti-allergy or exclusion diet, all the lectin-laden breakfast cereals, toast, rolls, sandwiches, cakes, hamburgers pizza, cookies, pies, pancakes and other trouble makers have to be removed. It is not difficult to make your own substitutes and in no time you will learn how to bake the Healthy Happy way and nobody will feel deprived.

These simple recipes are easy and quick to make and you select the ingredients according to your blood type, allergies and food budget. They do not contain any eggs, wheat, dairy products, margarine or baking powder. Substitutes have been suggested for brown sugar and grains that contain gluten such as wheat, barley, oats and rye.

First refer to the baking list on page 11

Make a shopping list of all the ingredients that are suitable for your blood type. Buy the recommended substitutes for sugar, margarine, baking powder and flour before you start baking. Most people will no longer be using wheat or sugar.

The basic muffin recipe has a very low Glycaemic Index and is suitable for diabetics and for controlling blood sugar imbalances. If normal meals are not on hand, use nutritious home bakes to stave off hunger and help maintain strength, energy and concentration during strenuous activity.

The high potassium and trace element content of natural ingredients can help to prevent blood pressure fluctuations, fatigue and dehydration during a long, tough day. The cookies are highly alkalising to the body and are a valuable source of soluble and insoluble fibres and lignin. The ground-up flaxseeds assist in the elimination of parasites and are very effective in relieving cases of chronic constipation.

Make a supply of power food

This easy new baking technique can be adapted to make muffins, cookies or a slab of dough that can be cut into squares. Enjoy munching them for breakfast or as snacks between meals. They are handy to keep at work, in the car or in your special snack box, should you be unable to eat a proper meal.

It is best to eat foods that contain starch separately. Chew them slowly and very well in order to mix the enzyme ptyalin from your saliva with the dry food. What a pleasure it is to have these cookies handy to do just that, when you need a quick food fix for low blood sugar or you have an attack of the munchies.

Walnuts and flaxseeds suit all blood types and add valuable Omega 3 essential fatty acids and fibre to food.

The all-type classic dough mix for muffins and cookies

These cookies are the ultimate in compact nutrition for sportsmen and the everyday person on the move, so start baking!
Yield: 24 muffins, or a tray 30cm x 45cm cut into 30 flat cookies
1 cup = 250ml. Pre-heat the oven to 180° C.
Alternative blood type ingredients are indicated by a slash (/)

Dry mixture:

2 cups oats (not O^2) / barley flour (not O) / rice flour (all)
1 cup rye (not B)/ soya (not B^2, O^2)/ yellow pea flour (all)
1 cup millet flour (all) / sorghum (only A, B^2)
½ cup ground-up flaxseeds
½ cup chopped walnuts / sunflower seeds (only A)
½ cup brown sugar / fructose / stevia equivalent
2 teaspoons bicarbonate of soda
1 teaspoon citric acid
1 teaspoon cinnamon powder (not B, O^2)
1 teaspoon ginger powder (all)
½ cup olive oil / canola oil (not B, O^2)
optional extra: 1 teaspoon cream of tartar (extra potassium)

Wet mixture:

100g chopped dates / raisins / dried fruit
200ml water or fruit juice
50ml blackstrap molasses

1 Mix all the dry ingredients together and rub in the olive oil.

2 Soak the dates / raisins / dried fruit and molasses in the water.

3 Pour the wet mix into the dry ingredients and stir well.

4 If the resultant mixture is wet and soft it can be spooned into the greased muffin trays. Adjust the consistency by adding more water if it is too dry and sticky; but for slab cookies , it must be dry.

5 For making a giant slab for cookies, the mixture must be quite stiff and sticky. If it is too wet, add another tablespoon or two of oats or rye flour to strengthen it. Spread out the mixture to a thickness of about 1cm onto a flat greased baking tray and cut into squares with a knife prior to baking. For round cookies, spoon out blobs of dough, leaving plenty of space and flatten out the tops.

The dough consistency will vary according to your selection of dry ingredients. If too crumbly or wet, adjust by adding more flour that binds, such as pea, soya or rye ; if too dry, add more water.

6 Sprinkle chopped nuts, sesame seeds or brown sugar over the muffins or cookies and bake them in the oven at 180° C for 10-15 minutes. Switch off the oven. Allow them to settle for a few more minutes till the muffins shrink around the edges before removing from the trays. Cool on a wire rack or in a flat basket. For a stronger more chewy cookie, leave the baking tray in the switched-off oven for at least an hour. They can stay in overnight for a harder, dry, crunchy biscuit.

Select and measure the dry ingredients and mix in the oil. Soak the wet ingredients with the fruit and add to the bowl.

Mix up and adjust the consistency. If too thick, add water; if too thin, add flour.

Whilst baking, roast peanuts, cook rice or make toasted granola breakfast cereals. (See pages 26 and 149.)

These two cookies have been made out of the same dough, but the one on the left was baked with bicarbonate of soda and cream of tartar and the texture is light and crispy. The other cookie has the same amount of dough, but no leavening.

Use grapefruit and lemons to revolutionise your baking

Grapefruit pith makes a wonderful baking ingredient. It adds pectin and special cancer-fighting bioflavonoids to your cakes and cookies. The peel is too bitter, so remove it.

Peeled grapefruit and whole, chopped lemons are processed in the blender with fruit juice or water. The pulp keeps well for a few weeks in the fridge. Use it to mix with your dry baking ingredients, as and when required.

You can keep a separate container of mixed dry ingredients and then mix in the pulp to make quick desserts or fairy cakes. They cook for a minute each in the microwave or bake a larger batch in the oven.

Grapefruit and lemon fairy cakes

These gorgeous golden cakes suit all blood types. The white pith of lemons and grapefruit are rich in phytonutrients like pectin and bioflavonoids that are now used for cancer therapy. This unique recipe uses this pith as a baking ingredient.

Mix up the dry ingredients with the oil:
½ cup rice flour (all)
½ cup yellow pea (all) / rye (not B) / soya (not B^2, O^2)flour
50ml brown sugar / fructose/ sweetener equivalent
1 teaspoon ginger powder / mixed spice
40ml olive / canola oil (not for B or O^2)

Other ingredients:
1 large or two medium fresh grapefruit
1 large or two small lemons
50ml sweet molasses / honey / brown sugar
1 teaspoon bicarbonate of soda

Remove the peel from the grapefruit (it is too bitter for baking). Squeeze out the lemon and grapefruit juice into an electric blender. Dice the grapefruit pith and finely slice the lemon rind and pith. Add them to the blender with the molasses. Process on high, then stir this smooth pulp into the dry ingredients. Add the bicarbonate of soda at the end to fluff up the dough. Spoon into fairy cake cases and bake in a hot (180-200° C)oven for 10 minutes. Microwave separate ramekins: 1 cake on full takes 1 minute. This makes a light, fluffy cake in a jiffy, and it works best in the microwave oven.

The secret to light fluffy baking without eggs

Usually eggs and baking powder make cakes light and fluffy. But you get far better results by using acid and alkaline combinations. Either make the dry ingredients alkaline, with bicarbonate of soda. Then mix in the wet ingredients with citric acid or lemon juice. If you make the dough acidic, like this recipe, add the bicarbonate of soda last to make it rise.

Rich fruit and nut cake or pudding

It takes time, practice and skill to turn out a light, fluffy, gluten-free, egg-free cake but here it is, after many attempts!
Preheat the oven to hot at 200° C.

Mix up the following wet ingredients and allow them to soak:
1 cup chopped dates / raisins / figs / dried fruit
1 cup boiling water (add ½ cup extra if using soya or pea flour)
50ml sweet molasses or honey / fructose / brown sugar

Mix up dry ingredients. Add oil and combine with the fruit mix.
1 cup rice flour
½ cup rye / barley / pea / soya flour
1 teaspoon bicarbonate of soda
1 teaspoon ginger / cinnamon / lemon zest
40ml olive oil / canola oil
Lastly, stir in 25ml lemon juice or 3ml citric acid to puff it up.

Spoon into 2 greased or paper-lined cake tins. The mixture must be light, fluffy and quite loose. Don't overwork the dough. Bake in a hot oven (200° C) for 10 minutes. Then switch off and allow the cakes to set in the middle. Cook other foods like rice and casseroles in the same oven to save time and energy.

When you cut rounds of greased or non-stick baking paper for cakes, leave on the corners to use as handles for easy removal.

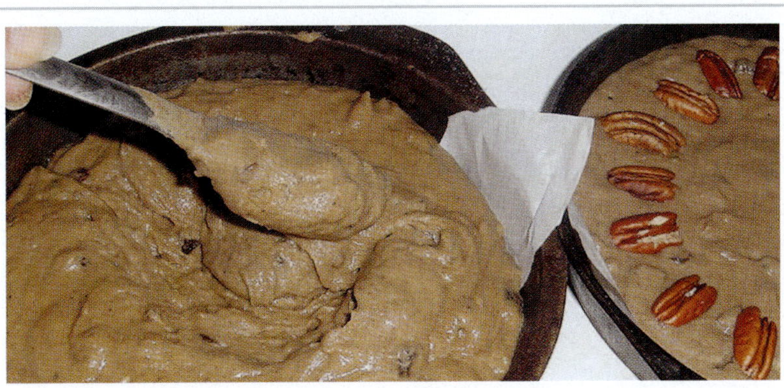

Baked apple dessert or a light "tipsy" pudding

Use half the quantity of the cake mixture to make an apple cake dessert. Peel and chop up some apples in a glass dish. Spread the cake dough over them and sprinkle with chopped nuts or brown sugar. To make a tipsy pudding, leave out the apples and add some chopped dates, soaked in juice or brandy. Pour brandy over the pudding while still hot, to remove the alcohol. Add cocoa for a chocolate pudding.

Bake in a medium oven for 20 minutes. Individual bowls in the microwave take 1 minute each. Enjoy hot or cold, with a little honey, cream, custard, yoghurt, tahini or soya ice cream.

Variations

Put aside a cup or two of the basic cake mix for making these chewy munch bars. Mix a few tablespoons of raw oats / barley flour / rye flour into the mixture and more chopped nuts, seeds, raisins and dried fruit until the dough is very firm but easy to form into small balls. Add more sugar or sweetener if you like.

Flatten the balls and bake them on a sheet of baking paper on a tray. Alternatively, roll out a slab of the stiff dough between two plastic sheets. Cut it into bars and bake in a medium oven. Add them to lunch and snack boxes.

The cake mixture can also be baked in fairy cup cases or in a muffin tray. For a brownie-type of flat cake, spread dough into a slab on a flat baking tray. Add cocoa, nuts, coffee or spices to suit.

Select the baking ingredients that suit your blood type

Almonds suit all except AB^1. Walnuts suit all blood types.

Hazelnuts and pumpkin seeds do not suit B and AB^2. Sesame seeds, chick peas, corn products and sunflower seeds are not for Blood types B and AB.

Peanuts only suit A and AB^2. However, first test all peanuts as they can cause inflammatory reactions in all blood types. They often contain moulds and aflatoxins. Sunflower seeds are only for blood type A.

If you have a gluten intolerance, avoid wheat, rye, oats and barley, regardless of your blood type. Use mainly millet, rice, soya, lentil or yellow pea flour according to what best suits your blood type.

Basic guidelines for happy baking

1 The amount of oil you add makes the dough more or less moist or tasty. Olive oil is good for all blood types. Always rub oil into the dry ingredients. To make savoury biscuits or wafers more crispy, add ground-up flaxseeds, sesame seeds, etc.

2 Liquids and water change the consistency of dough. Cookie dough should be like stiff cement, muffins need more water and should be baked at a higher temperature, for less time than cookies. Cakes require a hot oven for a longer time. Add a little more water to cake dough if it feels too heavy and sticky. Leaving biscuits in the oven after switching off will make them harder and stronger. Biscuits and savoury crisps need just enough water to make a putty-like ball.

3 The quantity of sugar also alters the taste and texture of your baking. Molasses is nice to add to the wet mix, producing a rich, dark colour. Honey should not be used for baking as heat destroys its healing properties. Pour it onto warm desserts after baking. Dates soaked in water and mashed are a good sweetener. Bananas are toxic when cooked.

4 Baking powder is bad for you. Substitute with 5ml bicarbonate of soda and 3ml citric acid or 20ml lemon juice for every 500ml of dry ingredients. A teaspoon of cream of tartar adds more potassium to the food value of the mixture. Add the bicarb separately: if the mixture is alkaline, add it to the dry ingredients. After adding the wet ingredients, you stir in the lemon juice or citric acid to make the dough rise up. If the mixture is acidic, as with using grapefruit and lemon juice pulp, add the bicarb last of all. If a cake mixture is too dry and stiff, the dough will be heavy, so add more water.

5 Soya, pea and rye flour make the dough more plastic and less crumbly, so add more when making biscuits that may fall apart. To make rice flour more plastic, mix it into a paste with boiling water and then knead in the dry ingredients.

6 Flaxseeds, millet, sorghum, rice flour and cornflour make a looser, crunchier texture. As they have no binding action, too much will make your cookies fall apart. We need to blend them with sticky flours like rye, soya, pea or lentil flour.

7 Yellow pea flour usually tests well for all blood types; you can buy it from health shops. Soya flour suits most blood types except O^2 and B^2. Lentil flour is good for A and AB, but not B and O^1. Chick pea flour is only for O^1. These flours are all gluten-free and low on the Glycaemic Index at values of 25 - 40. Rye flour is not for B. Oats are not for O^2. Try to avoid wheat. It can be tolerated by A^1 and AB. Barley is good for all types except O. Make a list of what type of flour suits you and your family. Use the table of baking ingredients on page 11 and adapt the basic recipes accordingly.

Dinner in the oven while you make snacks and cereals

Energy-saving tips for baking sessions

Cook other dishes like rice, curries or casseroles in the oven when you bake cakes and cookies to save time and energy. Try at least once a week to bake biscuits, muffins and cookies when you are using the oven. You can also make the breakfast cereals for the week, toast some crunchy snacks or roast your own peanuts. It is best to buy raw peanuts and roast them yourself.

Oven-baked breakfast cereal

Fill a baking dish with 4 cups of raw oats and mix in a few tablespoons of olive or canola oil and a little brown sugar. For those who tolerate soya, add 1 or 2 cups of soya mince (TVP granules). Bake in the oven at low heat or leave for a few hours or overnight. If you are baking in a hot oven, check every few minutes and stir as soon as the edges begin to brown. When cool, add chopped dried fruit, raisins, nuts, sunflower or pumpkin seeds.

The mixture can be blended with cooked soya flour or sorghum cereal for a more satisfying combination. Blend it according to your blood type. Add a cup or two of puffed rice if you want a lighter texture. Type A[1] can add corn flakes. This mixture makes a nutritious breakfast cereal or it can be chewed dry as a snack.

Dinners to bake at the same time

1 Roasted vegetables mixed with herbs, onion and spices and tossed in a little olive oil. Place the roasting pan on a lower shelf in the oven while you carry on with the family baking.

2 Rice is easy to cook in the oven. Place 1 cup of rice to 2 cups of cold water and a pinch of salt in a covered dish and bake it in the oven. Add sausage and veg for a Chinese hotpot. The whole dish will be ready after the cookies are done!

3 Curries, casseroles, roast chicken (not B!) or lamb dishes can also share the same oven.

4 Bake a few whole sweet potatoes. Make a slit and stuff them with chopped pieces of feta cheese and onion or leftovers from the fridge.

Crispy rice and corn nibbles

Place a few cups of puffed rice in a baking dish and blend with a few teaspoons of olive oil and a sprinkling of herb salt and curry spices. Toast in the warm oven when you switch it off after baking. For A[1], you can do the same with ordinary corn flakes for a savoury snack. Combine cornflakes with peanuts and sunflower seeds for a delicious crispy snack blend for blood type A[1].

Pop up the popcorn, especially for A[1]

Make popcorn for parties. Although corn is not a recommended food for most of us, A[1] children can have plenty of it at parties. Pop it fresh with olive oil and sprinkle with herb salt.

Savoury crisp fried rice noodles

This is a substitute for chemical-laden chips and salty nachos, etc. Any rice or mung bean noodles can be deep-fried in the same way as you fry prawn crackers. If you don't want them to swim in cooking oil, take the broad, flat Thai rice noodle and fry it in 1cm of hot olive or grapeseed oil. Work quickly as they curl and puff up in a jiffy and need to be rapidly removed onto a paper towel to drain. Fry up a good supply and sprinkle with herb salt. They are also nice with Indonesian or Chinese food.

Chocolate suits all blood types, but not the milk and sugar

It's good news that chocolate is neutral for all blood types, being highly beneficial as a heart medicine, a mood enhancer, an aphrodisiac, a wonderful tonic and helping to focus the brain.

The caffeine in cocoa is relatively low at 5-10mg per cup, as opposed to 60-120mg in a cup of tea or coffee. But we are not talking about commercial products laden with sugars, fats, milk, flavours, additives and other gremlins. Buy yourself some pure, natural alkaline cocoa powder that is free of additives and get to work on your chocolate cravings. Have a natural high with these delicious alternative chocolate goodies.

All these recipes are free of wheat, dairy, eggs and trans-fatty acids. The sugar content is greatly reduced but acceptable sugar substitutes are recommended. Learn to make chocolate treats that are rich in essential Omega 3 and 6 fatty acids, lecithin and other cholesterol-busters such as soya, millet, oats, barley and flaxseeds. These ingredients help to lower the Glycaemic Index to below 30 in some of the recipes, as a safer option for diabetics and I sugar junkies or chocoholics.

Chocolate for dipping or mixing with fruit and nuts. Melt cooking chocolate in a double boiler with the same quantity of olive or canola oil. Add more cocoa powder. You can also add a few spoons of lecithin granules, soaked in water, to emulsify the chocolate.

Rich, dark chocolate custard

Combine in a small pot (or a glass jug for the microwave):

1 tablespoon cocoa powder
1 tablespoon brown sugar (or fructose or stevia equivalent)
1 tablespoon olive oil
2 cups boiling water
½ cup rice flour (stirred briskly into the boiling water)
optional extra: 1 tablespoon lecithin granules

Heat up the pot of ingredients and keep stirring to thicken the custard. For the microwave, stir a few times at half minute intervals. When thick and creamy, whisk in a bit more olive or canola oil. Add more cocoa powder to taste. You can add 1 or 2 teaspoons of flaxseed, pumpkin or walnut oil to a serving to enhance the Omega 3 content, but this is an acquired taste.

Use as a sauce or a hot pudding, or pour into a pie crust made from ground-up soya TVP, mixed with melted butter and brown sugar. Grate over some baking chocolate or sprinkle with chopped nuts. Other flavours: 1 teaspoon Jamaica Ginger or ½ teaspoon ginger powder (ginger helps to thin blood and prevent it from clotting). Try a pinch of cinnamon. Serve with a hot sauce made from orange marmalade and a little boiling water.

Chocolate treats to make and enjoy

Chocolate mix for muffins, cakes or puddings

This mixture can be made and kept in the fridge. When you need to bake in a hurry, all you do is add some water.

1 cup breakfast oats (not for O^2) / oat bran (all types)
½ cup millet / rice / barley flour
½ cup ground-up flaxseeds
½ cup soya / pea / rye flour
½ cup brown sugar / fructose
2-3 tablespoons cocoa powder
1 teaspoon bicarb. soda plus ½ teaspoon citric acid
1 teaspoon ginger or cinnamon if desired
Rub in ¼ cup olive or canola oil to make fine crumbs

When ready to bake something, mix water or fruit juice into the dry mixture at a ratio of 1:1 for cookies and slightly wetter for muffins or cakes. Spoon into greased cake or muffin trays. Bake in a hot oven for 10 minutes. For a microwave test, place half a cup of dough into a small ramekin dish and you should have a perfect, fluffy cake in 1 minute. If the mixture is too dry, it will not rise sufficiently. If too wet, it will be sticky and crumbly.

Serve as a hot or cold dessert with chocolate custard or a hot fruity sauce. Poke a few broken pieces of bitter Albany chocolate into the raw dough before baking or add chopped nuts or fruit. Prior to baking, sprinkle on a layer of brown sugar, mixed with ground-up spices to make a nice saucy topping.

Cookies and biscuits with the same mixture

Use the same basic mix, it's so handy. For cookies, add another ½ cup of soya, pea or rye flour and make a stiffer dough. You can add chocolate chips or chopped nuts and raisins or extra cocoa to make rich chocolate cookies. Place spoonfuls of the mixture onto a baking sheet. Sprinkle on the sugar and spice mixture. Bake at 180 °C for 12 minutes.

Chocolate biscuits can be made in the same way, but with less water to make a stronger, more plastic dough. Dip fingers into oil or flour while you work if they get sticky. Dough can be rolled between two sheets of thin plastic, or use more flour. Thinner biscuits take less time and need a lower heat for baking. They can be topped with some instant chocolate spread, using the recipe on this page.

Instant chocolate spread

This one's a killer as it destroys all chocolate cravings. What's the secret? The high intensity of phytochemicals from all the pure cocoa, combined with the Omega oils. They hit the neuro-receptors in the brain and send you on an ambient buzz. You have been warned, so only take it in small doses! After a good binge, you will feel well satisfied, with no more cravings.

1 tablespoon soft butter
1 tablespoon sweet molasses
1 tablespoon olive oil
2 tablespoons pure cocoa powder

Work this mixture into a thick, dark and bitter paste. Some people prefer canola oil with a teaspoon of flaxseed oil. You can spread it on bread or biscuits or eat it neat. The paste freezes well and it remains soft and creamy on frozen food.

Hot chocolate with no milk

Add 1 teaspoon of pure cocoa to a cup of boiling water. Try drinking it neat with a dash of cinnamon or a tiny splash of milk. If too bitter, add a little brown sugar, molasses or stevia for sweetening. It's a good deterrent to eating chocolate!

As you can see, healthier versions of your favourite chocolate goodies are waiting for you to enjoy!

Use the natural colours of fruit, especially beetroot

Beetroot juice provides a magnificent range of pinks and reds and there is no need to use chemical colourants and food dyes. Make some very concentrated beetroot juice in the electric blender and strain it. If you do not have a blender, then soak grated beetroot in a little water. Use the juice to colour milk, yoghurt, soya milk, etc. Juice from oranges, plums, peaches, carrots, pineapple or mango have beautiful colours. Vitamin C can be added to the sweeter juices, to give a sharp tang.

A pink health drink that children will love

Beetroot juice is rather bland so add a pinch of vitamin C powder or a crushed 250mg tablet of ascorbic acid to each glass of juice. You can use lemon juice instead, if available. Sweeten with a little honey, stevia or a teaspoon of brown sugar. Float a few chunks of fruit or some grapes in the juices for fun. Add funky plastic straws and festive garnishes. Pink herb teas can be enjoyed hot or cold, with chunks of fresh fruit.

Water ices are lovely for parties or hot summer days

Pile some crushed ice into a glass and pour the juice over it. For a really special frozen slush, freeze some juices or sweetened herb teas, keeping them in separate tall plastic containers. Buzz these with a hand-held blender and spoon into tall glasses, using different layers of coloured ice. Do not overfreeze the juice as it may become too hard to blend. Juices react differently; some juices freeze up very hard, whilst others, like grape juice stay soft. Use the hard-freezing juices to make ice lollies.

Ice cream is not a health food, so find alternatives

Ice cream is not for lactose-intolerant individuals. They can try frozen yoghurt or soya equivalents. Make your own frozen joghurt ice by mixing plain yoghurt with concentrated fruit juice and freezing it for a few hours. Then process with a hand-held blender and serve immediately. Use beetroot juice for a pink colour. Make toppings for ice cream by mixing cocoa powder with butter, honey, tahini, etc. Peanut butter is delicious for blood type A or AB[2]. Try the new soya nut butter (not O[2], B[2]).

Make all your own drinks and desserts from fruit

A riot of natural colours and flavours for parties

All the party desserts and drinks you see above are free from preservatives, artificial colours or flavours. Natural sweeteners such as honey, molasses, mashed bananas, dates or stevia are used in moderation. This spread of party treats is loaded with healthy natural ingredients. Before serving fruit ices to guests, try out the basic techniques yourself so you can perfect the timing and presentation.

How to make creamy dreamy fruit ices

Banana freeze: mash 2 or 3 ripe bananas and mix with a teaspoon of lemon juice. Bananas freeze well and can be kept in the freezer for a few days. When ready to serve, process with the hand-held blender or mash till smooth and creamy. Serve as is, or use as a substitute for cream. Variations: chocolate banana ice is gorgeous. Add a few teaspoons of cocoa to the mashed bananas before freezing and leave out the lemon juice. Serve with a dark chocolate sauce made from a mixture of cocoa, honey and a little soft butter. Sprinkle with grated chocolate.

Mango freeze: peel and slice a few fresh mangoes and freeze them in a plastic container. Process with a hand-held blender. Make sure you use the hairless variety of mango! This idea comes from a delightful book of blood type recipes from two ladies in Paris. See page 160.

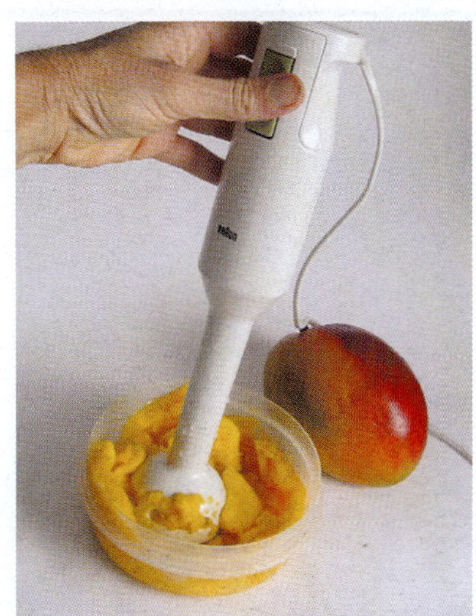

Peach freeze: keep cans of peaches, pears or apricots handy. Place the drained fruit in a 5cm layer in a plastic container and freeze it. When you have a dessert emergency, whizz it up and serve with yoghurt mixed with honey and tahini (sesame paste) or some suitable crushed nuts.

Pineapple and pear freeze: freeze up some peeled and diced pineapple with slices of fresh or canned pears. Serve with other fruit ices.

Make a variety of fresh juices

See the index for more about juices. Grapes and pineapple make good party blends. Freeze juices into ice cubes, especially beetroot for colour.

Sweet and healthy treats made to suit

Watch out for the sugar

Check the lists on page 11. To lower the Glycaemic Index, add nuts, oats and wholegrains or olive oil. (See page 43.) Use alternative sweeteners like stevia, fructose or liquorice powder.

Roly-poly munchies: a good standby for diabetics

Use a large heavy pot or pan and turn the heat to high, then add:

30ml olive oil
½ cup lentil / soya / yellow pea flour (suits all)

Stir together till absorbed and bubbling, then add:

50ml sweet molasses / fructose / stevia equivalent
50ml chopped dates, soaked in 100ml boiling water

Stir till the mixture is bubbling, then turn the stove to low and add:

1 cup oat / barley flour / oat bran (suits all)
½ cup ground-up flaxseeds
½ cup chopped nuts or seeds
½ cup raisins and chopped dried fruit
For a chocolate flavour: 1 tablespoon cocoa powder

Turn the heat off and stir well to mix all the ingredients till a firm mass is formed. Tip out the mixture onto a plate. Divide into 8 balls. Roll them into sausages or form into flatter bars. It is best to leave the rolls to dry out overnight in a switched-off warm oven or out in the sun. Wrap in cling film or attractive cellophane packages. They keep well and are useful as a snack or quick meal replacement.

Nibble these rolls slowly when the hunger pangs attack you. The natural fibre and essential fatty acids as well as the low sugar content make this type of food suitable for diabetics or people with low blood sugar, known as hypoglycaemia. These people must avoid white sugar, glucose and refined starches like white flour.

This munchy mixture can have endless variations, according to your blood type and nutritional needs. The bars or rolls can be kept in your bag or in the car.

Fruit balls, dipped chocolate

Soak and mash some dates and blend in nuts, seeds and dried fruit. Make a very stiff, strong paste by adding ground-up nuts and seeds. Add cocoa as a variation. Roll the balls in cocoa powder or sesame seeds. Alternatively, insert a toothpick and dip into the melted chocolate mixture on page 150. Try dipping fruit in this mixture or clustering nuts into blobs of the melted chocolate.

Healthy Happy sweets to make for nutritious snacks and treats

Always begin by heating up the sweet molasses till it bubbles, then turn down the heat or it will burn. Brown sugar and water can also be used for a toffee base. Boil 1 part sugar to 2 parts water.

Add seeds and nuts to the bubbling molassses and immediately remove from the heat. If you want to stretch out the mixture, then add some rice crispies. Add even more rice crispies or some oats to make a breakfast cereal.

Spread the hot toffee onto a greased surface and cut into squares while it is warm. Allow the toffee to cool down. You can also fill cookie cups with the mixture or spread it onto rice cakes.

Seedy nut toffee base for:
seed bars, nut clusters and toppings

This toffee base makes a good alternative to peanut brittle.

In a heavy bottomed pan, heat up the following till bubbling:

100ml sweet (desulphured) molasses

Then add the following ingredients:

1 cup chopped nuts and seeds like:
sunflower, sesame, walnuts, almonds, etc.

Flavour option: add 1 tablespoon of cocoa or carob powder or 1 teaspoon of instant coffee powder.
Extra choices: ½ cup raisins or some chopped, dried fruit.
Turn off the heat and keep stirring till the toffee becomes sticky and smells like caramel. Be careful not to burn it.
Optional: add 1 cup of rice crispies or oats to make cereal.

Tip out the mixture onto a greased tray and spread into a slab. As it cools and hardens, slice it into squares. Wrap in cellophane. Alternatively, spoon this mixture into small paper cookie cases.

Toffee and nut rice cakes

This mixture is nice to crumble onto desserts like stewed apple with yoghurt or homemade banana ice cream. (See page 153.)
For an extra treat, spread a tablespoon of the hot mixture onto a rice cake. If it gets too sticky, dip a fork in water to spread it evenly. As the mixture cools, it can also be rolled into balls.

From left: nutty seed bars, chocolate and nut clusters, chocolate coated dates, chocolate discs with walnuts, date balls, seed and nut toffee in paper cases and rice cakes topped with toffee.

What a delicious load of treats to make!

The sweetest part is knowing that they will suit the whole family as they are free of harmful fats, preservatives and chemicals. This selection is made out of foods that are high in natural fibre and oils. The chocolate treats have been modified to contain less fat and sugar. To make them, see page 150 for the chocolate dip recipe. Dip dates, dried fruit and nuts in chocolate or make nut clusters by adding nuts to the chocolate mixture and spooning into clusters.

Healthy party treats for children with allergies or intolerances

Chewy seed bars and rice cakes with seed and nut toffee. Make party sweetmeats a few days in advance. (See pages 154 and 155.)

You need to serve alternatives to dairy ice cream like tofu ice cream or frozen yoghurt. Make your own frozen yoghurt. (See page 153.) Make chocolate and nut sauces. Try using the new soya nut butter instead of peanut butter.

Most commercial peanuts are laden with aflatoxins and the oils have gone rancid. Rather roast your own or serve other nuts. Sprout some chick peas and yellow peas and roast them in olive oil with a little herb salt. Add spices that your children like and serve them with your selection of salty snacks.

Make fruit juices and ice slushes. Also freeze juice in ice cubes and lolly moulds. (See pages 89-91.) Frozen fruit desserts are made a few days in advance from fruits like mango, banana, pineapple, pear or canned peaches, apricots or apple. (See page 153.)

Some supermarkets sell gluten-free or wheat-free cakes. They can be sliced and decorated with chocolate health icing, candles, etc. (See page 151 for chocolate spread.) Make chocolate milkshakes out of rice milk, soya milk, oat milk, cocoa powder, bananas, honey, etc. This will depend on individual blood types and allergies.

Use all-type baking for cakes, fairy cakes and cookie bases. (See pages 144-148.) Try individual cakes with their own candles. Let the children decorate them.

Make savoury treats and try them out well in advance on your children. Recipes for toasted spicy rice pops, fried rice noodles and roasted peanuts are on page 149.

Mix up sweet or savoury dips. Slice up fruit and vegetables or offer rice crackers for dipping. Get the children to help you make dips they really like, using natural ingredients such as yoghurt, tahini, honey, etc. (See pages 114 and 115.)

Popular party themes

Arty-crafty parties

Prepare trays of gorgeous ingredients and let the children decorate the cakes, mix the dips and pretend to be chefs. They can also make the hats and decorations.

Adventure parties

A survivor-type of theme is the ultimate for hyperactive, energetic children with a sense of adventure, especially O types! Make them work for their food packages and they will appreciate every mouthful. Have team games, challenges and some exciting new physical "survivor" activities!

Fun and games

Not all children like hectic activity and may feel self-conscious. Make a carnival theme, where they can do activities like fun races, throwing balls, painting faces or dressing up from boxes of old clothes.

Magical parties

Harry Potter is an inspiration to all children and now that they love reading, make a magical party where children have to solve puzzles, riddles, etc. to gain access to maps, showing where the food and treasures are hidden. Let them dress up.

Toy parties

Try teddy bears' picnics, Barbie dolls, Lego and whatever their latest favourites are.

Picnic and adventure parties

Pack up the food and go somewhere nice and wild. Wear old clothes, play with water and mud and come home exhausted, filthy and totally played-out.

A Healthy Happy Birthday for all of us

The secret of successful parties for children

Most parents who have young children at school will encounter the party syndrome: the hype-up, the hype-down, all the work and fuss and finally a big mess to clear up. But take one look at the faces of your delighted children and their guests and of course, you will do it all again next year, but in a healthier way!

Allergies, ADD or ADHD, leaky-gut problems

These words cast a cloud over an invitation to a party. The standard birthday party fare will definitely be poisonous to sensitive constitutions. Nobody wants to be left out but the problem begins by letting your child go to a party, hoping that all will turn out fine. It doesn't, and you are stuck with hype-problems, mucous and asthma, skin rashes, indigestion and upset blood sugar problems. You have two choices: either the children take along their own food or you have a serious chat to the party hosts. If all the parents of a group of party-goers agree to cut out the junk, the children will no longer be under peer pressure.

Bright colours, party treats, fun and excitement

Healthy does not have to be boring. There are plenty of ideas you can adapt for party foods that will provide not only gastronomic delight, but adequate and balanced nutrition at the same time. Use the recipes and suggestions in this book. Always make food attractive and exciting at every meal.

The Healthy Happy Eating Revolution

We become addicted to junk food for a good reason. In a recent investigation it was made known that manufacturers of famous brands of foods spike the ingredients with extra fats, sugars and chemicals to keep people coming back for more. This food has an addictive effect on the brain and body. Most people far exceed their daily kilojoule requirements, yet still crave food because of the poor nutrient content. Rather change over to nutritious party foods with taste and colour sensations that satisfy your little customers so they no longer crave artificial colours, condiments and "empty, foodless" foods.

Index

Bibliography

Balch M.D. James, Balch C.N.C. Phyllis:
Prescription for Nutritional Healing
Barefoot Robert R, Reich M.D. Carl:
The Calcium Factor
Bell,Emslie-Smith & Paterson:
Textbook of Physiology
Blackie Margery:
The challenge of Homeopathy
Boericke M.D. William, Dewey M.D. Willis:
The Twelve Tissue Remedies of Schussler
Prof. J. Foster-Powell, Leeds DR. Anthony:
The Glucose Revolution
Brookesmith Peter:
Future Plagues, Biohazard, Disease & Pestilence
Budd Martin: Low Blood Sugar
Carper Jean : The food pharmacy
Chapman Esther: How to use the 12 Tissue Salts
Chapman M.D. J.: Dr Schuessler's Biochemistry
Chevallier Andrew: Encyclopedia Medicinal Plants
D'Adamo: Dr Peter, Catherine Whitney: Eat Right 4 Your Type, Live Right 4 your Type, Blood Type Encyclopedia
Davis Adelle: Let's get Well
Diamond Harvey & Marilyn: Fit For Life
Du Randt Dr Charl: Demonised Doctoring
Eheret Dr. Arnold: The Mucusless Diet
Grewal Dr. Iqbal: Home Remedies
Glenville Dr. Marilyn: Natural alternatives to Dieting, Natural Alternatives to HRT
Holford Patrick, Neil Kate:
Balancing Hormones Naturally, Optimal Nutrition, Natural Highs
Hovannessian A T : Raw - Eating
Kenton Leslie: Passage to Power, Raw Energy, Detox Now, Juice Blitz
Liebermann Sam:
D.I.Y. Fasting, Healthy/ Unhealthy Water
Lockie Dr. Andrew: Family guide to Homeopathy
Medical Research Council Traditional Medicines, Research Group of the University of Cape Town and The University of the Western Cape: South African Primary Health Care Handbook
Mindell Earl: The Vitamin Bible
Monte Tom , Editors of East West Natural Health:
The East West guide to healing your body
O'Mathuna Ph.D. Donal & Larimore M.D. Walt:
Alternative Medicine: The Christian Handbook
Parkhill Joe M: Wonderful World of Bee Pollen
Prevention Magazine Health Books:
The Doctors Book of Home Remedies
Reader's Digest: The Body Book
Regher Clark Ph.D, N.D. H: The Cure For all Diseases
Roberts Margaret: Tissue Salts for Healthy Living
Sears Barry: The Zone, Anti-Ageing zone
Serfontein Prof. Willem: Your Gateway to Health and Wealth, New Nutrition for the New Millenium
Speroff, Glass & Kase:
Clinical Gynecologic Endocrinology and Infertility
Stone Dr. Randolph:
Health Building. The conscious art of living well
Treben Maria: Health through God's Pharmacy
Walker Dr. Morton: Olive Leaf Extract
Wallach BS DVM M. D. Joel: Dead Doctors Don't Lie
Weiner Michael, Goss Kathleen:
The complete book of Homeopathy
Wingate Dr. Peter: The Penguin Medical Encyclopedia, W H O:
The use of Traditional Medicine in primary health care

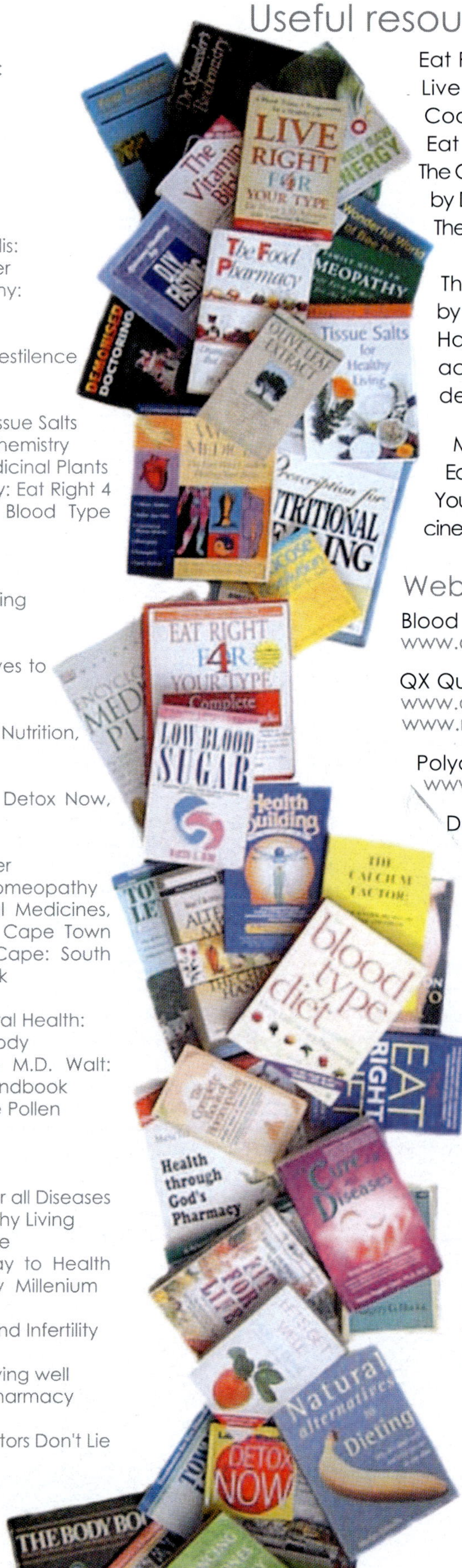

Useful resources and websites

Eat Right 4 Your Type
Live Right 4 Your Type
Cook Right 4 your Type
Eat Right 4 Your Baby
The Complete Blood Type Encyclopedia
by Dr. Peter, D'Adamo
These are the best reference books.

The Blood Type Diet Cookbook
by Karen Vago and Lucy Degremont
Handy hints and case histories to accompany the wide variety of delicious family recipes.

Medicams Index
Editor: Dr Peter. R. Smith
Your guide to complementary medicine: A concise, practical handbook.

Websites and addresses

Blood type research and help
www.dadamo.com

QX Quantum Xrroid Analysis
www.quantumlife.com
www.metabole.com

Polycystic ovarian syndrome
www.pcos.com

Dark field blood analysis
www.sevenpointfive.co.za

Water website
www.watercures.co.za

Townsend letter references
www.tldp.com
tldp@olympus.net

Medicams Index
www.medicamsindex.co.za

Author's website
www.naturefresh.co.za
info@naturefresh.co.za

Dear Readers,

Plese keep in touch with me for the lastest news, recipes and updates. Use the free search facility, diets and site links. I hope you all enjoy reading this book over and over again.

A special thank you to all the wonderful, patient people who have helped me to produce this book.

Regards, Sue Visser